"This delightful book is both intelligent *and* wise. It is full of insights that trigger just the right kind of reflection and soul-searching. Anyone serious about becoming more effective at work (or anywhere in which interactions with other people matter) will benefit by reading this book and taking its insights to heart. Marcum and Smith do a beautiful job describing ego's strengths and pitfalls, and they guide us gently, with care and empathy, toward practices that help tame the ego to get it to work for us rather than against us. To do this, they integrate established social science research with their own experiences, and the result is a seamless readable journey that experts and novices alike will enjoy."

—Dr. Amy C. Edmondson, Novartis Professor of Leadership and Management and chair, Doctoral Programs, Harvard Business School

"I love this book. From Freud to modern neuroscience, we've been told that it's our ego, the monitor of good and bad judgment and decision making, that determines our fate and future. This book reveals in depth and originality how to deploy this basic force for self-development and for the common good. A book every leader should read."

—Dr. Warren Bennis, Distinguished Professor of Business, University of Southern California, and author of *On Becoming a Leader* and coauthor of *Geeks and Geezers: How Era, Values, and Defining Moments Shape Leaders*

"*egonomics* is great medicine for those of us who manage knowledge workers—people who know more about what they are doing than we do! Marcum and Smith show you how to get ahead without letting it get to your head. The book is filled with great learning and, at the same time, great fun. This book addresses the greatest challenge faced by successful people. A wonderful book."

—Dr. Marshall Goldsmith, *New York Times* and *Wall Street Journal* bestselling author of *What Got You Here Won't Get You There: How Successful People Become Even More Successful!*

"What a brilliant and vitally important book! So true and so pragmatically necessary. Ego is the opposite of conscience. It never sleeps. It micromanages and disempowers. Ego interprets all of life through its own agenda. It is only when conscience and humility tame ego and channel its strength that it can be used for good. Then, humble confidence and the ambition only to significantly contribute matter, which in turn produce constant improvement cultures and synergistic relationships. Integrity then becomes a higher value than loyalty, in fact becomes the essence of true loyalty."

—Stephen R. Covey, author of *The 7 Habits of Highly Effective People and The 8th Habit: From Effectiveness to Greatness*

"This book is quite an accomplishment. *egonomics* addresses an incredibly important aspect of work life (and all of life) that gets very little systematic attention and sustained implementation in the business world. Marcum and Smith's practical approach may just save you from the blindness of your most mindless self and tap those elements of heart and mind, native intelligence, and our capacity for wise action that can make a huge difference to the effectiveness of an organization and the quality of its corporate culture. It reminds us where our truest self and self-interest as leaders might be found. Such embodiment will make for happier stakeholders all around, and for the best reasons."

—Jon Kabat-Zinn, Ph.D., professor of medicine emeritus, University of Massachusetts Medical School, author of *Coming to Our Senses: Healing Ourselves and the World Through Mindfulness,* and leader of the University of Massachusetts Medical School's *The Power of Mindfulness* retreats for leaders and innovators

"After the extraordinary hubris of recent business history—the Enron scandal, the Donald Trump TV shows—it's so refreshing to read *egonomics,* which makes a compelling case for the practical importance of humility and veracity in the business realm."

—Alan Deutschman, senior writer, *Fast Company;* author of *Change or Die: The Three Keys to Change at Work and in Life* "*egonomics* quickly focuses your mind on the need for personal improvement and does so through the principles it teaches—humility, curiosity, and veracity. It is a riveting assessment of every leader's daily challenge for real and perceived ego balance in a journey characterized by permanent white water. *egonomics* is the critical ingredient for the quality and sustainability of any organization's value system and economic profit."

> —James C. Thyen, president and chief executive officer, Kimball International, Inc.

"This book is about a subject that has received little attention for far too long. True, it deals with an important aspect of leadership that is difficult to discuss comfortably, much less to solidly research. Marcum and Smith have done a scholarly job of both. They not only recognize and clearly explain the significant problems and opportunities EGO brings to great leadership, but they motivate you to do something about it and explain how it can be done. It's good reading for every executive and could result in enormous rewards."

> —Dr. Jack R. Wentworth, professor dean emeritus of business administration, Kelley School of Business, Indiana University

"This book is terrific! *egonomics* provides grounded, practical approaches for those trying to lift their organizations from the strangleholds of runaway egos. Marcum and Smith's perspective on 'veracity' should be required reading in every MBA program."

> —Christine M. Pearson, Ph.D., professor of management, Thunderbird School of Global Management

"Marcum and Smith's well-written, engaging, and useful work identifies early warning signs of ego and principles to avoid excessive ego (humility, curiosity, veracity). They document that when leaders act purely out of ego they make costly and ill-advised decisions. Leaders may maintain self-confidence without the downside of ego by being aware of the early warning signs Marcum and Smith identify and the principles they advocate. The book is well documented, easy to follow, and filled with specific ideas that can be helpful for leaders at all levels of a company."

—Dave Ulrich, Ph.D., professor, Ross School of Business, University of Michigan; partner, the RBL Group; and coauthor of *The Leadership Brand*

"*egonomics* brings a new significant leadership resource—moving us from experiencing ego as a liability to appreciating ego as part of the power of personal humility. *egonomics* enhances the language of the leader of the future."

—Frances Hesselbein, chairman of the board, Leader to Leader Institute (formerly The Peter Drucker Foundation)

"Individual success depends on ability, drive, and creativity. These same qualities often produce strong egos, which often undermine the ability of an organization to leverage the diverse skills, ideas, and perspectives of its employees. Blending ideas from cutting-edge research with the wisdom that can only be acquired from being in the game, *egonomics* shows leaders how to recognize ego's cost and how to control their own egos and manage those of others. A must read for any manager or business leader. The smarter you think you are, the more you need to read this book."

lol

—Scott E. Page, Ph.D., professor of complex systems, political science, and economics, University of Michigan, Ann Arbor; external faculty, Santa Fe Institute; and author of *The Difference*

"With stunning examples, Marcum and Smith's *egonomics* shows how the ego needs of executives, managers, and key others can sabotage corporate and personal success. Marcum and Smith chronicle the difference between strong and needy egos, and chart the early signs of formal leaders' ego deficiencies and defenses. I applaud their psychological knowledge of self-defeating behavior, their Rogerian applications, and their ability to show how humility, curiosity, and truth can restore the self, the confidence of others, and the corporate bottom line."

— Dr. Carol Hoare, professor of human development and human resource development, George Washington University

"Finally a book that tackles the toughest problem in business today: the inflated egos of the players, especially top management. Marcum and Smith deliver a wealth of helpful advice on how to deal with your own ego as well as the egos of those you work with. A brilliant and badly-needed book."

— Al Ries, coauthor of *The Origin of Brands*

"Marcum and Smith have identified an important yet unexplored facet of the power of individual differences at the workplace. They provide convincing evidence that harnessing the power of ego will provide new levers for enhancing organizational effectiveness. This book provides practical wisdom that will be essential to understanding and motivating the high potential workforce of the future."

— Terri A. Scandura, Ph.D., professor of management and psychology, University of Miami

"We have come to think of 'ego' as the source of major problems in life and in organizations. Marcum and Smith show, in clear language and practical detail, how to make ego into a force for positive change—for personal and organizational success. This book will prove to be a valuable resource for managers, executives, and anyone who wants to find more productive ways to fulfill what psychologists call 'ego needs.'"

— Marshall Sashkin, Ph.D., professor of human resource development, Graduate School of Education and Human Development, George Washington University

"*egonomics* is a very interesting and unique approach to helping people learn to steer their behavior more productively in the workplace. It is certain to be widely used, especially now that so many businesses understand that their primary competitive advantage is people and culture."

—Rosabeth Moss Kanter, Ph.D., professor, Harvard Business School, and bestselling author of *Confidence: How Winning Streaks and Losing Streaks Begin and End*

"*egonomics* is a breakthrough work much needed in a time when we are bombarded with quick fixes of marginal relevance. It is a carefully considered and wide-ranging work that provides excellent guidance for managers at all levels as well as serving as a blueprint for researchers interested in fully understanding organizational behavior. This volume is well written and interesting. The flow carries the reader along with minimal effort so that you don't want to put it down. The concepts are concise and clearly explicated so that the logic is easy to follow and the conclusions equally easily accepted. I highly recommend *egonomics* to managers, researchers, and students. Each of them will appreciate the implications and importance of this work."

—Dr. David D. Van Fleet, professor of management, School of Global Management and Leadership, Arizona State University

"David Marcum and Steven Smith's new book, *egonomics,* addresses head-on the delicate and subjective nature of ego. This readable book develops in a compelling fashion, and provides insightful guidance about how to confront and master ego—largely neglected as a crucial element of successful performance—to drive individual and enterprise performance."

—Herbert S. Wander, Katten Muchin Rosenman LLP, Chicago, Illinois

egonomics

what makes ego our greatest asset
(or most expensive liability)

david marcum & steven smith

A Fireside Book
Published by Simon & Schuster
New York   London   Toronto   Sydney

FIRESIDE
A Division of Simon & Schuster, Inc.
1230 Avenue of the Americas
New York, NY 10020

First Fireside hardcover edition September 2007

FIRESIDE and colophon are registered trademarks
of Simon & Schuster, Inc.

Designed by Mary Austin Speaker
Interior graphics by Terral Cochran

Manufactured in the United States of America

1   3   5   7   9   10   8   6   4   2

Library of Congress Cataloging-in-Publication Data
Marcum, David.
Egonomics : what makes ego our greatest asset (or most expensive liability) /
by David Marcum & Steven Smith.
p.   cm.
"A Fireside Book."
1. Success in business—Psychological aspects.
2. Ego (Psychology).   3. Leadership—
Psychological aspects.   4. Humility.
5. Self-confidence.   I. Smith, Steven.   II. Title.
HF5386 .M30873   2007
658.4'09019—dc22   2006101638

For information about special discounts for bulk purchases,
please contact Simon & Schuster Special Sales at 1-800-456-6798
or business@simonandschuster.com.

ISBN-13: 978-1-4165-3323-8
ISBN-10   1-4165-3323-0

Dedicated to the final ten percent

contents

1
ego and the bottom line   1
why managing the power of ego is the first priority of business

2
the ego balance sheet   21
the four early warning signs that ego is costing your company,
and the three principles of egonomics that turn it around

3
early warning sign 1–being comparative   38
how being too competitive can make us less competitive

4
early warning sign 2–being defensive   55
the difference between defending ideas and being defensive

5
early warning sign 3–showcasing brilliance   74
how intelligence and talent can keep the best ideas from winning

6

early warning sign 4—seeking acceptance   89

how our desire for respect and recognition gets in our way

7

humility   100

opening minds and creating opportunity for change

8

humility, part II: intensity and intent   137

*using humility as a bridge to turn silence
or argument into vigorous debate*

9

curiosity   168

how different types of curiosity unlock our minds and conversations

10

veracity   199

*how to make the undiscussables discussable, and closing the gap between
what we think is going on and what's really going on*

appendix   229

notes   235

acknowledgments   249

index   251

1
ego and the bottom line

Every good thought that we have, and every good action
that we perform, lays us open to pride, and thus exposes us
to the various assaults of vanity and self-satisfaction.

WILLIAM LAW

Ego is the invisible line item on every company's profit and loss
statement.

And because ego's subtly out of sight on the P&L, that's precisely
why for decades, if not centuries, we've become no better—and
maybe no worse—at managing the most pervasive, powerful force
inside every person in every company.

Chances are when you read the opening line of this chapter, the
idea that ego is *profitable* wasn't exactly the first idea to catch your
attention. But despite the negative reputation of ego, it isn't purely
a *loss*. On the profit side, ego sparks the drive to invent and achieve,
the nerve to try something new, and the tenacity to conquer set- ⎫ positives
backs that inevitably come. Surprising as it may sound, many people
don't have enough ego, and that leads to insecurity, hollow partici- ⎭
pation, and apathy that paralyze cultures and leaders.

Invested into every team meeting, boardroom debate, performance review, client conversation, contract negotiation, or employment interview is the potential for ego to work for us or against

us. If we manage ego wisely, we get the upside it delivers followed by strong returns. But when that intense, persistent force inside manages us, companies suffer real economic losses.

Over half of all businesspeople estimate ego costs their company 6 to 15 percent of annual revenue; many believe that estimate is far too conservative. But even if ego were only costing 6 percent of revenue, the annual cost of ego—as estimated by the people working to produce that revenue—would be nearly $1.1 billion to the average Fortune 500 company. That $1.1 billion nearly equals the average annual profit of those same companies. But whether ego costs us 6 percent of revenue or 60, when people estimate those costs, what are they thinking of? Usually the last time they crashed into someone's ego or the latest headlines.

Under the leadership of David Maxwell and then James Johnson, Fannie Mae delivered unmatched performance from 1981 to 1999, beating the general stock market 3.8 to 1. Fannie Mae was listed as one of only eleven companies in Jim Collins's study of 1,435 companies in *Good to Great* that created and sustained unparalleled performance, with leaders to match. On January 1, 1999, however, Franklin Raines replaced Johnson as CEO. Five years later, under pressure from Fannie Mae's board of directors after questionable accounting practices, Raines resigned. "By my early retirement," Raines claimed, "I have held myself accountable."

Ironically, four years earlier, in 2002, Raines was asked to testify before Congress about the collapse of Enron. "It is wholly irresponsible and unacceptable for corporate leaders to say they did not know—or suggest it is not their duty to know—about the operations and activities of their company," Raines told lawmakers, "particularly when it comes to risks that threaten the fundamental viability of their company." Raines walked away from Fannie Mae with a retirement package potentially worth $25 million and total compensation of nearly $90 million during his tenure. He was replaced on December 22, 2004, by Daniel Mudd.

As we were writing this chapter, a colleague emailed us a news release. The headline announced, "Fannie reaches $400 million settlement." The first line of the release read, "Fannie Mae's '*arrogant* and unethical' corporate culture led to an $11 billion accounting scandal at the mortgage giant, federal regulators said Tuesday in announcing a $400 million settlement with the company." [emphasis added] Daniel Mudd's leadership was also questioned. "Fannie Mae thought itself so different, so special, and so powerful," wrote Bethany McLean of *Fortune*, "that it should never have to answer to anybody. And in this, it turned out to be very wrong." It took Fannie Mae almost twenty years to move from good to great, and less than five years to go from great to good to . . . only time will tell.

The risk in the headlines of ego out of control, or the brutal impact of a long buildup of an egotistical culture, is that we can say to ourselves, "We would *never* do that. We're just not that bad." That's true. Ninety-nine percent of us will never be Dennis Kozlowski (Tyco), Ken Lay and Jeffrey Skilling (Enron), Bernie Ebbers (WorldCom), or Martha Stewart or earn a nickname like "Chainsaw Al" (attached to fired Sunbeam CEO Al Dunlap). We won't go to prison or single-handedly cause the collapse of our companies— and that's the trap.

Because those stories are so extreme, rarely do they cause us to ask, "Is *any* part of that true of *our* company?" "What about *my* team?" or "What about *me*?" That's when we tune out, and we miss the behaviors that never get that severe but subtly and surely undercut our ability. As authors, we can tell you from experience and our research that ego-driven behaviors rarely feel extreme at any one moment in time. "We started great," as one Fortune 50 manager said to us. "Over time that greatness led to ego, which then led us back to good, and now we find ourselves needing to start over. We were blind to how our egos were escalating along the way."

Organizations are rarely short of people with enough talent, drive, IQ, imagination, vision, education, experience, or desire. As consultants, in our conversations with leaders and managers following failed projects or average results, we've often heard, "He's very innovative, but . . ." or "She has incredible vision, if she could only . . ." or "We were on the right track, and then all of a sudden . . ." The exceptions to the praise are consistently tied to the escalation of one thing—ego. So if the costs are so deep and persistent, why do people hold on to ego so tightly and, in some cases, even fight for it? That's a question that, early on, we couldn't answer ourselves.

liability or asset?

We started our research with the premise that ego was negative and needed cold-blooded elimination—at least from a business perspective—because it was a hidden cost with zero return. In fact, the working title for this book for a very long time was *egoless*. For nearly two years into this project, that view seemed justified by both micro and macro egonomics. At the micro level, Roy Baumeister of Florida State University and Liqing Zhang of Carnegie Mellon University conducted a series of experiments designed to reveal what kind of financial decisions people would make when their ego was threatened.

In one experiment designed to examine how ego would affect participants' decisions, the researchers assigned people to one of two groups: the "ego-threat" group or the "non-ego-threat" control group. In each of the experiments, participants stood to win money, lose money, or break even to varying degrees. Both groups were given the same instructions: you're about to take part in a "bidding war" similar to an auction, but with only one other person, whom you're obviously trying to beat. The auction is for one dollar. Your goal is to get that dollar for less than a dollar, but you can spend up to five dollars to get it. But each person in the ego-threat group was told privately before starting, "If you're the kind of person who usually chokes under pressure, or you don't think that you have what it takes to win the money, then you might want to play it safe. But it's up to you."

As the bidding soared in the experiment, the people who received the ego "threat" let their bids escalate higher in almost every instance than those who weren't trying to protect their ego. After a drawn-out bidding war, those whose egos had something to prove spent up to $3.71 trying to buy one dollar. In fact, the higher their "self-esteem," the more money they lost. The experiment illustrated how ego entraps people in costly, losing ventures. When participants were interviewed afterward, those who spent more money to "win" in the experiments not only didn't feel good about the money they had spent to win, they felt worse about their own self-esteem. In other words, they lost money *and* self-confidence.

seems ridiculous total lack of common sense.

Because of ego, "people tend to become entrapped . . . and throw away good money after bad decisions," said Baumeister and Zhang. "They get locked into uncompromising career choices, supervisors become overcommitted to those employees who they had expressed a favorable opinion in hiring decisions, senior executives in banks escalate their institution's commitment to problem loans [because *they* approved the loan to begin with] and entrepreneurs and venture capitalists become entrapped in unprofitable projects." The conclusion of their extensive research was that when people feel their ego is threatened, people make "less optimal decisions as judged from the standpoint of financial outcomes."

always use common sense

At a macro level, business performance suffers when ego negatively impacts the *way* we produce. Dr. Paul Nutt of Ohio State University conducted more than two decades of research with hundreds of organizations on why business decisions fail. In examining why 50 percent of decisions fail, he discovered three key reasons:

- Over one-third of all failed business decisions are driven by ego.

- Nearly two-thirds of executives never explore alternatives once they make up their mind.
- Eighty-one percent of managers push their decisions through by persuasion or edict, and not by the value of their idea.

Over the last two and a half years we searched 2,190 news articles (mainly business-related) that used the word *ego* in any way. Eighty-eight percent of the time *ego* was used negatively, usually followed by suggestions on how and why people should get rid of it, and what would happen if they didn't. News articles berate ego-trippers with headlines like "Don't Let Ego Kill the Startup" from *BusinessWeek* or "Ego Slams T.O." (Terrell Owens, NFL wide receiver) from *USA Today*.

Over the last five years, we surveyed thousands of people who attended our leadership sessions and asked them to write down the first words that came to mind as they were shown random words. If the word *ego* flashed in front of you, what would *you* write? Ninety-two percent of the first responses were negative. "Arrogant" is the first word mentioned by almost 5:1, followed by "self-centered," "insecure," "close minded," "defensive," "conceited," and "condescending," if we keep the list clean. Just listen to how people talk about ego—especially someone else's—and it's easy to get the message that ego is the enemy.

For example, if you're in a one-hour meeting and at minute forty-three of that meeting someone lets their ego take control, which minute will be remembered? What effect does that minute have on the previous forty-two? At worst, they're erased. What happens to the next seventeen minutes? At best, they're tainted. And how much time will be wasted after the meeting talking about what happened in the meeting? We may not remember that exact minute, but we will live with the impact. If ego doesn't crash the meeting, it certainly leaves a dent.

As we continued our search for answers, we interviewed, surveyed, and observed people across industries and disciplines to find out why they do what they do. While we scoured hundreds of business articles, periodicals, and a wide range of psychology journals, we also reengaged in a study of leadership and management literature from as early as 1944, when Peter Drucker first began to raise awareness about the modern-day need for a different kind of management. Even though many books had interesting ideas, by our criteria only a handful qualified as landmark books—books whose ideas were so powerful, they changed the way people thought about business.

These well-researched books—such as *The Effective Executive; In Search of Excellence; The Change Masters; Built to Last; First, Break All the Rules*—marked what separates one category of leader or company from the typical. As we examined those themes piece by piece, most outlined techniques, strategies, and tactics for change, but the theories and practices didn't account for the difference between what we read and what we saw in action when ego was in play. By almost all accounts, ego seemed to stake its claim on the business world's most-wanted list.

But there's another side to the story.

ego 2.0

The word *ego* comes from Latin, where it means "I, myself." What people usually mean when they talk about "ego" is that someone *else* is so me-myself-and-I absorbed, that person can't see anything else. Yet "I, myself" isn't always self-absorbed. Open a dictionary or psychology textbook to the entry "ego," and "an inflated sense of self-importance" is quickly followed by the definition "self-confidence." With those same surveyed audiences mentioned earlier, ego also has a positive meaning; 8 percent of the time words surface like "self-confidence," "self-esteem," "open-minded," and "ambitious," with "confidence" cited nearly 10:1. **The further our investigation went, the more it appeared there was an irony about ego: it is both a valuable asset, and a deep liability.** With that dual nature in mind, we turned our search to what moves ego one way or the other.

As fate would have it, one of the most prolific business authors of the last fifty years, Jim Collins, appeared to be on a parallel track to our early work. Collins noted in his *Good to Great* research that two-thirds of the companies that didn't make the leap from good to great were weighed down by the "presence of gargantuan personal ego that contributed to the demise or continued mediocrity of the company." For the eleven companies that made the cut, Collins discovered two unique traits of their leaders: 1) intense professional will, and 2) extreme personal *humility*. He called the rare combination "Level 5" leadership.

Good to Great

As Collins described his findings to a group of executives before his book was released, a newly appointed CEO spoke. "I believe what you say about the good-to-great leaders," she said, "but I'm disturbed because when I look in the mirror, I know that I'm not Level 5, not yet anyway. Part of the reason I got my job is because of my ego drives. Are you telling me I can't make this a great company if I'm not Level 5?" Avoiding a definitive yes, Jim simply pointed to the evidence validating the findings. The group sat quietly for a moment, and she followed with her next question, "Can you learn to become a Level 5?"

He answered that there are two categories of people: those who have it and those who don't. "The first category consists of people who could never in a million years bring themselves to subjugate their egoistic needs to the great ambition of building something larger and more lasting than themselves," said Collins. "The second category of people—and I suspect the larger group—consists of those who have the potential to evolve to Level 5; the capability resides within them, perhaps buried or ignored, but there nonetheless. And under the right circumstances—self-reflection, conscious personal development, a mentor, a great teacher . . . they begin to develop." That's where Collins's answer to her question stopped.

To answer that CEO's question with any degree of hope, a series of questions had to be asked and answered—questions we've been asking for years: What is it about ego that allows leaders to take their organizations to good, but without humility never allows them to move to great? Why does it appear that ego is something we must have if we want to succeed, but having it often interferes with the success we pursue? Are there habits we can develop that manage the drive of ego? Should it be managed in the first place? If humility is so powerful and a necessity for Level 5 leadership, why don't more of us have it? Can we learn to be humble? If ego and humility can't coexist, what has to give, and what change is required? *Egonomics* is the result of the answers to those questions. We believe these findings are the difference between ego working against us as a liability or for us as an appreciating asset. If we know how to use it effectively, the upside of ego is just as powerful as the downside. The first step toward increasing ego's return on investment comes from understanding what "ego" is in the first place and how it works.

[handwritten margin note: dual nature of ego]

egonomic health

To get a clear understanding of the way ego works, picture the way our bodies work. To keep our body healthy, our immune system creates molecules called free radicals that fight viruses and bacteria. However, when environmental factors such as pollution and pesticides cause free radical production to become excessive, the molecules attack not only viruses and bacteria but good cells and vital tissue as well, causing illness, premature aging, cancer, and other diseases.

Ego is a free radical.

In the right amount ego is inherently positive and provides a healthy level of confidence and ambition—driving out insecurity, fear, and apathy. But left unchecked, it goes on a hunt. The primary "cells" ego attacks are our talents and abilities—either through overconfidence and giving the false illusion we're better than we actually are, or by robbing us of confidence so that we lose trust in our ability to use those talents to capacity. **Ego's power is pervasive and relentless but never neutral in how it affects our performance.** Drawn from decades of personality work by experts including Katharine Cook Briggs and Isabel Briggs Myers, Carl Jung, and Taylor Hartman, listed below are talents and traits that cover most personality types. In the boxes, check three to five of your greatest strengths:

1. ☐ assertive
2. ☑ analytical
3. ☐ flexible
4. ☐ charismatic
5. ☐ committed
6. ☐ decisive
7. ☐ dedicated
8. ☐ directive
9. ☐ passionate

10. ☐ dependable
11. ☐ optimistic
12. ☐ open-minded
13. ☑ discerning
14. ☐ loyal
15. ☐ trusting
16. ☐ strong-willed
17. ☐ pragmatic
18. ☑ self-confident

19. ☑ straightforward
20. ☐ alert
21. ☐ diplomatic
22. ☐ determined
23. ☐ courageous
24. ☐ innovative
25. ☐ disciplined
26. ☑ smart
27. ☐ independent

Each of those strengths contributes to who we are. Keeping those traits true to form makes us employable and promotable and allows us to make unique contributions to the companies we work for. If we were to get rid of ego, we would lose what ego provides—the confidence and ambition to build on and take advantage of our talents and traits. But those strengths don't always work to our advantage when we lose control of ego.

from talent to traitor

When we don't manage the intense power of ego effectively, it damages our strengths and turns them into weaknesses. Through ego's overconfidence, overambition, insecurity, or me-centered agenda, our talents take on a slightly different appearance but have a significantly different impact. Looking at the same list of strengths as before, find those you previously checked and transfer them to the list below.

ego-balanced return	egotistical risk
1. ☐ assertive	pushy
2. ☑ analytical	pessimistic
3. ☐ flexible	pushover
4. ☐ charismatic	manipulative
5. ☐ committed	overbearing
6. ☐ decisive	hasty
7. ☐ dedicated	stubborn
8. ☐ directive	dictatorial
9. ☐ passionate	overzealous
10. ☐ dependable	rigid
11. ☐ optimistic	unrealistic
12. ☐ open-minded	indiscriminate
13. ☑ discerning	judgmental
14. ☐ loyal	blind
15. ☐ trusting	naive
16. ☐ strong-willed	inflexible
17. ☐ pragmatic	uninspired
18. ☑ self-confident	self-absorbed
19. ☑ straightforward	inconsiderate
20. ☐ alert	anxious
21. ☐ diplomatic	political
22. ☐ determined	stubborn
23. ☐ courageous	reckless
24. ☐ innovative	impractical
25. ☐ disciplined	restrictive
26. ☑ smart	know-it-all
27. ☐ independent	detached

The point here is not simply that we all have strengths and weaknesses: "I can see the big picture, but I'm not very good with details," or "I'm good with numbers, but I'm uncomfortable with people." That's typical. The crucial point is that when ego isn't balanced (with *what* we'll discuss in depth later), it turns our strengths not into polar opposites but into close counterfeits. That subtle modification becomes the ultimate blind spot, because our weaknesses feel almost the same to us as our strengths. While the difference isn't discernible to us, it is clear to others. When we spot those weaknesses in ourselves or the work culture we're in, we can be confident negative ego is the culprit. The table below shows how strengths turn to weakness and put the value of our talents at risk.

strength	return	costs
charismatic	Paints a vision. Inspires others, attracts talent, keeps people motivated.	Manipulates bad ideas to sound good. People overlook substance for style.
dedicated	Produces. Doesn't let obstacles overcome the end in mind. Finds a way to get things done. Makes no excuses.	Won't consider alternatives. Resists change, even when change proves a better outcome. Cuts off creativity in the name of "getting things done."

strength	return	costs
optimistic	Isn't frozen by "reality," especially when it's negative. Can help people get through difficult times without losing sight of better times ahead. Keeps things in perspective.	Won't listen to bad news. Thinks a positive mental outlook can overcome anything. Rejects bad news as a lack of faith or vision or the pessimism of nonbelievers.
straightforward	Provides a clear path, confronts brutal realities, eliminates guessing.	Creates anxiety, uses little tact and so offends people. Intimidates. Generates gossip.
diplomatic	Invites diversity. Understands the dynamics of group process and facilitates discussion. Works to include those needing inclusion.	Becomes political. Creates divisions and sets people against each other to promote own ideas. Manipulates the process. Focuses more on who wins than on which idea is the best.

(handwritten margin notes: "stubborn" beside the optimistic row; "people need to learn to take the truth" beside the straightforward row)

Note: The complete table of each strength, and its returns and costs, can be found by going to www.egonomicsbook.com.

losing control of ego

In 1996, two rival expedition companies ran separate but concurrent treks to reach the summit of Everest. In that pursuit, nine people died. Even if you've already read the account, the lessons are still relevant. Both fatal expeditions were led by well-seasoned Everest climbers: Rob Hall from New Zealand and Scott Fischer from the United States. Both had the aid of expert guides. Each had led successful expeditions before. Despite unequaled track records, even they weren't immune from the human frailties of confidence turned into a sense of infallibility and of resolve turned into denial. Jon Krakauer, a journalist who signed on with Hall's expedition to do a story for *Outside* magazine, recaps his experience:

> With so many marginally qualified climbers flocking to Everest these days, a lot of people believe that a tragedy of this magnitude was overdue. But nobody imagined that an expedition led by Hall would be at the center of it. Hall ran the tightest, safest operation on the mountain, bar none. So what happened? How can it be explained, not only to the loved ones left behind, but to a censorious public? Hubris surely had something to do with it. Hall had become so adept at running climbers of varying abilities up and down Everest that he may have become a little cocky. He'd bragged on more than one occasion that he could get almost any reasonably fit person to the summit, and his record seemed to support this. He'd also demonstrated a remarkable ability to manage adversity. . . . Hall may well have thought there was little he couldn't handle.
>
> [In addition] the clock had as much to do with the tragedy as the weather, and ignoring the clock can't be passed off as an act of God. Delays at the fixed lines could easily have been

avoided. Predetermined turn-around times were egregiously and willfully ignored. The latter may have been influenced to some degree by the rivalry between Fischer and Hall. Fischer had a charismatic personality, and that charisma had been brilliantly marketed. Fischer was trying very hard to eat Hall's lunch, and Hall knew it. In a certain sense, they may have been playing chicken up there, each guide plowing ahead with one eye on the clock, waiting to see who was going to blink first and turn around.

Most of us don't lose our lives when we momentarily lose control of ego—but we lose a lot: trust, respect, relationships, influence, talent, careers, clients, and market share. Each of us has occasionally, perhaps unknowingly, let ego weaken our talents despite our qualifications, expertise, charisma, track record, or remarkable ability. Carly Fiorina, former CEO of Hewlett-Packard, engineered the highly publicized merger between Compaq and HP. When the signs became evident that the merger wasn't working as planned, one executive remarked, "She's a very, very smart, competent, talented executive. She cannot bite the bullet and say 'We lost.' Other businesspeople can do that and move on. She can't." Fiorina's great determination and optimism served HP well in the beginning. She was ranked as the most powerful woman executive in the United States by *Fortune* magazine. But over time, ego appeared to work against her, and Fiorina's exceptional determination and optimism were too often reduced to inflexibility and denial. Less than three years after the merger she championed, Fiorina was fired. Ego—for good or bad—is so deep-seated in each of us, and therefore embedded in the way we use our talents to lead, manage, think, talk, listen, decide, and take action, it deserves our unqualified attention as a first priority.

[handwritten margin note: always be aware of how you are perceived]

r.o.i.

When an organization invests in us for our talents, it also inherits the potential counterfeits of those talents. "The great organization must not only accommodate the fact that each employee is different, it must capitalize on those differences," wrote Marcus Buckingham and Donald Clifton in *Now, Discover Your Strengths*. "It must watch for clues to each employee's natural talents and then position and develop each employee's natural talents so that his or her talents are transformed into bona fide strengths." Equally important to that development is to watch for early warning signs of ego that signal when natural talents have become natural enemies.

warning signs

When ego works against us, these four early warning signs indicate we're losing value: 1) being comparative, 2) being defensive, 3) showcasing brilliance, and 4) seeking acceptance. When those signs appear, rest assured we're losing talent. The greater the intensity or frequency of the early warning signs, the steeper the decline in value. How effectively we manage ego determines the "risk, reward" ratio for each of us—whether we're the most valuable asset to the business, or the reddest cost.

To gauge that ratio, the next logical question we wanted answered as authors was how often people observe that individual strengths and organizational value evaporate in the name of ego. If the evaporation rate was low, we were ready to check ego off as an interesting but only mildly impactful topic and move on. Currently, 63 percent of businesspeople say ego negatively impacts work performance on an hourly or daily basis, while an additional 31 percent say it happens weekly. Even if we recruit the best and brightest people on the market, once we have that talent on the payroll, we don't *really* have it when ego interferes with the way we work. In getting full access to that talent, measuring ego's cost by the clock may be more accurate than by the calendar. Any way it's measured, performance takes a hit: 35 percent of managers who take new jobs fail and either quit or are asked to leave within eighteen months.

talent supply and demand

Companies not only can't afford for individual talents to weaken from ego, they can't afford egocentric cultures. One Fortune 1,000 CEO we interviewed for this book was giving us background on his company's progress. After praising two specific competitors, he ended his comments by saying, "They're operationally excellent, and I do think their *current* performance is sustainable," he said, "but they can't keep people. Their culture isn't healthy, and I would probably describe their culture as a little egotistical. I believe that will keep them exactly where they are." Companies like that stagnate as their people check out by walking out the door or divesting mentally, and the reputation of the company in the labor market suffers.

[handwritten: egotistical culture]

Those same organizations then have to attract talent primarily by pay, missing the opportunity to attract talent by the opportunities for growth the company provides or the desire people have to work there. When people work hard to stay employable, they won't bet their career on a company where prospects for personal growth look weak and employment is unstable. In turn, talent looks for a home somewhere else. The ripple effect is that companies become less competitive and are marginalized by the lack of talent.

[handwritten: Google. why do ppl want to work there? Self-growth and focus on employees' wellbeing]

If those cultures are as prevalent as most think they are, then we shouldn't be surprised that 65 percent of those currently employed are looking for new jobs, and 28 million people every year leave where they work. While there are certainly other factors that affect those numbers, at $50,000 per employee in hiring and training costs across all jobs and industries, that's $1.4 trillion annually, or $7.5 million for the midsized company of one thousand employees with annual turnover of 10 percent. Losing talent is an increasingly unaffordable cost. "After 500 years or so—the scarcest, most valuable resource in business is no longer financial capital. It's talent," said Geoffrey Colvin of *Fortune*. "If you doubt that, just watch how hard companies are battling for the best people . . . there isn't nearly enough of the very best stuff."

By the year 2010, over half of all U.S. workers will be over forty, and the decades ahead will see baby boomers (born between 1946 and 1964) being replaced by Gen Xers (born between 1965 and 1981) and millennials (born between 1980 and 2000). That shift will create a supply and demand gap of over ten million workers within the next 2,700 days. To make matters worse, when 2,900 HR executives and managers were interviewed, only one-third were confident they would have enough talent in the pipeline to keep their businesses moving forward as the workforce changes.

"There's an imminent leadership crisis at many big companies," said Paul Terry of the consulting firm Novations Group, who worked on the survey. "They have less management bench strength than at any time in memory." Bench strength can be lost by the lack of numbers. The same bench is also weakened by the talent lost to ego. The principles of egonomics aren't the only route to maximized talent and leadership bench strength, but these assets are at high risk without them.

the bottom line

Often the hardest side of business to master is the human side, and nothing is more human than ego. How we manage ego on the human side affects everything we do on the business side, one way or the other. It's up to each of us to shift the momentum of the one thing that shifts the energy of everything else we do. That shift requires each of us to take a piercing look at the way we work—conversation by conversation, proj-

reflections

ect by project, meeting by meeting. There are three principles of egonomics that, when fused together, make that shift: 1) humility, 2) curiosity, and 3) veracity. These three principles not only require us to *do differently*, they require us to *be different*. To the degree we change, our talents are liberated to the strategic benefit of our companies and careers, and the way we work is not only more effective, it's easier. As a result, organizations become capable of:

- building an open-minded culture where change and new ideas aren't resisted, and business agendas aren't overshadowed by personal agendas.
- maximizing individual talent and organizational strengths by capitalizing on the strengths of ego and minimizing its weaknesses.
- creating intense business debate about ideas with the intention of progress without the drag of conflict and premature judgment.
- cultivating relationships strong enough (and cultures safe enough) to share watercooler honesty and nontraditional thinking during meetings, rather than after—or never.
- effectively dealing with the ego of others when it's hurting performance or preventing/slowing innovation.

culture of the workplace idea Google culture

We know we're not offering a "final" answer; we don't believe anyone has a final answer. We *do* hope to ignite a conversation long overdue that can subtract the needless work and talent depreciation caused by ego that undermines corporate performance and careers. In the next chapter we'll highlight the four early warning signs that signal ego is becoming a liability—to your company, your career, or even just a conversation. We'll follow that with the three principles of egonomics that tap the power of ego and keep it squarely in the asset column of business.

1: ego and the bottom line | key points

- Ego is the invisible P&L line item. Currently, 51 percent of businesspeople estimate that ego costs their company 6 to 15 percent of annual revenue; 21 percent say that the cost ranges from 16 to 20 percent.

- Ego is both a liability *and* an asset: ego works for us and against us, depending on how it's managed.

- Ego gives us confidence to use our greatest strengths, but it also turns them into weaknesses that counterfeit those same strengths.

- Currently, 63 percent of businesspeople say ego negatively impacts work performance on an hourly or daily basis, while an additional 31 percent say it happens weekly.

- Organizations where ego is poorly managed then have to attract talent primarily by pay, missing the opportunity to attract talent by the opportunities for growth the company provides or the desire people have to work there. The ripple effect is that companies become less competitive and are marginalized by the lack of talent.

- When an organization invests in us for our talents, it also inherits the potential counterfeits of those talents. When ego's working against us, four early warning signs indicate we're losing value: 1) being comparative, 2) being defensive, 3) showcasing brilliance, or 4) seeking acceptance.

- To counteract the four early warning signs of ego, there are three principles of egonomics: 1) humility, 2) curiosity, and 3) veracity.

2
the ego balance sheet

Ego is our silent partner—too often with a controlling interest.

CULLEN HIGHTOWER

In a typical business meeting it can take as little as five minutes to determine if ego is lessening the honesty of what's said, lowering trust, diminishing the sincerity with which people listen, clouding the accuracy of assessments, and altering the openness of debates. When those warning signs appear, ego is becoming a liability rather than an asset. Those signs are 1) being comparative, 2) being defensive, 3) showcasing brilliance, and 4) seeking acceptance. The earlier we see the signs, the faster we can take action to correct ourselves or lead others to self-correct, and lessen the damage ego does. Here's a summary of each sign, which we will cover thoroughly in later chapters.

early warning sign 1—being comparative

Ironically, being too competitive makes us less competitive. By fixating on someone else, we lose unrecoverable time that could be devoted to becoming uniquely great; we give up our potential in the name of becoming "better than" or at least "as good as" someone else. "Better than" is a strategy for ordinary. "The competitor to be

focus not on others, but yourself.

feared is one who never bothers about you at all," said Henry Ford, "but goes on making his own business better all the time."

Excessive comparison also turns colleagues into competitors, and competitors aren't effective collaborators. A meta-analysis of 265 studies over fifty-six years found there was almost no task on which competitive or individualistic efforts were more effective than collaborative efforts. The rare exceptions were physical tasks that required little thought and no collaboration. In addition, when we're comparative, either we tend to pit our strengths against another's weaknesses, which may lead us to an exaggerated sense of confidence, or we compare our weaknesses to their strengths, which can cause negative self-pressure.

collaboration vs. individualism

in either case, comparing leads to failure.

When we're too comparative, the goal we reach for is someone else's standard of success. While under the influence of comparison, we don't discern whether the standard is so low that in leaping it we barely tap our potential, or is so unrealistic that we fail and become discouraged trying to achieve something we can't, or isn't the best use of our talents. In any case, we accomplish less.

early warning sign 2—being defensive

There's a vital difference between defending an idea and *being* defensive. The motive behind defending an idea is to let the best argument win. Because nobody is all-knowing, the best decisions are the result of rigorous independent thinking followed by passionate, collaborative debate. To cover every angle of a debate before we make key decisions, we lay out our best thinking and defend it passionately. Because the intent is progress, we are equally interested in hearing opposing arguments. In fact, in the true spirit of real debate, we may even create counterarguments when others agree too quickly. That openness lets the validity of an idea win or disappear—either outcome being equally okay, regardless of the intensity with which we make our case.

decision making

(handwritten margin notes: ideas vs. self / when ego takes over. / negative results)

But when we cross the line from defending to being defensive—even momentarily—seeing our idea "disappear" isn't an option. When we can't "lose," we defend our positions as if we're defending who we are, and the debate shifts from a we-centered battle of ideas to a me-centered war of wills. With the change of intent, we focus on proving our case and deflecting differing points. At our defensive worst, we refuse to be influenced at all, regardless of gaps in logic or inaccuracies—which we no longer see. We resist feedback, brush off mistakes, withhold apologies, and our discussions become superficial exercises.

In refusing to change our minds or see things differently, we emerge from debates with ultimatums rather than options, and we rely on political power or positions of authority to force our agenda whenever we can. As for those being forced by our egocentric will rather than persuaded by the merit of ideas, they will offer only half-hearted support, and the desired change or adoption of the ideas never genuinely occurs. As we'll discuss later, research shows that while people believe they are open to feedback on ways they can improve and listen without being defensive, the people who work closely with them disagree.

early warning sign 3—showcasing brilliance

At face value showcasing brilliance, or highlighting our talent, seems like something we would want to do. If we hide our talent, what good does that do the company or our career? None. But showcasing isn't about making our brilliance visible. It's about making it the center of attention and unduly occupying time and energy. The more we want or expect people to recognize, appreciate, or be dazzled by how smart we are, the less they listen, *even if we do have better ideas*. "We should take care not to make [brilliance] our god," Einstein reminds us. "It has, of course, powerful muscles, but no personality. It cannot lead, it can only serve."

When we allow showcasing to occur, the casualty is collective wisdom. As we'll cover later, studies prove collective intelligence outperforms the brightest individual in everything from bean-counting contests to stock market performance to complex problem solving. The people we already have in our companies are exactly what we need. Together they possess the knowledge needed to solve the problems we face or to innovate and seize new opportunities.

early warning sign 4—seeking acceptance

Leadership is best reserved for those who don't need positions of leadership to validate who they are. Being aware of what people think is a sign of great leadership. Becoming oversensitive to what people think of us keeps us from being true to ourselves. That in turn places speaking our mind behind personal promotion or public opinion. Acceptance and respect are among the most fundamental needs we have. But when we equate acceptance or rejection of our ideas with acceptance or rejection of who we are, we "play it safe." We tend to swim with the current and find a slightly different way of saying what's already been said as long as acceptance is the outcome. That makes us not only a bland follower but an uninspiring leader.

One of the main risks of seeking acceptance is that it drives intellectual diversity and independent thinking underground. Group applause and universal harmony don't make for the best decisions. The first rule of making good decisions is to not make a decision unless there's been vigorous debate and differing points of view—which, if done well, is likely to have included some disagreement. Seeking acceptance may be the most subtle of the early warning signs because it's so "nice" and doesn't draw attention to itself.

[handwritten margin notes: fragile equilibrium; ideas vs. self; decision making. also balances accountability; Akash.]

from business to home and back again

The early warning signs that ego is working against us rather than for us aren't limited to business. John Gottman is a world-renowned research scientist on marriage and family at the University of Washington. We recently spent a weekend with John and Julie Gottman at their marriage retreat in Seattle. For thirty years Gottman has tracked the correlation between certain marital behaviors and marriage satisfaction and longevity. Watching and listening—second by second—to over three thousand couples in three separate studies at a place affectionately known as "the Love Lab," his research team records everything from a couple's heart rates to facial expressions to stress levels as they communicate. It is the largest scientific study of marriage ever undertaken.

Though Gottman refers to his work as "extremely simple-minded science," the revelations from his work are anything but ordinary. After only three minutes of observation he can predict with 96 percent accuracy whether a marital discussion will resolve a conflict. He can predict divorce rates with 91 percent accuracy after as little as five minutes of observation. His remains the highest prediction rate ever for a scientific study of relationships. His remarkable accuracy isn't driven by what couples argue or talk about, their personality differences, or—believe it or not—how often or even how intensely they argue.

He primarily looks for behaviors driven by excessive ego. He calls these behaviors—stonewalling, defensiveness, criticism, and contempt—the "four horsemen of the apocalypse." The result of his research allows him to help couples improve—and save—their marriages. Gottman's marital therapy relapse rate is only 20 percent, while relapse rates nationwide run between 30 and 50 percent.

Every couple experiences the "four horsemen of the apocalypse" now and then. That's normal. If those signs appear, it doesn't mean a relationship is doomed, unless the couple does nothing about the problem. What's sad is that couples don't recognize the signs until it's too late. "Only after the papers have been signed, the furniture divided, and separate apartments rented," says Gottman, "do the exes realize how much they really gave up when they gave up on each other. There is a remarkable similarity between what makes a marriage work and what makes a business relationship work.

If you recognize in yourself any of the early warning signs we've mentioned above (being comparative, being defensive, showcasing brilliance, and seeking acceptance), that's normal. It doesn't mean you're doomed, unless you don't take action. When it comes to ego, you can take small steps that stop the damage. But you'll never take those steps if you can't see the warning signs in the first place. Since awareness is crucial to the cure, we explore each warning sign in depth.

We will point out the reasons the warning signs show up and when they're most likely to appear. It's important to know that for each sign, there's a precise amount of that behavior that's healthy. For example, when managed effectively, comparison pushes us to reach our best and motivates us to change. But despite the benefits connected with each sign, there's a tipping point where they become destructive. (Later we will cover those tipping points for each of the early warning signs.) When we see, hear, or feel the early warning signs of negative ego—in ourselves or others—there are three principles that keep individual talents and organizational performance from oxidizing.

three principles of egonomics

For a moment, let's return to the analogy of ego as a free radical. To keep our body's free radical count in balance, our body produces antioxidants. Those antioxidants act as hunters that track down excessive free radicals and neutralize them, keeping us and our immune system healthy. Our body doesn't produce enough antioxidants on its own, but a diet rich in vitamins A, C, and E helps the body protect itself against the destructive effects of free radicals.

In matters of personal ability, the same principle of a balanced diet applies. The health of our company's culture, our conversations, and our careers relies heavily on three key "antioxidants" that track down excessive ego free radicals (the early warning signs) and neutralize them, allowing our talents to stay true to form and our company's culture productive. The three principles of egonomics that keep ego working as an asset rather than a liability are 1) humility, 2) curiosity, and 3) veracity. Here's a preview of each one we will explore in depth later in the book.

1. humility

Humility is the first principle of egonomics because of its unique ability to open minds. Until we're ready to listen and learn, curiosity and veracity are never invited on stage. But as crucial as an open mind is, that may not even be the most essential characteristic of humility. Humility is a means to an end, and that end is the progress of the business. [Discussions and debates that facilitate true progress require we temporarily suspend what we think is best for *us* to consider what's in the best interests of the *business*.] From a business perspective, humility doesn't lose sight of "me," but it also doesn't let our own needs interfere with open dialogue and intense debate. With that intention of progress, we discovered a characteristic of humility we came to call "constructive discontent." — *productive debate*

Without losing confidence in who we are or lessening the importance of what we've achieved, humility has the unique ability to create a craving to reach the next level of performance. Without an open mind, no questions are asked about what that next level might be. And even when questions are asked, without humility we hear

only selective replies. Humility swallows excessive ego and chan-
nels our ambition into the business success of "we" rather than a
selfish, short-lived agenda of only "me." Humility doesn't replace
"me" with "we" but places our focus in the proper sequence, for the
right reasons, and at the right time.

In one survey, *Fast Company* asked 1,665 respondents to rate
leaders in various types of organizations on their ability to lead. Of
the abilities they saw in their leaders, characteristics like being passionate about work or ruthless for success rated high. Unselfishness
rated dead last. In one of our surveys, nearly eight out of ten people
wished their organizations were more humble. Interestingly, when
we're teaching those same people and we begin the discussion of
becoming more humble, there is hesitancy until we explore what
humility really means As a trait, humility is the point of equilibrium between too much ego and not enough. Humility has the
reputation of being the polar opposite of excessive ego. In fact, the
exact opposite of excessive ego is no confidence at all. Humility
provides the crucial balance between the two extremes. To borrow
a phrase from Alcoholics Anonymous, humility requires not that
we think less of ourselves, but that we think of ourselves less often.
Humility is not the equivalent of being weak, ignored, indifferent,
boring, or a pushover. If it is to be a point of equilibrium, humility
must include confidence, ambition, and willpower.

Without a clear understanding of what humility is, it can be
seen as a trait best left to special causes and religious leaders, not
businesspeople If humility seems to be an outdated concept in a
fiercely competitive world, it's because humility is misunderstood,
understudied, and underused—and, consequently, underesti-
mated. As an indispensable trait of great leadership, humility must
make its way past the pulpit of Sunday sermons and into cubicles
and boardrooms. Humility should be our first reflex, not our regret
once the moment has past.

passed.

2. curiosity

Once humility creates an open mind and a deep commitment to progress, curiosity is the active ingredient that drives the exploration of ideas. Curiosity gives us permission and courage to test what we think, feel, and believe to be true, reminding us we don't know everything about anything. If we lead with questions rather than answers, curiosity can strip us of an agenda and stop us from holding so tightly to our own ideas and beliefs that we aren't able to consider others'. The good news is that most everyone is curious, so we have a head start. But there is a difference in the type of curiosity we have and the degree to which we're curious. That difference is a vital answer in determining the value we create. Highly curious people are different than you might imagine; they have a unique ability to bring both openness and order to conversations, not excluding either in the way they think.

Curiosity is so potent that just extending the invitation to be curious makes a difference in performance. A group of business students at the University of Michigan was split into two teams and given an identical business case to solve. The instructions given to both groups were also identical, except for two small words; group two was told to "be creative." Thirty-nine percent of students in group one solved the case successfully, while 52 percent in group two solved it successfully. Creativity springs from curiosity, and something as simple as reminding people to be curious makes a difference. We'll take the discussion beyond a reminder by exploring different types of curiosity and show how it unlocks minds and conversations.

3. veracity

Veracity is the third principle of egonomics that keeps ego working for us rather than against us. *Veracity* is the English word for the

Latin term *veritas*, which means "truth." But why would truth be an antioxidant of unhealthy ego, and why not just say the word *truth* if that's what we mean? *Truth* essentially refers to facts or reality; it implies accuracy and honesty. Veracity, however, differs slightly from truth; veracity is the habitual pursuit of, and adherence to, truth. Veracity differs from truth in action, not in value.

So why is veracity an "antioxidant"? Who doesn't want the truth? It's not that people don't want the truth, but we don't always want all of it. What part wouldn't we want? The part that's hard to hear. What fraction of the truth wouldn't we want to address? The portion that's hard to say. There is a point and time in almost every important business discussion where we might be curiously exploring or intensely debating, and we stumble upon brutal facts. Humility's constructive discontent almost always brings to the surface a truth difficult to hear. "Truth," said Oliver Wendell Holmes, "when not sought after, rarely comes to light." If openness and progress are the outcome of humility, and innovation is the aim of curiosity, then veracity is the light that exposes the truth hidden in the shadows of habits and comfort zones. As we discuss later, veracity is as important to leadership as vision, strategy, integrity, execution, or passion.

a study of moments

Very early in my career, I (Dave) was asked by a mentor what I thought the difference was between a very good leader and an exceptional one. Wanting to give an impressive answer, I pointed to several key characteristics. He said, "I believe it's different than all of that. It's about ten minutes." What he meant by "ten minutes" is that in a typical day we make decisions in a moment. The decisions from those moments throughout a day carry us down a path and we reap the results. The difference between very good and exceptional is the humility, curiosity, and veracity that drive our decisions in those ten minutes when our decisions are made—moments that can appear anywhere and at any time.

During dinner with a friend, a moment appeared for me. Unexpectedly my wife turned and began asking my friend Todd questions about a digital camera she wanted to buy. The questions were perfectly normal. But that's not what the little voice inside my head was saying. "Why is she asking him and not me? We haven't even talked about this before. Why is she bringing it up now?" Startled at what was happening inside my head, I lost track of their conversation in favor of the one I was having with my ego.

As I analyzed what was happening, I asked myself these questions: "What's going on down deep that made me ask that question? What's wrong with her asking Todd? I don't know much about digital cameras. Why do I even care if she asks him?" Wrapping up my silent conversation I smiled, realizing how easy it is to go on an ego trip. After all, as a man I'm capable of pretending to have an answer when I haven't a clue. "What are you smiling about?" Karen asked after Todd left. I wanted to quickly get past it, so I said, "Oh, nothing." "Was there anything wrong with my questions?" she asked. "No, not at all," I replied. Then she followed with a question I wasn't ready for. "Did it bother you I asked Todd before I asked you?" Everything inside me wanted to say, "No big deal." But that wasn't true. I confessed.

My ego tripped me in a moment during a simple dinner conversation about something as trivial as a camera. **In a fifteen-minute conversation, we might spend fourteen minutes with our ego balanced and checked—but it only takes one moment to undo the previous fourteen.** A variety of situations, people, and moments will test us differently. Those moments may come unexpectedly and pass quickly, defining the difference between what we are and what we could be.

perfect moments, not perfect leaders

Everyone has their defining moments. In 1994, Jeffrey Immelt was vice president and general manager of GE Plastics Americas. Instead of hitting his 20 percent profit growth goal, he delivered 7 percent—a net miss of $50 million. At the annual GE leadership meeting, Immelt used his most creative strategies to avoid running into Jack Welch, GE's famous CEO. Immelt would arrive late to group dinners and leave early, and strategically place himself in meetings on the opposite end of the room from Welch. On the last night, halfway to his escape to the elevator, Immelt felt a hand on his shoulder. It was Welch. "Jeff, I'm your biggest fan, but you just had the worst year in the company. I love you," said Welch, "and know you can do better. But I'm going to take you out [of your position] if you can't get it fixed."

Imagine that moment if you were Immelt. He could take the one-on-one opportunity with Welch to justify the performance. Any one or all of ego's early warning signs could have surfaced. He might have defensively complained about a lack of support, shifted responsibility to others, faulted changing market conditions, or pointed to government interference. He could have compared his track record to others to minimize the deficit, or used his intellect to create compelling justification from industry trends. He'd been given an open invitation for an ego trip. But that's not what happened. "Look, if the results aren't where they should be," said Immelt, "you won't have to fire me because I'm going to leave on my own."

Even though Immelt's job was in jeopardy, that response revealed his agenda: a concern for the company first, himself second. Immelt wasn't fighting to protect himself or his job. It's not that he lost sight of himself; he simply had the right perspective. Three years later Welch appointed Immelt as president and CEO of GE

Medical Systems, a division of GE. Four years after that promotion, GE's board of directors appointed Immelt as the replacement for Jack Welch as CEO.

We asked Welch what impression that brief elevator meeting with Immelt had left him with. He didn't remember the incident specifically, but then followed with something that made us think: "I probably thought Jeff's response was typical Jeff." And that's the point: what's typical? For each of us, in the most difficult moments, what would someone say is *typical* of us? Without a specific memory, what would people assign to us by default because of the way we've responded in our tests of leadership? How we act in those moments steadily adds up to typify our careers. In that pursuit, we will each make mistakes along the way—plenty of them. We can't let imperfection discourage us.

In the search for people who perfectly balance ego with humility, curiosity, and veracity, we came up short. We can't point to one person in history and say without reservation, "Look to her," or "Emulate him." Despite some inspiring examples, there was always more than one "yeah, but . . ." along the way. As much praise and credit as great leaders like William Hewlett and David Packard of HP, Darwin Smith of Kimberly-Clark, or Colman Mockler of Gillette deserve for being humble, determined leaders, our discussions with people who worked with them revealed they were human.

Among presidents and prime ministers, civil rights leaders, inventors, and entrepreneurs, whether public servants or private citizens, close inspection always revealed imperfect moments. That discovery only gave us more hope for what's possible in spite of our imperfections. Egonomic success doesn't require anyone to be superhuman—just determined.

There have been critical moments in the lives of all great leaders—in fact, in all our lives—when we didn't let our ego inappropriately drive our response or the agenda, and that choice made all the difference. *Egonomics* is an examination of what those moments reveal. But unless we're willing to open our minds and take an inventory of ourselves, this book will be nothing more than an intellectual tour of ideas. It can be tempting to think of who else needs to read this book. Don't wait for others to change first; most won't.

You can—one moment at a time.

Small changes in the way we think and behave make a surprisingly big difference in making the most of those moments. History shows there will be a few who succeed, and greatness is usually found in small numbers.

momentum

As we were completing this book (Steve recalls), a friend of mine died in a tragic plane crash. Unable to cancel a client engagement, I missed his funeral. Upon arriving home, I drove to his gravesite. The marker with his name on it was surrounded by dozens of bouquets. I stared at the freshly cut grass placed over his casket. I placed my hand on the turf and expected to find a conclusion. Instead, I felt suffocated—barricaded from one more chance to interact with him. I couldn't understand why. I expected a period to the sentence of this episode, and instead I found another comma. Unresolved that evening, I asked my wife, Kitty, what the funeral was like. The church where they held his services had been filled to overflowing. My friend's wife delivered the eulogy. Kitty described the delivery of his eulogy and the entire experience as "educational, uplifting, and filled with hope."

My friend taught people how to be producers in society, not just takers. In that church were hundreds of people who had been profoundly affected by his message. At the instant Kitty shared the feeling at his funeral, I felt the momentum of his life. The energy of his message wasn't extinguished by his death. He was gone, but the momentum of his life continued through other people.

Each of us is like my friend. We are momentum creators. What momentum we create is up to each of us, but it won't be stolen by death. That momentum will be shaped by the next conversation we have or the next decision we make. The word *momentum* is related to the word *moment*, and those moments for humility, curiosity, and veracity present themselves every day, in every meeting, with every person. Those moments aren't meant to weigh us down with the pressure of perfection; rather they give us the opportunity to live and lead a little better today than we did yesterday.

2: the ego balance sheet | key points

- In a typical business meeting it can take as little as five minutes to determine if ego is negatively affecting a discussion or a decision.

- **early warning sign 1—being comparative.** Ironically, being too competitive makes us less competitive. By fixating on someone else, we give up our potential in the name of becoming "better than" or at least "as good as" someone else.

- **early warning sign 2—being defensive.** There's a vital difference between defending an idea and being defensive. The motive behind defending an idea is to let the best argument win. When we're defensive, we defend our positions as if we're defending who we are.

- **early warning sign 3—showcasing brilliance.** Showcasing isn't about making our brilliance visible—it's about making it the center of attention. The more we want or expect people to recognize, appreciate, or be dazzled by how smart we are, the less they listen, *even if we do have better ideas*.

- **early warning sign 4—seeking acceptance.** Leadership is best reserved for those who don't need a leadership position to validate who they are. Being aware of what people think is a sign of great leadership. Becoming oversensitive to what people think of us keeps us from being true to ourselves.

- **Humility** is the first principle of egonomics because of its unique ability to open minds. Humility is a means to an end, and that end is the progress of the business. Another characteristic of humility is constructive discontent. Without causing loss of confidence or lessening the importance of what we've achieved, humility craves the next level of performance.

- **Curiosity** is the active ingredient that drives exploration of ideas. Curiosity gives us permission and courage to test what we think, feel, and believe to be true, reminding us we don't know everything about anything.
- **Veracity** is the habitual pursuit of and adherence to truth. It helps make the undiscussables discussable and closes the gap between what we think is going on and what's really going on.

3
early warning sign 1

being comparative

Every man in the world is better than someone else and
not as good as someone else.

WILLIAM SAROYAN

We make comparisons every day: prices, candidates, car lanes,
diets, job offers, movie reviews, wines, restaurants, temperatures,
and on and on. Comparison is a necessary, natural, minute-by-
minute part of our lives. As an unconscious habit it can be either an
effective tool or a weapon that turns against us.

A frequent companion of comparison is competition—preached
as the capitalist way of life. As Andrew Carnegie said, "[Competi-
tion] is here; we cannot evade it; no substitutes for it have been
found; and while the law may be sometimes hard for the individual,
it is best for the race, because it ensures the survival of the fittest in

every department." Because we're immersed in competition, and the competitive spirit pushes us to do better, we hardly notice when it makes us worse.

are you a turkey?

In his famous fable "The Fox and the Turkeys," Jean de La Fontaine tells of a group of confident turkeys who suffered the consequences of being preoccupied with an opponent. The fox in the story is determined to make a group of turkeys his feast. But using the high perch of a forest tree as their haven from the fox, the turkeys stay out of reach and mock the futile attempts of the fox to reach them. After hours of jeering and taunts, the fox changes his strategy. Rather than keep trying to get to the turkeys, he gets the turkeys to come to him. On the stage of the forest floor beneath the spotlight of the moon, the fox entertains the turkeys throughout the night.

The turkeys find the fox's antics so amusing, they can't take their eyes off him the entire night, despite their need for sleep. Eventually they grow tired, drift off to sleep, and fall from their perches. Then the fox fills up on turkey dinner and saves the leftovers. De La Fontaine closes his fable:

> A foe, by being over-heeded,
> Has often in his plan succeeded.

By not watching modern-day foxes too closely, *CSI* executive producer Anthony Zuiker created the most successful crime drama in television history. Currently, all three *CSI* series (*CSI, CSI Miami, CSI New York*) are in the top ten on Nielsen's television ratings. When asked how he manages to keep producing *CSI*s without diluting the brand, Zuiker responded, "The thing I'm most proud of is that *we didn't react to the competition*. Some of the other crime shows have added labs and are doing more forensics, and there have been all kinds of knockoffs watering down the market, but we've held true. You need to evolve, but you don't need to evolve defensively. That's a classic mistake." [emphasis added] Ironically, we lose our competitive edge when we cross the line and become *too* competitive.

But where is that line?

Let's explore where that thin line is, how deeply it divides healthy from unhealthy comparison and competition, and how to recognize that line before crossing it.

mirror, mirror, on the wall

Sometimes we're hardly aware we've crossed the line. In one study, researchers asked people to rank how much they liked ordinary, everyday items like a drink holder, comb, stapler, and so on. But the survey had a catch: each person was given one of the items on the list as a gift *before* they were asked to rank their preferences. As trivial as the gift seems, people ranked the gift they received higher when comparing and then ranking the twenty items. If it's ours, it *must* be better!

In another study, researchers found that we're influenced by something as simple as the letters in our name. The results showed there is statistically an overrepresentation of Georges in Georgia, Virginias in Virginia, and Marys in Maryland. There are more lawyers named Lawrence, dentists named Dennis or Denise, and hardware stores owned by people whose names begin with the letter *H* than would normally be represented. In the normal course of life, even the smallest details create bias that makes us less objective without any awareness on our part, and therefore less effective in our comparisons. But even when we are aware, our self-bias plays a sizable role when judging ourselves against others.

U.S. News & World Report asked one thousand people how likely particular celebrities were to reach heaven. The choices included people like Oprah Winfrey, Dennis Rodman, Mother Teresa, Mi-

chael Jordan, Bill Clinton, and Princess Diana. The winner was
Mother Teresa: 79 percent believed she was heavenbound. That
question was followed by asking readers how likely *they* (the readers) were to go to heaven. Eighty-seven percent of respondents
voted themselves into heaven. So, according to the survey, if there's
only one lot left in heaven, and God has to choose between us and
Mother Teresa, we believe the divine real estate is ours. If Mother
Teresa doesn't win by comparison with us, you might guess that
neither does anyone else.

The tendency to see ourselves through rose-colored glasses
doesn't stop with our views of the afterlife. We surveyed nearly
1,800 people to ask how confident they were in making good decisions. Eighty-three percent rated themselves as very confident or
confident. When we asked how confident they were in the ability of
the people they work most closely with, confidence dropped from
83 percent to 27 percent. Can we really be that good, and everyone
else that bad? When we weigh ourselves against others through the
eyes of pure ego, we're likely to favor ourselves. When that favorable view isn't validated by performance, excessive comparison
justifies the gap. Maybe they were lucky. Maybe they had an advantage we didn't know about. Maybe we didn't do as well as we normally do. Maybe all of that is true. Maybe it's not.

True or not, excessive comparison drives us to search for areas
where others don't match up to us, and we breathe a competitive
sigh of relief when we find the gaps. For example, Andrew Oswald,
a professor of economics at the University of Warwick in the United
Kingdom, surveyed over 16,000 workers in eight hundred organizations and found salary has little impact on job happiness. That
finding isn't surprising or even new. But what is surprising is how
much we rely on comparison for satisfaction. When Oswald looked
at an employee's position in a company, rank influenced how proud
people were with their professional achievements. In fact, rank in-

creased happiness 50 to 60 percent, even when compared to the size of their paychecks.

In other words, when we're too comparative, ranking higher than someone else matters more than how much money we earn or what we've actually achieved. In a second experiment, Oswald asked students how satisfied they would be with a job offering a yearly salary of $32,000 after graduation. Some were told the salary was the second lowest in the firm, while others were told it was the fifth from the bottom. The higher the salary ranked, the more satisfied students were with their prospective job—regardless of the offer itself.

Research on social comparisons show the more uncertain we are about who we are or what we have, the more automatic and persistent our comparisons become. **Unfair or inaccurate comparison not only steals credit from the person we're comparing against when they deserve credit, it interferes with the opportunity to make the most of our situation—independent of anyone, or anything, else.** Then we stall, waiting for luck or destiny to find us and deliver our portion of comparative success. The tax we pay emotionally on comparison doesn't help us or change anything.

When trapped by comparison—even temporarily—we're not nearly as interested in helping others advance as we are in advancing ourselves. There is in most of us a fierce desire to be "better than"—more valued, loved, rewarded, and respected. "Pride gets no pleasure out of having something," wrote C. S. Lewis, "only out of having more of it than the next man." It's very different to think "I'm better than he is" versus "I'm better than I was." Perhaps more important, mistaking the two makes us discouraged when we shouldn't be.

oprah versus *bride of chucky*

In 1998, Oprah Winfrey released her first film as a producer, *Beloved*. She considered the film one of the greatest accomplishments of her life, in a life with quite a few achievements. The movie grossed $23 million at the box office: by Hollywood's standards, it tanked. In box office revenues, her film was beaten by *Bride of Chucky*'s opening weekend. In her own words, she was "disheartened and depressed." But the reason she felt disheartened wasn't really the movie's performance; it was an unfair and ineffective comparison. Working through her disappointment, Oprah lamented one evening to her close friend Gary Zukav. Zukav asked her a profound question that brought her comparison to an accurate view: "What was your intention?"

"My intention," she replied, "was to create a movie so powerful that it would allow people to feel, not just see, what it meant to overcome slavery and be able to love—and to reconstruct a life. My intention was for people to realize that this wasn't just a 'period' in history, that these were real people, my ancestors, who had fought their way back to some sense of humanity in ordinary and extraordinary ways." "Well," he said, "you did that." In that moment she released unrealistic, unfair expectations for box office numbers and looked honestly at the film for what it truly was.

Her film wasn't only about box office success or beating *Bride of Chucky*. The film's real objective—lost temporarily in the web of comparison—was to be a message of strength, history, courage, and humanity. By comparison, her film was a failure; by intention, it was a success. Imagine, however, if she had made the film only to compete, to produce revenue and beat films like *Bride of Chucky*. The vision for her film would have been misdirected from the beginning. Comparison often clouds the clarity of our vision.

the "more or less" campaign

When competition blurs our focus, we cross the line of healthy comparison by placing a single person, group, or company at the center of our attention. Then comparison gets personal—"you versus me" or "us versus them." In the "you versus me" game, the level of internal competition leads to behaviors that make companies less effective. In four different group experiments, team members withheld accurate information from the team leader assigned to make a decision. They also gave *inaccurate* information to the decision maker when they perceived the decision maker as ultracompetitive. When asked why they misled or withheld information, they answered it was because of the decision maker's greed and competitiveness, or the fear of being mistreated. Being competitive, without letting it suck us into being counterproductive, isn't easy.

In a world that constantly judges who finishes first, second, and third, it's hard not to judge ourselves or others as more or less smart, innovative, insightful, talented, or successful. There's a constant stream of messages reminding us that who we are and what we achieve isn't enough. We're flooded with images that give the illusion certain people have it all, and select organizations are idolized as near perfect. The truth is no one has it all and perfection is an illusion.

But the "more or less" commercials of competition that surround us distract from who *we* are and what we *do* have. If others seem to have more or are larger in our limited view, it doesn't mean we must therefore be smaller. With a surplus of comparison, multiplied by excessive competition, our view gets tilted. When competitive challenges consume us—even momentarily—combined with the bias of our comparisons, we get sidetracked in three ways: 1) we set goals we shouldn't set to begin with, 2) we set the bar higher than is reachable or realistic, or 3) we get comfortable where we are.

1. the wrong goal

Constantly looking over our shoulder at what others are doing takes our eyes off what's ahead of us. Then our goals are set not by what's possible or relevant but by what someone else is doing. In that case, we're not even setting our goals; someone else is. A preoccupation with comparison pushes us to measure success against accomplishments that have little or nothing to do with what we're uniquely suited for. Envy is a strong motivator but a weak navigator.

In the late 1980s, the satellite communication company Iridium got locked in a duel to beat its competitors to get a new product to market. The company was the first to develop a satellite phone that would allow you to talk from Mount Everest to Los Angeles static free and with no dropped calls. The only problem was handsets cost $3,000 each and per-minute charges ranged from $3 to $8. "What it looks like now," said Chris Chaney, an analyst for A.G. Edwards, "is a multibillion-dollar space project." When we talked with people who worked at Iridium, it was clear the leaders of the company were preoccupied with comparisons to a specific competitor. As a result, their commitment to the new product escalated into heavy, hurried investments and rushed execution despite warnings that signaled dramatic changes in cellular and wireless technology. While the two competitors raced each other toward a nearly irrel-evant finish line, market-relevant competitors passed them by. In 1999, Iridium crashed and became one of the twenty largest bank-ruptcies in history. A group of private investors later bought the company and its sixty-six satellites for only $25 million.

When companies are fixated on competitors—where they're going, what they're doing, who they're doing it with, when they're doing it, or what their next move might be—business IQ drops. And we become less competitive. "Competition whose motive is merely to compete, to drive some other fellow out, never carries very far," said Henry Ford. "The competitor to be feared is one who never bothers about you at all, but goes on making his own business better all the time. Businesses that grow by development and improvement do not die. But when a business ceases to be creative, and it believes it has reached perfection and needs to do nothing but produce—no improvement, no development, it is done."

When we fixate on what others achieve, we overrespond to their every move. "If you base your strategy on what competitors are doing," said Amazon.com CEO Jeff Bezos, "then—because the competitive environment changes so rapidly—you'd have to change your strategy all the time." In an interview with *Business 2.0*, Google CEO Eric Schmidt was asked to respond to a statement from a Microsoft leader about Google, hinting Microsoft was now the "underdog." "He's welcome to say whatever he'd like," said Schmidt. "I'm happy to talk about Google." His comment wasn't competitive naiveté but an appropriate view of, and reaction to, the competition.

Many of the smartest business ideas today (such as eBay, Home Depot, iTunes, Whole Foods, Skype, Progressive Insurance) were created through uniqueness, not competitive sameness. Marketing experts Seth Godin and Jack Trout stress that the greatest chances for success in marketing are in being a one-of-a-kind brand or product. Godin calls that uniqueness a "purple cow." Trout simply says, "Differentiate or die." Not only can comparisons hurt the creativity that leads to uniqueness, they may spur us to prematurely abandon the truly unique creation. "Everyone engaged in creative work is subject to persecution by the odious comparison," said the brilliant architect Frank Lloyd Wright. "Odious comparisons dog the footsteps of all creation wherever the poetic principle is involved because the inferior mind learns only by comparisons; usually equivocal, made by selfish interests each for the other. But the superior mind learns by analyses." **The search for uniqueness compels us to innovate, not impersonate.** But strategies driven purely by comparison are set because of the pressure—which is frequently imagined—we feel from competition, not because those goals are relevant or unique.

2. the cow jumped over the moon?

In addition to setting the wrong goal, the second way comparison sidetracks us is by inducing us to set an unrealistic goal. For example, in 2001, then CEO Dick Brown of EDS decided that 2002 revenue had to grow by nearly 60 percent and committed to that number to the board of directors. Given the fact it took over forty-two years to get to $21.1 billion, increasing revenue by $13 billion in one year was no small feat. One of the primary strategies to hit the revenue goal was to grow the sales force by 50 percent. One of the sales vice presidents confided that regardless of whether they believed the candidates were qualified or would be successful, they were required to hire a certain number by a specific date. EDS paid big signing bonuses, agreed to higher salaries than they would have otherwise, and covered moving expenses.

What were the results of this grand strategy? Revenue for 2002 grew by 2 percent. Operating margin fell by 2.4 percent. Earnings per share fell by $.53. The total value for contracts signed fell by $7 billion. Within twenty-four months, nearly 95 percent of newly acquired sales talent left the company. And what happened to Dick Brown? In March of 2003 he was fired. When the bar is out of reach, we set ourselves up to fail. Worry and frustration follow. The warning here of setting unrealistic goals is far from an endorsement of complacency. Attuning to reality first before setting objectives shouldn't be confused with fear of setting ambitious goals or construed as not trying anything new. But while ego-driven, unrealistic goals might be temporarily motivating, it's not long before they're discouraging and expensive.

3. sit back and relax?

The third detour of comparison tricks us into complacency. When our comparison finds performance that doesn't match ours, we get satisfied. **While there's nothing wrong with satisfaction, comparison makes us *completely* content. Even though we're capable of more, comparison lulls us into a state of comfort, and our contentment to simply be "better than" turns out to be the enemy of what's possible.**

In an article on the United States' disappointing showing in the 2006 World Cup, writer Ives Galarcep spoke of the comfort of star U.S. player Landon Donovan. "If anything, Donovan provided clear-cut evidence that it is time for him to pack his bags, sell his beachside condo in California, and go back to Europe," wrote Galarcep. "He has sold us on a bill of goods for more than a year about being a better player when he is comfortable. Being comfortable doesn't make you a better player. Being comfortable makes you a comfortable player. Donovan—and any soccer player worth his golden spikes—needs pressure to evolve. Pressure makes diamonds, busts pipes, and turns soccer players into big-game stars. The World's best players, be they European or South American, live a life of continuous pressure to perform. . . . [Does] he want to be remembered as an amazing soccer player who made the most of his talent, or does he want to be remembered as the incredible talent who cared more about being comfortable than being great?"

Under the anesthesia of comfort, when we see a gap that suggests we're not as elevated as we once thought, we search for reasons to stay satisfied, rather than wake up. For example, I (Steve) recall that when my son Caden was little, he wouldn't sleep in his own bed. Because he was afraid of monsters under his bed or in his closet, no matter how hard we tried, begged, cajoled, pleaded, prayed . . . he refused. We read child psychology books, watched documentaries on child behavior, and waited for Dr. Phil to do a show on it. Nothing seemed to work. One night as I was lying down with Caden, waiting for him to doze off, I had an idea. In desperation, I decided to appeal to his fierce sense of competition.

"Cadybug—Nicky, your *little* brother, sleeps in his own bed. He's not afraid." "Dad," he said, "Nicky is only three. He's too *stupid* to be scared of monsters!" Resisting the urge to give him a lecture on name-calling, I thought the next logical comparison would convince him of his error. "Well, Alec, your *older* brother, isn't afraid to sleep in *his* own bed." "Dad," he said with a sigh of frustration, "Alec is nine. Do you know how old that is in dog years? He's like . . . thirty-three. He's *way* too old to be scared." The comparison had come full circle. Either way, Caden remained—in his own mind—the perfect sleeper in no need of a change by comparison to those lesser sleeping intelligences called his brothers. For him, it was quite comfortable to have Mom or Dad sleeping in his room until he gave them permission to leave.

better than . . . until

In business we can get distracted by gazing on those "below" us, and if the gap is big enough, we stop paying *any* attention to them and get comfortable. Before we know it, they—or someone else—pass us. The Sony Walkman was certainly "better than" every other portable, personal stereo. Until iPod. Sears was "better than" every other retailer in the world. Until Wal-Mart. GM and Ford were definitely "better than" every other automobile company. Until Toyota, which is currently on track to be the world's largest automobile manufacturer. Day-Timer was "better than" the average calendar. Until Outlook . . . until Palm . . . until BlackBerry . . . until

Motorola's Razr. There's always an *until* waiting for each of us if we drift off to sleep under the fleeting warm blanket of contentment, leading to faulty assumptions, mediocre performance, and sometimes career-altering decisions.

first among . . . ?

Molly is a bright, vivacious friend of ours who teaches global business at a university. Early in her career, she had a career-altering experience with comparison. In 1986, at the encouragement of friends, she trained for her first triathlon in Chicago. To finish in a respectable position, she spent months of free time swimming in Lake Michigan, riding her bike up and down Lake Shore Drive, and running all over the suburbs. Race day came and she placed in the top 20 percent for her age group. Falling in love with the sport and her placement, she shifted not only her personal goals but her professional ones as well to concentrate on training for other triathlons. She joined a local club, subscribed to every available running magazine, and signed up for as many races as she could. For the next year and a half, she worked full-time and trained at night. By the end of the next year she had ten more races under her belt and some encouraging successes.

To get to the next level, she thought it would be helpful to train and race in an environment swirling with triathlon fever. So she moved to Atlanta and got a job with a sporting goods firm. In her first summer in Atlanta she raced in seven triathlons. She achieved a significant milestone when she won the Georgia state championship for her age group. In doing so, Molly qualified for the USA Triathlon's National Championship to be held in Chicago. Qualifying gave her an incredible rush of confidence and power. Feeling as if she had found her life's calling as a professional triathlete, she quit her job in a well-paid management position and began to train full-time. The national championship features the best athletes in the triathlon world. By qualifying for this race, she would be set to compete alongside all the marquis names.

Then race day came.

She lined up with her fellow "champions" in her brand-new Speedo triathlon suit and ran into the water to start the swim. No more than a few seconds into the swim she felt a hand push her under the water and an arm in her side. She was literally tossed, turned around, swum over, and pummeled. Her normally fast swim time turned into a struggle to survive. "Who are these women?" she kept thinking. "This is awful!" The conditions didn't get any better. After forty-five minutes in the water, and the age groupers' coming from behind and passing her, she dragged herself to the bike. Again she felt a leg on the side of her, this time kicking her bike, and another body pushing so close to her that she crashed.

Discouraged and thinking she would be lucky to finish in the championship group, Molly pulled herself up and slowly spun through the rest of the bike segment. By the time she ran the last twenty-five miles, she had completely lost the championship group, had been passed by age groupers, and was now among the normal Joes of Chicago running their first triathlon. She was embarrassed, especially since her number of 28—versus 8,476 or some other high number—indicated she was in the championship group. People who saw her knew she was supposed to be *much* farther ahead. When she crossed the finish line, she could see her mother's and sister's worried looks. "We *wondered* where you were!" they said. "Everyone else in your group finished *ages* ago."

What does Molly's story have to do with the bar comparison sets for us? Maybe it was just a bad race. Maybe she simply needed to train harder. Perhaps this was simply an obstacle on the road to greatness. Looking back, Molly said she tricked herself by comparison into a feeling of superiority. "Some 'gift to triathlon' I turned out to be," she told us—at times smiling widely, and at other times shaking her head. "When I look back on the experience, I realize I never really did very well in any race. I placed in my age group when there were no other people *in* my age group, and I 'won' the Georgia state championship because the only other women in my age group didn't finish. (One dropped out and the other had an accident!) My 'success' and my decisions were based mostly on inaccurate comparisons, and I let it go to my head. I was humbled so completely in Chicago that I gave up triathlons as anything other than a hobby from that time forward. It was a hard lesson to learn. I wish I could have learned the 'easy' way, but life doesn't always deliver easy lessons. Since that time, I'm careful about what comparisons I make."

Being our competitive best requires a clear view of ourselves. We all tend to see ourselves in some areas a little better than we are, and occasionally worse than we are. We can't be our best if we're mistaken by excessive comparison about who we are and what abilities we have or don't have. We shouldn't eliminate competition or stop challenging ourselves. But we can't afford to cross the line and let unwarranted comparison and competition lead us down an irrelevant, frustrating, or mediocre path.

Falling into the comparison trap usually precedes and triggers the other three early warning signs: being defensive, showcasing brilliance, and seeking acceptance.

Breaking the habit of any early warning sign requires we examine beliefs that drive those behaviors. Our beliefs are based on a mathematical equation—a series of "this plus this equals this" or "if-then" logic. But the math we do in our heads doesn't always add up—the beliefs we have may be anything but true. If we can identify the faulty equations in our minds, we can break bad habits.

There is also often a difference between what we say or do and what we're thinking or feeling. Even though we might say the right words, sometimes we feel different. While what we feel or think can be masked by the right words or actions, our intentions and feelings are always true, although not always revealed. What we or others are feeling lets us know if we're managing ego effectively.

In appendix 1, we've listed key beliefs, healthy and unhealthy, for each early warning sign along with questions we can ask to challenge unhealthy beliefs to overcome that early warning sign. Also listed are primary emotions and attitudes related to each of the four early warnings signs we can watch for in ourselves and others. A more comprehensive list may be found at www.egonomicsbook .com.

3: being comparative | key points

- Comparison is such a necessary, natural, minute-by-minute part of our lives, it's an unconscious habit. That habit is either an effective tool or a weapon that turns against us. A frequent companion of comparison is competition. Because we're immersed in competition, and the competitive spirit pushes us to do better, we hardly notice when it makes us worse.

- An appropriate view of competition resists the temptation to make comparisons that turn colleagues into competitors. We make better choices by not attempting to become someone, or something, else.

- We lose our competitive edge when we become *too* competitive.

- When we're too comparative, ranking higher than someone else matters more than how much money we earn or what we've actually achieved.

- Research on social comparisons shows that the more uncertain we are about who we are or what we have, the more automatic and persistent comparisons become. Unfair or inaccurate comparison not only steals credit from the person we're comparing against, it interferes with the opportunity to make the most of our situation—independent of anyone, or anything, else.

- When excessive comparison comes into play, judgments that follow prevent us from reaching our potential by satisfying us with status quo or distracting from the performance itself.

- When competitive challenges consume us, combined with the general inaccuracy of our comparisons, we get sidetracked in three ways: we set goals we shouldn't set to begin with, we set the bar higher than is reachable or realistic, or we get comfortable where we are.

4
early warning sign 2

being defensive

Men often oppose a thing, merely because they have had no agency in planning it, or because it may have been planned by those they dislike. But if they have been consulted, and have happened to disapprove, opposition then becomes, in their estimation, an indispensable duty of self-love. They seem to think themselves bound in honor, and by all the motives of personal infallibility, to defeat the success of what has been resolved upon contrary to their sentiments.

ALEXANDER HAMILTON

The second early warning sign that ego has moved from an asset to a liability is defensiveness. On the one hand, there's absolutely nothing wrong with defending an idea. Vigorous debate and the clash of different points of view are requirements for letting the best ideas win. An idea that is able to withstand scrutiny warrants support, and if it can't, we should be equally happy with that as an outcome. Being passionate about an idea isn't the same as being right, and disagreement doesn't equal negativity. "I look for bright people with strong personalities who will argue with me," said Massachusetts governor Mitt Romney. "I like discussing both sides of an issue and I'm comfortable with controversy." That's a rare approach for a Republican in a heavily Democratic state. In fact, it's uncommon practice in most any arena—business, school, politics, or home. Yet if our intent is to let the best ideas win, we can take *any* stance, on any topic, in any arena to test the strength of what we're debating. But there's a difference between defending a position and *being* defensive.

When my daughter Lindsay was in high school (Dave recalls), she frequently left the garage door open after she got out of her car, even though we had given her several reminders to close it before she came into the house. One evening, as I went out to the garage to get something from the freezer, I noticed she had left it open—again. I wanted to make the point clear that she usually forgets, and I thought this was the perfect opportunity:

DAD: Lindsay, is there a reason you don't close the garage door when you come home?

LINDSAY: I'm not the only one that leaves it open.

DAD: Yes, but you just came home ten minutes ago and it's open. Jeff and Spencer are both gone, so it couldn't have been either one of them. And I didn't go open it up just so I could get you in trouble. If the garage door is left open, the wind blows dirt, leaves, and trash into the garage. Then someone has to clean it out, and that someone is usually me. I want you to remember to close it when you come home.

LINDSAY: Why do you only get after *me?* When the boys come home
from school, they leave the garage door open all the time
and you don't say anything to them. I've even seen you and
Mom leave your garage doors open. I'm not the only one
that does it. Besides, I might leave to go somewhere later.

In any situation, when the power of ego surges, our intent
switches from honestly defending our point to proving our case
exclusively; we refuse to be influenced, regardless of gaps in logic
or inaccuracies. In the relentless effort to be "right," we make excuses, find fault with others, even if our faultfinding is unrelated to
the discussion at hand. Or we simply deny any wrongdoing. Sometimes we excuse mistakes by saying, "That's just the way I am." Occasionally we go to extremes to make the point we disagree with
seem far-fetched and therefore irrelevant.

The exchange of extreme ideas quickly turns into an exchange
of intellectual or emotional blows, and small things become big
things. To justify our switch from defending to defensiveness, we
may feel righteously indignant or that we're the innocent victim.
And when a simple acknowledgment of being wrong would move
everyone toward openness, oddly enough we use apology as another weapon of defensiveness. Defensive "apologies" are so common, they merit elaboration.

i'm sorry, but was that an apology?

"I'm sure that I'm supposed to act all sorry or sad or guilty now
that I've accepted that I've done something wrong," said Pete Rose
when he admitted to betting on baseball. "But you see, I'm just not
built that way. So let's leave it like this: I'm sorry it happened and
I'm sorry for all the people, fans, and family it hurt. Let's move on."
If you're an avid baseball fan, is his apology acceptable? Defensiveness doesn't allow a genuine apology; we go through the motions.

In an article for *Governing* magazine, Alan Ehrenhalt identifies a second strategy—the "I'm right, you just misinterpreted me" strategy. Ehrenhalt describes how Massachusetts state representative Ellen Story got herself into hot water for saying the state underfunded mental health because of the "predominance of Irish Catholics in authority." She said the Irish deemed retardation to be God's will. After colleagues called her view "bizarre," she apologized to "anyone I offended" by the "poor choice of words." The warmth of her apology? Thirty-two degrees Fahrenheit.

The final defensive maneuver in the form of an apology is an unwilling about-face. On the campaign trail several years ago, presidential hopeful Howard Dean said he wanted to be the candidate for "guys with Confederate flags on their pickup trucks." After getting blasted in the press for the next twenty-four hours, Dean did a one-eighty: "I think I made a mistake. I apologize for it. I think it's time to move on." Was he truly sorry? The Reverend Al Sharpton told Dean: "You are not a bigot, but you appear to be too arrogant to say, 'I'm wrong,' and go on." When asked why he didn't apologize earlier, Dean said, "I tend to be somebody who, under pressure, tends to fight back." But insincerity only serves to keep everyone as unforgiving, unapologetic, and entrenched in their opinion as they were before.

In time, we become more insensitive to our mistakes and develop a natural inclination to "fight back." Unfortunately, we fall back on that inclination not only when faced with outright challenge or accusation, but when someone is trying to help us.

can I give you some feedback?

When someone tells us they want to give us feedback, we don't usually think, "*Yes.* I've been hoping for someone to point out a blind spot. I can't wait to hear what they have to say!" The word "feedback" has become code for "Can I tell you what's wrong with you?" Even though it *sounds* courteous, we expect to hear unpleasant news, and it's easy to be defensive, even if only on the inside. In fact, if we're feeling defensive and someone suggests we're being defensive, our typical response is to say, "No, I'm not." We're even defensive about being defensive.

In his work based on *The 7 Habits of Highly Effective People*, Stephen R. Covey has conducted over 150,000 360-degree assessments in the last decade. In an analysis of those assessments, of the seventy-eight items included in the survey, "Receives negative feedback without becoming defensive" and "Seeks feedback on ways he/she can improve" rank dead last when people are evaluated by their colleagues. Ironically, those same two items show up in the top ten when people rank themselves. If we don't "mind the gap," we stay mired in ineffective habits we can't even see.

What is it about feedback that makes it so hard to take? We know we're not perfect. Even so, feedback isn't easy when a flaw is exposed, especially when someone else reveals it. There are two major reasons for our defensiveness: the image we want others to have of us, and the image we need to have of ourselves.

the burden of perfection

We want and need others to have a positive image of us—who we are, what talents we have, what we're like to work with, whether we can be trusted, whether we're competent, whether they should follow our lead, and so on. As a result, it's natural that we project our best possible image. But when someone has feedback to share, we fear our image has been tarnished, or will be if we don't defend it. We don't want to look as if we're not all we should be or as if we have a chink in our armor. That would make us look foolish for not recognizing and addressing an apparent weakness. So in response to that pressure, we rally our own personal PR firm to manage perceptions and defend our reputation. We could be defending our identity—who we are and what we stand for—our behaviors, or our ideas. But when we attempt to manage perceptions through defensiveness, the effort is transparent.

In a televised press conference on the Watergate scandal in 1973, President Nixon forcefully resisted admitting mistakes as he defended his record in the Watergate case. "I am not a crook," he said. "[I]n all of my years of public life I have never obstructed justice. People have got to know whether or not their president is a crook. Well, I'm not a crook. I've earned everything I've got." Nine months later Congress impeached Nixon and forced him to resign the presidency. And who could forget President Clinton's infamous 1998 grand jury testimony when he said, "It depends on what the meaning of the word 'is' is." America rolled its eyes in disbelief. Whether we're in a public political position, a visible corporate leadership role, or a simple everyday encounter, when we try to escape responsibility for mistakes, to hide the truth, or when we agree we've made mistakes but discard them as trivial, people usually see through our defensive ploys.

Not surprisingly, the more visible we become, the more we're expected to be "perfect." It's almost as if to qualify as a leader we aren't allowed to have flaws. The social pressure makes it even harder to admit mistakes. At a press conference on April 13, 2004, John Dickerson of *Time* magazine asked an unexpected question of President George W. Bush: "You've looked back before 9/11 for what mistakes might have been made. After 9/11, what would your biggest mistake be, would you say, and what lessons have you learned from it?"

The president's response was indicative of not just a political propensity but a human tendency to hide frailty. "I wish you would have given me this written question ahead of time, so I could plan for it," President Bush said. "John, I'm sure historians will look back and say, gosh, he could have done it better this way, or that way. You know, I just—I'm sure something will pop into my head here in the midst of this press conference with all the pressure of trying to come up with an answer, but it hasn't yet." Then the president went on to explain his reasoning for the things he believed he had done *right*—from Afghanistan to Iraq. He closed by saying, "I hope I— I don't want to sound like I've made no mistakes. I'm confident I have. I just haven't—you just put me under the spot here, and maybe I'm not as quick on my feet as I should be in coming up with one."

President Bush was quicker on his feet a month later. At a White House correspondents' dinner he was asked about that unforgettable question. "It's an excellent question that totally stumped me," Bush admitted. "I guess looking at it practically, my biggest mistake was calling on John." Perhaps President Bush would lose with a yes or no answer. If he answers yes, his opponents and the press have new ammunition. If he answers no, he looks arrogant. How refreshing it would have been to hear something like this:

John, that's not an easy question to answer. Admitting mistakes is hard, whether it's to the nation or to my wife. I believe that's a human tendency each of us is susceptible to. To make matters worse, politics has become a place where admitting mistakes is a sign of weakness, and an opportunity for others to jump on and amplify those mistakes. In spite of that, I have made mistakes. For example, I was convinced it was in the best interests of our national security to [fill in the blank]. But because there are variables no one controls, it didn't play out the way I thought it would. Now, with better information, looking back on it, I wish I had done differently.

With that said, I ask the American people to forgive me for those mistakes—and the mistakes I'm certain I will yet make. I'm not under the delusion I'm perfect, and I know the people in this room aren't under that delusion about me either. There's

no such thing as a mistake-free presidency: it hasn't been pos-
sible for the forty-two presidents who preceded me. Those who
don't learn from history are bound to repeat the same mistakes,
and that applies to me, you, and each American citizen. I know
I can do better. Thank you for the honesty of your question.

Maybe President Bush lost an opportunity to shift the discussion from party politics and brazenness to candor and humility. His predecessors have certainly had opportunities to make that same shift and passed them up. Only forty-three people in the history of the United States have been asked such questions from the podium of the White House press room, and it's easy to give advice from the sidelines or to criticize. **The point is, our defensiveness, often seen as evasiveness, only serves to indict us, regardless of the truth of the accusation, the sincerity of the question, or the nature of the feedback.**

happy go (un)lucky

Another reason we resist feedback is that we want and need to hold a positive image of ourselves. An accurate, healthy self-image is an essential pursuit of life and a prerequisite to making a positive contribution. Anything counter to that positive image can be seen as a threat to our identity. In fact, there's an argument to be made against feedback—that a dose of reality when it's negative isn't healthy medicine.

Research by Shelley Taylor at the University of California and Jonathan Brown of Southern Methodist University showed that the more positive we are about ourselves—even if our perception isn't tied to reality—the happier, harder-working, more benevolent, and more determined we are. So why in the world would we want feedback that could shatter our rose-colored glasses? And when we get feedback, why not simply dismiss it if we're happier without it?

The answer is that those findings are incomplete. In the long run we wouldn't actually be happier, harder-working, or more productive. Mark Leary, professor and chair of psychology at Wake Forest University, has conducted years of research that suggests the danger of an overly positive self-view:

> Holding an overly flattering view of one's personality, abilities, and other attributes is often a recipe for disaster. Success in life comes largely from matching one's abilities, interests, and inclinations to appropriate situations, jobs, and relationships. To the extent they misperceive who or what they're really like, people are more likely to make bad decisions. How many people are in jobs, relationships, and lives for which they are unsuited simply because they perceived themselves inaccurately? When self-serving illusions blind people to their shortcomings and weaknesses, they are unlikely to try to improve.

If hearing feedback from someone is painful, the alternative—ignoring it—appears even worse. Being defensive doesn't erase the truth; instead, it only protects our illusions that block progress. "We defend our enslavements," said an unknown philosopher, "as if they were our freedoms." Freedom comes from inviting reality checks while at the same time holding a positive self-view. The feedback we get won't always be accurate; the data we receive filters through the biased lens of the one giving it, as well as the one on the receiving end. But what other people tell us does represent their perception of us, and we should remember that their perception *is* their reality. So if we want to work effectively with them, we must understand their reality. We're not saying it's a joy to hear about our imperfections, but if we resist the feedback, then we're bound to live with the flaws. One of the flaws we should examine that may help us to stay open to feedback is the logic underlying our defensiveness. As it turns out, it isn't very logical at all.

logically illogical

The logic behind defensiveness doesn't stack up. If we're wrong, do we really want to defend a bad idea or position? If we're right, will being defensive increase or decrease the strength of our position? Will it hurt or help the odds that others will give up their position in favor of a better way? Will defensiveness foster better listening, on either side? Will our defense or denial of our weaknesses make us stronger? While there's no rationale behind the tactic of being defensive, there's plenty of emotion. Fear is the mortar that holds together the wall of defensiveness. We fear that

- we weren't smart enough to see it first.
- we risk losing what we have or who we are if we change.
- if we admit we're wrong, we'll lose face.
- the world is changing and we don't want it to—so we defend the "old world," under the illusion that if we hold to our position long enough, the world will adjust to us.
- the past has been different from what we thought it was, and the future might be different from what we want it to be.
- we *are* the feedback we're getting.

If we're defensive whenever others give us feedback, they stop giving us input, even when it's in our best interests. They're more than willing to become spectators and let experience teach us a lesson. "You can't shut out the world," said Arnold Glasgow, "without shutting yourself in." One of the preferred means we use to shut the world out is what we call spin.

spin doctors

During a political debate, each candidate's camp is abuzz with staff members analyzing what is said by the candidates, gauging how the public will react, and, if necessary, manufacturing corrections. Immediately after the debate is over, each side eagerly and passionately claims victory and assures the pundits that their candidate delivered *the* message the public resonates with. What often gets shared after a debate isn't always an accurate assessment but a carefully crafted spin that makes one candidate's points look dead-on and the opponent wrong or out of touch. People good at this are dubbed spin doctors. Our guess is that if you reviewed postdebate rhetoric, it would appear not one candidate ever lost a debate.

Spinning was an art originally designed to polish a clear, accurate message so people could understand it quickly. Now it's the ability to manufacture a one-sided version of the truth, and too often to make weakness look strong and fallacy seem factual. The final report of the U.S. House of Representatives investigation into the Katrina disaster states, "Critical time was wasted on issues of no importance to disaster response, such as winning the blame game [and] waging a public relations battle." In other words, defensive spin.

Spin isn't reserved for politicians, media personalities, or congressional inquiries. It doesn't matter if it's the Oval Office, a Fortune 500 boardroom, a meeting room, or a living room; we've each learned to shape our side of the story to show ourselves in a positive light. While there's nothing wrong with our side of the story, the wheel of spin has four major spokes that lead to bias and error:

- **Exaggerate.** Inflate information beyond its actual significance
- **Understate.** Filter, minimize, or block out certain information
- **Manipulate.** Twist and re-form information
- **Fabricate.** Create information that has no basis in reality

When defensive, we're inclined to use spin tactics to suffocate good information and advance our cause. Unfortunately, defensiveness doesn't always show up in our words.

he (really) said, she (really) said

We're not only defensive when someone challenges us or gives us feedback. We can be defensive in simple interactions because of previous exchanges, and yet defensiveness isn't always apparent on the surface. Consider a meeting where the right words are being said, but defensiveness still spins how information is shared and received:

what's being said	what's really being thought/felt
MELISSA: I appreciate everyone taking the time to listen to this proposal again. If we didn't really believe in the idea, we wouldn't be asking for you to reconsider it.	MELISSA: This is going to be a waste of time. The last time I shared this idea, Craig totally shut it down. He shouldn't even be on this budget approval committee. His closed mind is killing innovation around here.
CRAIG: Well, we're always willing to take a second look if the business case justifies the time.	CRAIG: I disagreed with their strategy the first time she presented it. Why are we going through this again?
MELISSA: That's good to hear because I think the business climate has changed from last year, and our strategy is better positioned for the changes we're seeing in the market.	MELISSA: That sounds more like a challenge than an invitation. The proof he expects is so over-the-top that I doubt anyone could jump that hurdle.
CRAIG: I'm all ears. What changes do you see?	CRAIG: No amount of changes will make her strategy any more appealing. She just doesn't want to give up on this because it's *her* idea.

what's being said	what's really being thought/felt
MELISSA: Let's start with the new market we're proposing we enter, and then tie what we've learned to our current target market.	MELISSA: He's not all ears— he's acting interested just to be politically safe. He won't really listen. His mind is already made up.
CRAIG: *(interrupting)* Why don't you think we should focus on our current market first?	CRAIG: Why are we going to go after a new market when we're getting pounded in the current market we're in? I think they're looking for the easy way out. They're in over their heads and don't know what they're doing.
MELISSA: Well, if you'll let me finish I was about to explain our rationale.	MELISSA: He's clueless. He can't let go of his own agenda.

As this conversation escalates, imagine the rest of it seesawing back and forth. Neither hears the other, because they're filtering everything through the spin inside their heads. On the surface we can use open, polite words, but the internal barriers that are constantly being fortified make honest, open conversation nearly impossible. When dead-bolted minds clash, the outcome is predictable.

A deceptively attractive quality of spin is how persuasive it can be. As an example, we once consulted with the CEO of a company that needed to change its corporate strategy. With hundreds of thousands of individual customers all over the world, and not much cash to experiment with, a change in strategy would have major implications. The following is the condensed version of the one-year conversation this CEO had with us and others. He was one of the best spin doctors we've run across.

US:	So, you've done market research?
CEO:	Yes.
US:	Where?
CEO:	L.A. and Boston.
US:	Good. Where else?
CEO:	Nowhere.
US:	Okay. How many customers in L.A. and Boston?
CEO:	Twelve.
US:	Twelve?
CEO:	Twelve.
US:	What kind of market research did you do?
CEO:	Focus groups.
US:	Who conducted the focus groups?
CEO:	Me.
US:	You?
CEO:	Me.
US:	Well, did they all like the new strategy?
CEO:	Yes . . . by the end of the day they all agreed it was a compelling strategy.
US:	What do you mean "by the end of the day"?
CEO:	Well, two of them liked it right off, but the others needed some work. They eventually came around.
US:	You're going to change the strategy of the whole company with hundreds of thousands of customers all over the world based on what you personally think and what twelve people said in L.A. and Boston?
CEO:	Yes.
US:	Uh-huh. (Check, please!)

Unknown or known to him (we couldn't quite tell), he was spinning to get what he wanted in the first place. He exaggerated the "market research" way beyond its intended significance, filtered out information and those who disagreed, modified data as it came in, and fabricated information that didn't exist. His spin started to infiltrate the culture, and we could see objectivity and openness evaporate. Marketing guru Al Ries told us, "You can't ever suggest that any decision made by the chief executive in the past was wrong. You can't get to be a chief executive or a CEO without a powerful ego. And people with powerful egos will never, ever admit they made a mistake. How then can you sell a new strategy unless you can convince the company that their previous strategy was wrong? You first have to tell them that their strategy was 'right for its time.' But today, times have changed; therefore their strategy has to change. No CEO has ever told me that he or she has ever made a mistake." When an individual leader is prone to defensiveness, it creates a defensive corporate culture.

not-so-happy meal

Consider the defensive canopy that once covered McDonald's. In 2001, McDonald's announced major restructuring after many quarters of declining profits, cutting corporate jobs, and consolidating service regions. A story for *BusinessWeek* by David Leonhardt pointed to a preceding decade of disappointing performance: much lower taste rankings than competitors, dissident franchisees, declining profits, low stock performance—especially for a brand that was sixth most recognized in the world—layoffs, and increasing competition. The company's response? Chairman and CEO Michael Quinlan was asked if change was needed. "Do we have to change? No, we don't have to change. We have the most successful brand in the world." The illusion of invulnerability and collective rationalization had crept in among smart, hardworking, dedicated people—and into the same CEO who earlier acknowledged they had "made some mistakes." There were other signs of cultural defensiveness.

Leonhardt wrote, "As the company's performance has deteriorated, top execs have tended to blame others. They have publicly blasted dissident franchisees, whom they dismiss as a small faction. Negative news accounts are chalked up to misperceptions by reporters. And one persistently critical Wall Street analyst—Damon Brundage, now at J.P. Morgan & Co.—was barred from the company's latest biennial briefing." Stereotyping outsiders as the enemy, McDonald's head of marketing pointed to the media for the company's brand problems. "If there were one thing I would want to change about McDonald's," said Senior Vice President Brad A. Ball, "it would be to correct the misconceptions and perceptions that have become so pervasive in the last few years." Defensiveness focuses on changing others, not ourselves. Eventually, the fog cleared for McDonald's with new leadership, fresh ideas, and an open mind.

shifting into high gear

In stark contrast to the defensiveness we frequently see, there's the example of Carlos Ghosn, a Lebanese Brazilian working for a French company (Renault), who went to Japan to turn around a traditional Japanese auto company—the perfect conditions for defensiveness on both sides. In 1999, Nissan was $22 billion in debt. It had inflated supplier costs, new product development was stuck in neutral, and only one out of the last ten years had been profitable. Daimler-Chrysler and Ford had both considered offers to buy Nissan but backed away. Renault stepped up, bought controlling interest, and asked Ghosn to lead the transformation. "The company was considered to be lost," Ghosn said. "When you are the last bidder, you know that you are going to have to make a difference or there is no future."

Today Nissan is in overdrive. Currently, Nissan is on track to sell 3.6 million units annually (a boost of 1 million in three years), with five-year sales growth nearly matching Toyota's and profit margins and return on equity to match *Fortune*'s most admired companies. With performance like that it's easy to credit Ghosn's clear strategy, market-driven designs, insistence on performance measurement, cost-cutting savvy, and cross-functional team approach. What's even more striking than Ghosn's success is the *way* he did those things, and *how* he was able to do them in the first place. In his speech to the team he brought with him from Renault to "fix" Nissan, his advice reveals his commitment to openness and unwillingness to spark defensiveness in others:

> *"You're not missionaries. You've come here not to change Japan, but to straighten out Nissan with the men and women of Nissan. We're the ones who have to assimilate with them—it's not up to them to adapt to us." A manager who worked closely with Ghosn said, "[his] idea was to tear down the walls, whether visible or invisible, that reduce a collective enterprise to a congregation of groups and tribes, each with their own language, their own values, their own interests. To compel people to talk to one another, to listen to one another, to exchange knowledge. That was the essence of their power."*

If we can drop our defensive posture and listen, it gives us power—power to be influenced and power to influence others. When Ghosn came to Nissan, he listened to as many people as he could. People gave him advice; they told him he couldn't close plants in Japan . . . or go fast . . . or reduce head count . . . or . . . "I listened carefully, even to the opinions that *totally contradicted my own beliefs,*" said Ghosn, "to make sure that when I made my decisions, I hadn't missed anything. I told my critics, 'Don't judge me on a good speech. Judge me on my results. *Be very cynical. Be very cold.* Look at the profits, the debt, the market share, the appeal of the cars. Then judge me.' "

Instead of moving away from or resisting what others were saying, he moved boldly toward it—even when he didn't like it. He didn't have to agree with it to understand it, but he did need to be influenced by it. And that made all the difference. Ghosn's approach allowed ideas to make their way from the watercooler—where ideas almost always evaporate—to Nissan's boardroom, where they could work *for* rather than against the company.

4: being defensive key points

- There's nothing wrong with defending an idea. If our intent is to let the best ideas win, we should be able to take *any* stance, on any topic, in any arena to test the strength of what we're debating. But there's a difference between defending a position and *being* defensive.

- When the power of ego surges, our intent switches from honestly defending our point to proving our case exclusively. We refuse to be influenced, regardless of gaps in logic or inaccuracies. In the relentless effort to be "right," we make excuses and find fault with others, even if our faultfinding is unrelated to the discussion at hand.

- Even apologies can be defensive.

- We resist feedback because we want and need to hold a positive image of ourselves. Anything counter to that positive image can be seen as a threat.

- The logic behind defensiveness doesn't stack up. If we're wrong, do we really want to defend a bad idea or position? If we're right, will being defensive increase or decrease the strength of our position?

- The wheel of defensive spin has four major spokes that lead to bias and error: 1) exaggerate: inflate information beyond its actual significance, 2) understate: filter, minimize, or block out certain information, 3) manipulate: twist and re-form information, and 4) fabricate: create information that has no basis in reality.

5

early warning sign 3

showcasing brilliance

This woman said I was acting like God. Therefore, I said
unto her . . .

WOODY ALLEN

In addition to being comparative and defensive, showcasing brilliance is an early warning sign that ego is eroding the bottom line.
Even though showcasing (showing off) brilliance is easy to spot for
those on the receiving end, perpetrators seldom see it. For example, while I (Dave) was managing a design team at a newspaper
early in my career, I watched the following exchange between two
colleagues:

SAM: Sarah, can I give you some feedback about this design?
SARAH: Um, *(pause)* yeah, go ahead.
SAM: I'm not trying to brag, but I think my creativity and ability

is as good as anyone's in our department. I've been doing this for longer than I like to admit and I think I have an eye for what looks good and what doesn't. To me this design is sloppy, boring, and . . . well . . . too predictable.

SARAH: Why do you say that? I've worked hard on this and I think it looks pretty good.

SAM: Well, for starters, how hard you work on a design isn't the point. Even though what you've done *is* creative, you've also created confusion with the main message that has to get through to the reader. The visual elements aren't balanced very well and distract rather than help. Plus you have to remember this is going to be in a newspaper environment where there are other ads and stories right next to it, on top of it, or on the opposite page. The goal is to create a stop sign for the reader, not a yield sign. If I were you I'd move this—

SARAH: *(interrupting)* Everyone's entitled to an opinion. This has already been shown to the client and they loved it. Thanks for your ideas, but I think it's just fine the way it is.

Later that afternoon, Sarah told me that "even though I think Sam has some good ideas and I respect his experience, I can't stand it when he talks down to me. It's as if he thinks he's above making those same mistakes, but he's not. Plus, he makes it seem like I should bow down and be grateful he took time out of his busy day to help the 'little people.' " As expected, the next day Sam complained to me about "how frustrating it is that people are so defensive when I give suggestions that could improve a design. Why don't people listen to someone with more experience? I'm only trying to help." **The more we expect people to recognize, appreciate, or be dazzled by our brilliance, the less they listen,** *even if we do have better ideas.*

When others stop listening, we isolate ourselves not only from their interest in our ideas but from *their* brilliance in making ideas better. Then we're left less informed and with less influence—the opposite of what we thought we were getting by showcasing. That's why showcasing is the ultimate irony; whether we dominate a conversation, grandstand to show how much we know, name-drop to dazzle, choose words or phrases to impress, pontificate to promote ourselves, or pay only superficial attention to what others say, the *more* we showcase, the *less* brilliance surfaces—and the less brilliant we're likely to be. There's nothing wrong with being brilliant or capitalizing on our talents. After all, what's the value of having brilliance if we don't use it? But we cross the line from sharing to showcasing when we use it to feed our ego.

you're really smart, but . . .

In the pursuit of brilliance, most of us want smart people around, but only under one condition: if they share their brilliance in a way we can take. When people move from sharing to showcasing, the smartest people are ignored—even when they're needed most. For example, if you were under pressure to get big-time results and were putting together your project team, would you choose someone you like who's not quite a genius but easy to get along with, or someone who's brilliant but hard to tolerate? The politically correct answer is "Hire the showcaser. We may not like him, but brilliance is hard to come by." It's hard to argue with that.

Except, when push comes to shove and we have to make that choice, we actually do the opposite. In a study of over 10,000 real-time working relationships, Tiziana Casciaro of Harvard Business School and Miguel Sousa Lobo of Duke University discovered that while people *say* they would choose someone who's "brilliant" but arrogant, they actually chose those they liked. One of the reasons we're excluded when we showcase is the trace of intellectual arrogance people feel from us. That separation "gives the segregator a false sense of superiority," said Martin Luther King, "and the segregated a false sense of inferiority."

As our perceived brilliance separates us from others, it leads to a one-way mind-set: everyone else is a student, and we're the teacher. Our impulse as the teacher is to have the first and last word, with as much stage time in between as possible. The students aren't excluded from participation, but they're not actively invited either. If you watch conversations carefully, you can see that showcasers can rarely tell the difference between obligatory tolerance by others and genuine interest. Dialogue becomes monologue, and blank stares are interpreted as engaged, attentive eyes. All the while, the teacher is clueless. "Intellectual arrogance," wrote Peter Drucker, "often causes disabling ignorance."

an identity crisis

The effects of showcasing steadily add up until they disable a career, even a culture. In the spring of 2003, the *New York Times*, one of the world's most important newspapers, was impeached. Jayson Blair, a reporter for the *Times*, resigned after an investigation revealed he fabricated or plagiarized dozens of stories. But Blair was only the tip of the iceberg. In his compelling narrative of what happened, journalist Seth Mnookin looked deep inside the culture of the *New York Times* and found the problems below the surface were as much to blame as the deception by Blair.

The cause of the mass below the surface was *Times* CEO Howell Raines, who had egomaniacally elbowed his way to the top. Soon after his ascent to executive editor, anyone with different views was treated as a dark cloud blocking the light of his vision. "He embraced his authoritative nature and began editing the paper according to his whims and predilections," writes Mnookin, "in the process embarrassing and marginalizing people who disagreed with him."

Responding to Raines's self-centered style, the *Times* culture deteriorated. Employees became unhappy, discouraged, and increasingly emotionally distant from the mission of the paper. In turn, that distance shaped the process and quality of their work. Key editors stopped talking to each other. Concerns, ideas, and problems were being saved for off-the-record conversations or simply withheld. "Everybody felt under siege," said Roger Wilkins, a former *Times* editorialist and columnist. "The instinct to cooperate and watch your buddy's back was diminished. When Thor is up there throwing thunderbolts, your happiest moments come when those thunderbolts hit someone else."

In spite of his talent, in twenty short months Raines's egotistical showcasing created chaos, tarnished the good reputation of a prestigious newspaper, and undid the years of personal effort and contribution that had qualified him for such an influential post. "[Raines] made the fatal mistake of many talented men and women who allow their rise to the top to be defined by ego and blind determination," writes Mnookin. "He confused his own identity with the company he led. In the end, this self-created man was done in by the need to see himself at the center of every story." What happened at the *Times* illustrates perfectly how one person's showcasing affects others. But showcasing isn't solely an individual problem.

cultural signs of showcasing

On February 1, 2003, during reentry into Earth's atmosphere, the space shuttle *Columbia* disintegrated. The disaster took the lives of the entire seven-member crew. In their investigation, the *Columbia* Accident Investigation Board reported that *the culture* at NASA "had as much to do with the accident as the foam." They wrote:

> *Many accident investigations do not go far enough. They identify the technical cause of the accident, and then connect it to a variant of "operator error"—the line worker who forgot to*

> insert the bolt, the engineer who miscalculated the stress, or the manager who made the wrong decision. But this is seldom the entire issue. When the determinations of the causal chain are limited to the technical flaw and individual failure, typically the actions taken to prevent a similar event in the future are also limited: fix the technical problem and replace or retrain the individual responsible. Putting these corrections in place leads to another mistake—the belief that the problem is solved.

Even after the loss of the *Challenger* space shuttle seventeen years earlier, NASA's belief that they were the "perfect place" and "the best organization that human beings could create to accomplish selected goals" created disabling ignorance. The "perfect place" was a reference by the board to work by Yale's Garry Brewer in which he writes that in such cultures, the ability to listen—*especially* to disagreement—requires "the shock of heavy cannon." The line that divides intellectual arrogance from confidence is a thin one.

the half-life of brilliance

When we begin our career, start work with a new employer, or take a new role in our current company, there's a learning curve. Because of that curve, we're not likely to be as relevant or valuable today as we will be in, say, six weeks or six months. No one expects us to be. But they do expect us to get up the curve as quickly as possible. In the figure shown below, the box represents our accumulated knowledge, experience, and competence. The size of that box varies for each of us, but regardless of its size, the curve represents the relevance of what's inside the box. The higher our position on the curve, the more indispensable we are to our company and the greater the demand for our services in the labor market. But there's a requirement for staying on top or moving toward the peak of that curve—keeping the lid to that box open to learn.

"The larger the island of knowledge," said Ralph Sockman, "the longer the shoreline of wonder." While Sockman's idea should hold true, we're susceptible to a delusion of adequacy. **When ego is out of balance, there is an inverse relationship between amassing knowledge and learning; the more we know, the more confident we become. When our confidence in what we know increases to the point where we think there's little left to learn, we're less open.** That's the point of danger; the lid to our box of knowledge begins to close. As it closes, new ideas have a harder time getting in, flawed ideas have a tough time escaping, and we slide down the other side of the curve. The faster the lid closes, the faster our descent.

The slide down the curve is evidenced in our vocabulary: "If you'd been here as long as I have . . ." or "I know my experience speaks for itself, but . . ." Down goes our relevance. Once the box is locked, we slide to the bottom on the other side of

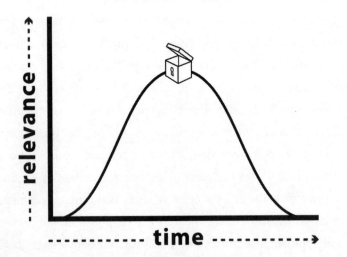

the curve—as relevant at the end of our careers as we were when we began. "In times of change, learners will inherit the earth," said philosopher Eric Hoffer, "while the learned will find themselves beautifully equipped to deal with a world that no longer exists." To which futurist Alvin Toffler added, "The illiterate of the 21st century will not be those who cannot read and write, but those who cannot learn, unlearn, and relearn." If we're to increase our knowledge and relevance, the first step of leadership literacy is learning.

To avoid the slippery slope of irrelevance, think of the knowledge we have in the same way scientists look at isotopes. One of the properties that govern isotopes is a phenomenon called half-life. The half-life of an isotope is the amount of time it takes for half of its atoms to decay. But as an isotope goes through natural decay, it doesn't just become less potent—it actually *loses* its original identity. For example, oxygen-17 decays first into nitrogen-17 and then fluorine-17. In much the same way, our knowledge has a half-life: it can actually lose its original relevance. "There's good evidence that once physicians leave their residency," says Larry Gruppen, PhD, a cognitive psychologist at the University of Michigan Medical School, "the currency of their information starts to decline fairly steadily." That decline isn't reserved for the medical field.

yours, mine, and ours

Keeping our own box of expertise open is vital. It's also not enough. In an organization, no one person is an island of brilliance, and no single box of knowledge is sufficient for progress. Unfortunately, the "lone genius" is the message that's sold and people are inclined to buy. Too many articles treat "the one" who gets the credit for a success as if such people were isolated from those who work with them. Who gets credit for inventing the assembly line? Henry Ford.

Who made flight possible? The Wright Brothers. And what about the telephone? Alexander Graham Bell. Who should we thank for the happiest place on earth? Walt Disney. Who made us fashionable? Liz Claiborne. Who ran the company that could sell you a refrigerator, a lightbulb, and a jet engine all at the same time? Jack Welch. Who has women driving pink cars? Mary Kay. Who does Windows? Bill Gates. The list could go on and on, and not surprisingly, people know the answers. But when one person gets the credit, it skews our perspective about what really happened behind the scenes. The question is how *alone* were the lone geniuses?

Research shows that brilliance doesn't spring from flying solo. Take one example from the list above: Henry Ford invented the assembly line, right? As it turns out, it wasn't originally Ford's idea. In 1799 Eli Whitney took an innovative approach to manufacturing. He used the ideas of division of labor and engineering tolerance to create assemblies from parts. Whitney's ideas just happened to be borrowed from political economist Adam Smith. Then in 1901, Ransom Eli Olds patented the first assembly line, which he put to work in his Olds Motor Vehicle Company factory.

Olds was the first company in America to mass-produce automobiles. But it was Henry Ford's engineers who perfected the assembly line concept. How? It was an evolution by trial and error, not any single event, idea, or person. More important, it was a *collective* effort primarily by Peter E. Martin, the factory superintendent; Charles E. Sorensen, Martin's assistant; C. Harold Wills, a draftsman and toolmaker; and Clarence W. Avery and Charles Lewis, first line supervisors. Among other improvements, they added a conveyor belt and built factories *around* the assembly line. With these improvements, in 1916 Ford cranked out over 700,000 Model Ts, which was twice the output of all competitors combined. The increased efficiency allowed Ford to cut prices in half, so that a car sold for $360 in 1916. By 1924 the price was down to $290. The old adage "Two heads are better than one" is true.

diversity: politically correct or necessary?

Not only are two heads better than one, research shows that many heads are better than two—but collaboration isn't practiced nearly as well as it's preached. The culprit may be misperceptions about how to get the most out of intelligence. The answers to the following questions may reveal the misconceptions. Consider the following scenario: you're faced with a big problem. If you get it wrong, you're fired. If you get it right, you're promoted. With X years of experience (you fill in the number), you probably could solve it on your own. But would you? Or—given that the stakes are so high—would you opt for collective intelligence just to be on the safe side? How would you include others: would you rather have a randomly selected team, or would you prefer to handpick the players personally? If you're in human resources, do you gather mostly HR types? Or if you're in sales, do you pull in the salespeople who are hitting the biggest numbers? Which approach is the safest bet for your career?

Scott Page, a political scientist and economist at the University of Michigan, answered some of those questions, and the answers aren't conventional wisdom. Page created an experiment where groups of people were challenged to solve the same complex problem. When people were isolated and worked on their own, as expected some were good at solving the problem, while others weren't as good. But the next step in his research didn't produce an outcome as easy to predict. Page teamed the good problem solvers with the not-so-good. What effect would the weakest link have on the collective ability to solve the problem? Would the good be dragged down by the not-so-good? Together, the mixed teams almost always did *better* than those who were good problem solvers on their own. But wait—what if you created a team made up of *only* those who were the best problem solvers on their own? Wouldn't that produce the best results? Actually, no.

Even when the "smartest" individual problem solvers were put on the same team, they weren't as good as the teams made up of both the good and not-so-good problem solvers. In other words, the people we already have in our companies are exactly who we need. "Together they possess the knowledge we need to solve the toughest problems we face, or to innovate and seize new opportunities," writes Page. "Our individual differences—the differences in how we think, in the cognitive tools we possess, in our perspectives—is far outside the mainstream in a society that prizes individual talent and achievement. It shouldn't be. Our collective ability depends as much on our collective differences as it does on our individual IQ scores. [Does] this logic imply that we should abandon the meritocracy? That we should remove those 'my child is an honor student at Neil Armstrong Junior High' bumper stickers from our minivans and randomly allocate spots in our top colleges? Of course not. Obviously, ability matters. But, here's the catch, so does diversity. [We're] limited in our abilities. Our heads contain only so many neurons and axons. Collectively, we face no such constraint." When showcasing interferes, collective IQ drops and diversity disappears.

Sometimes the disappearance of diversity is due to subtle showcasing. The subtle version can be brought on by a promotion or a position in an organization. With perceived power comes the temptation to see things from a self-referenced vantage point. "After all," we might feel subconsciously, "I wouldn't have this position if I didn't already know, or wasn't smart enough to figure out, this on my own." The way we do it in this case is in not going out of our way to seek the perspective of others.

In a series of studies on power and perspective taking, researchers wanted to study the link between people in power and their
ability to see things from a different perspective. In one study, they
asked participants to draw the letter *E* on their foreheads. The researchers theorized that if a person wrote the *E* in a self-oriented
way, he or she would view the world from his or her own perspective. If, however, a person wrote the letter so that *others* could
read it easily, it was an indicator that that person was considering the perspective of others. The results showed that those in
the "high-power group were almost three times more likely to
draw a self-oriented *E* than those who were assigned to the low-
power condition," wrote *Science Daily*. "The researchers found that
power leads individuals to anchor too heavily on their own vantage
point, thus leaving them unable to adjust to another person's
perspective and decreases one's ability to correctly interpret
emotion."

"The research has wide-ranging implications, from business to
politics," wrote Adam Galinsky of Northwestern University. "Presidents who preside over a divided government (and thus have reduced power) might be psychologically predisposed to consider
alternative viewpoints more readily than those that preside over
unified governments."

In *The Wisdom of Crowds*, James Surowiecki takes the idea of collective intelligence and different perspectives much deeper. He
cites dozens of studies that prove the many are smarter than the
few. In researching everything from bean-counting contests to
stock market performance to predictions about which actors will
grab a coveted Oscar, it is the collective intelligence of people that
makes the best decisions, not the lone genius. Surowiecki points
out that as long as people think through ideas independently first,
even the method we use to make decisions doesn't matter much, as
long as we're tapping the collective wisdom of the crowd. To put it

another way, a discovery-driven process that explores what's happening from a variety of perspectives—rather than an idea-driven process by an individual—increases the odds of making the best decision by 50 percent.

There are, of course, exceptions to the rule that collective brilliance trumps individual genius. But those exceptions are rare. If a theatrical play was written by a committee, you wouldn't expect it to reach Broadway, let alone win a Tony. Poetry is most likely beautiful when penned as a solo effort. But you probably *do* want computer viruses tackled by a team (letting the best idea win) rather than a lone genius. You *do* want medical science teams solving the dilemmas of disease. You *do* want government by the people and of the people. But in business, even when the *one* outdoes *everyone*, what happens when the one leaves or runs out of relevance? The culture is empty of any collective history, habits, or ability to innovate. Increasing the odds of brilliance is an interdependent task.

In the arithmetic of true brilliance, any number (you) multiplied by only one (your solo effort) is only equal to the original number (you, by yourself). The likelihood of success for that equation requires once-in-a-lifetime brilliance—which isn't a sound strategy. **While great ideas will continue to spring from the minds of the brilliant few, the vast majority of smart ideas and excellent execution are waiting for the rest of us.** Being smart will, as long as the group is diverse, contribute to brilliance. Laboring to be the smartest person in a room of smart people won't.

The fact is there are dozens of people behind the faces of lone geniuses responsible for an organization's success. In an issue of *Fortune* that explored the performance of Apple, Steve Jobs's picture is on the cover, but the picture inside shows six people sitting *next* to him—not behind him or in front of him. The article refers to them as the "brain trust"—a *collective* brilliance. And for every person sitting next to Jobs, there's another picture worth taking that would include the people who sit next to them. Working with people—not above, below, or around them—is where true genius is consistently found.

5: showcasing brilliance | key points

- Even though showcasing brilliance is easy to spot for those on the receiving end, perpetrators seldom see it.

- The more we expect people to recognize, appreciate, or be dazzled by our brilliance, the less they listen, *even if we do have better ideas.*

- Showcasing is the ultimate irony; the *more* we showcase, the *less* brilliance surfaces—and the less brilliant we're likely to be.

- When people move from sharing to showcasing, the smartest people are ignored—even when they're needed most.

- When ego is out of balance, there is an inverse relationship between amassing knowledge and openness to learn; the more we know, the more confident we become. When our confidence in what we know increases to the point that we think there's little left to learn, we're less open to learn. That's the point of danger; the lid to our box of knowledge begins to close and we lose relevance.

- Research shows that brilliance doesn't usually spring from one person flying solo. A discovery-driven process that explores what's happening from a variety of perspectives—rather than an idea-driven process by an individual—increases the odds of making the best decision by 50 percent.

6

early warning sign 4

seeking acceptance

> Here is a secret that no one has told you: Life is junior high.
> The world that you are about to enter is filled with junior
> high, adolescent pettiness; pubescent rivalries; the insecu-
> rities of 13-year-olds; and the false bravado of 14-year-
> olds.
>
> TOM BROKAW

If you had the chance to go back and relive junior high school, would you?

At 7:26 a.m. on a cool September morning we boarded the yellow school bus and did exactly that. Although we were a few decades removed from the right age, our visit to a junior high school quickly jolted our memories. Do you remember the peer pressure, cliques, and preoccupation of trying to fit in? It's still there. Every comment, question, and move seems to be instantly weighed against acceptance from peers. Some kids work to draw attention to themselves, while others avoid it at all costs—both extremes used to keep acceptance high. At times they tear each other down or withhold their approval so no one gets a popularity advantage or appears more acceptable than they themselves are.

Junior high is our first real introduction to the high-stakes art of seeking acceptance—what will "they" think, what did they say, what did they mean by that, what should I say, how should I act, what should I wear, what's everyone else wearing, who's hanging out with whom? While some of these concerns are driven by massive amounts of hormones—and not every attitude or behavior is dysfunctional—they're all around.

i double-dog dare ya

Formal research seems to back up our observations at school. Nearly three hundred adolescents were surveyed in the United States and Ireland to find out how many take unnecessary risks to impress their friends. Twenty-five percent admitted to driving dangerously. One-third of male students said they had done stupid stunts simply to make an impression. The compelling need for approval leads children to become ultra-self-conscious. The more self-conscious they become, the less likely they are to perform well. Performance on video games drops by 25 percent when game players are told they're being watched.

As fathers, we've seen the need for approval preoccupy our own children. More than once we've arrived home from work to have one of our children say, "Dad, come outside and watch me do a cartwheel!" Often the kids are so concerned with whether we're watching or not that their newfound skill momentarily escapes them. When children care too much about what others think and how others will react to their show, they lose sight of the performance itself. We happily ended our nostalgic day at the local junior high school just before lunchtime—which is another memory in itself. What a relief it is to be past the consuming desire to win the approval of others.

Only we're not past it entirely.

When ego isn't managed well, we don't grow out of the junior high need for acceptance, we grow into it as "grown-ups." According to one study, 30 percent of men admitted they've lifted too much weight to make an impression on their friends. Twenty-seven percent of women admit to overexercising in front of others to impress them. When running with others, runners often run faster and longer than they should. The same desire for acceptance that leads us to overexercise also leads to poor decisions and weak cultures.

junior high business

Jenny Chatman of the University of California at Berkeley's Haas School of Business studied 120 Northwestern students interviewing for jobs. Those who told corporate recruiters what recruiters love to hear, such as "Your company has a reputation for being team-oriented, and that's something I truly value," landed jobs at twice the rate of their more reserved but equally qualified or more qualified peers. While telling interviewers what they want to hear may get us a job, it may also put us in the wrong job. If you're a recruiter influenced by praise, you're likely to hire the wrong person. Whether we're on the receiving or giving end of acceptance, when we're too anxious for it, we are susceptible to insincere comments or artificial information. We're also prone to say whatever we think will get us the acceptance we need, which ironically increases the chances we'll get rejected.

In the early eighties, a good friend of ours was a partner in a small computer software firm in Boston. The Foot Locker invited his company to propose on a large retail software contract. To his surprise, they were one of only two finalists invited to make a final presentation. The other finalist was IBM. The morning arrived to make their presentation, and they delivered their best business case to the executive committee. When they finished their presentation, the CEO asked, "How big is your company?"

Privately, the size of their firm was our friend's biggest concern—especially when compared with IBM, who had already made their presentation. They were convinced they would lose the sale if they appeared too small to handle the business. One of the partners began describing how much experience they had collectively, how many clients they had done work for, how big some of the projects were they had successfully completed, and how happy those clients were with the results. He shared every ounce of information that would convey the message that they were big—at least big enough. "I was even mesmerized with his answer," said our friend. "We sounded *big*."

After seeking the CEO's acceptance, they sat down, waiting for the CEO to give it—and it came. He congratulated them on their success and then added, "For us, it's also disappointing. The last time we worked with a big, experienced company like yours, they were so unresponsive that we could never get what we needed when we needed it," he said. "Given what's at stake for us, we can't afford that kind of response again. For this purchase, we need to work with a small, responsive, entrepreneurial company. I think we're going to keep looking, but thank you very much for your presentation and interest in our project." Even when seeking acceptance does work, that doesn't mean the acceptance we flattered our way into isn't without risk.

my, what lovely teeth you have

For some, giving acceptance is a way of getting it in return. Have you seen somebody "kiss up" to someone hoping to receive approval in turn? It's a marvel the boss doesn't see through it. In an article on the finer points of giving false praise, Kim Girard of *Business 2.0* gives some suggestions for lines you can use:

"I'm really excited about your proposal. What an original idea." (Hyperbole should be down-to-earth.)

"It's like you said in last week's meeting: The brand is everything." (Bosses like to hear themselves quoted.)

"You look great. That Zone diet is really working." (Personalize your compliment so it sounds sincere.)

"Got it. Great idea. I'll do it that way, and you said you want it tonight, right?" (Show you listen intently.)

Parrot key ideas or slogans. Using the boss's pet phrases in meetings, reports, and memos shows that you're getting the message, you respect her opinions, and you firmly grasp what she wants from you on the job. This doesn't take practice, just shamelessness. *lol,*

Be aware of your manager's interests. Those pictures of your manager's dopey-looking kids cover her desk for a reason. Ask how they're doing. Does the boss love tennis? Suggest a match after work. At the very least, ask the boss to lunch. Talk about her, not you.

There's nothing necessarily wrong with the ideas above, provided the intent prompting them is genuine. But what this article seems to suggest is: lie—but don't let it look like a lie. Fake your sincerity. The tactics are nothing more than tips for deceiving people you work with who may be craving acceptance. That way of doing business needs to be undone. **The question is, what value is someone adding, and what value is the company getting, if the leader is personally craving acceptance? If a person wants to be told only what makes him or her feel good, how close to reality could that person possibly be in making decisions?**

when being nice isn't nice

When we favor popularity over candor, conversations are artificial and reality goes under the table. Isabelle Royer of the University of Paris at Dauphine researched project success in organizations. After discovering that a majority of new projects fail, she wondered why more people didn't speak up when dubious ideas were proposed, given the high failure rate and heavy cost. In an article for the *Harvard Business Review* she wrote, "Exit champions [people who have evidence that a project should be killed] need to be fearless, willing to put their reputations on the line and face the likelihood of exclusion from the camaraderie of the project team."

Bad projects don't always fail because we can't see the problems with the project. They sometimes fail because we trade candor for camaraderie or popularity. Cultures that encourage people to not speak their minds cost organizations time, money, and talented people. We asked 1,123 businesspeople, on a scale from one to ten (with one being poor and ten being great), how well their companies were doing in creating a culture where people felt free to speak up and weren't overly concerned with seeking acceptance. Here's how they rated their companies:

- People share concerns directly with people in a meeting rather than with "others" later after the meeting—5.4.
- People are not intimidated by others who are in more "powerful" positions in the organization—5.9.
- People share candid thoughts and feelings even when they'll be seen as unpopular—5.9.

Halfway to ten may not seem like it's such a bad score. On second thought, imagine that a good friend wants to set you up on a blind date. A little hesitant, you ask your friend to give an overall rating of the person's looks, personality, sense of humor, intelligence, background, interests, etc., on a scale from one to ten. If your friend answered, "Oh . . . well . . . I'd say maybe a six," would you be excited to go? The same can be said for companies; when we have level-six cultures, people aren't excited to go to work or fully engaged when they arrive.

why we do it

Most people think when someone has a problem with ego, they have too much. Seeking acceptance can be an early warning sign we have too *little* ego, which is equally ineffective. Though most people don't typically think of seeking acceptance as a sign of poorly managed ego, it may be the most common sign of all. The reason we don't see seeking acceptance as a more prominent sign is because *genuine* acceptance is so valuable. But how can seeking something so meaningful be an early warning sign? It's not—until your motive changes.

Everyone needs to know they matter—that they're worth something. Everyone is. We need love and respect. From the time we're born, we look for it, and in doing so learn that others give us acceptance based on what we do or say. When we sing our first song, say the alphabet for the first time, or take our first steps, people around us react. We interpret their reaction to what we do or say as acceptance or rejection, as approval or disapproval, or as good or bad. These reactions help us learn which beliefs and behaviors we should or shouldn't adopt. Unfortunately, there's also a misleading interpretation.

Under the influence of seeking acceptance, we believe others' reactions endorse us as acceptable or not. We don't separate our actions from who we are—intrinsically valuable human beings deserving of love and respect. To be more acceptable, we strain to project a positive image that reflects what we believe *others* think we should be, rather than the person we truly are. "If I tell you who I am," said John Powell, "you may not like who I am, and it is all that I have." When we fear rejection, being liked less, or losing acceptance, we trade authenticity and self-confidence for approval from those around us.

self-respect and acceptance

There's a vast difference between wanting respect and recognition and being desperate for it, even momentarily. **When too little ego deprives us of a healthy sense of self, getting approval from others is our primary motive and a consuming distraction to making a contribution.** We then seek acceptance because we believe if we get the approval of others, it will feed our ego what it's missing. But those are empty calories. If we're hypersensitive to how others react to the words we say, the possessions we have, the thoughts we share, or the actions we take, we give control of how we feel about ourselves to others.

When others are in the driver's seat of our self-confidence, we shape our thoughts and actions to what we believe will be endorsed by others; we become pleasers and don't offer what's on our minds. People then get good ideas from us—but sadly, not our best. Ironically, when they don't get our best, they're less likely to give us the acceptance we deserve. Somewhere deep down, we know we could have given our best and usually regret we didn't. That disappointment eats away at our confidence, and our ego is weakened.

When our desire for acceptance is healthy, love and respect are still important to us, but they aren't our solitary goal. We can want acceptance without letting it affect our self-worth or authenticity. When our desire for recognition and respect is balanced, we draw a clear distinction between who we are and what we do. We may not have been as creative as we would have liked in the last meeting, but we can still value our creativity: one stifling day doesn't mean we've lost it. We may have offered an irrelevant thought, but who doesn't? We're still capable of generating a thousand other relevant thoughts. **Ironically, the less we're worried about maintaining an ideal self-image and being endorsed by others, the more genuine acceptance and real confidence come our way.**

three principles of egonomics

We've discussed four early warning signs that indicate that the power of ego is costing us: 1) being comparative, 2) being defensive, 3) showcasing brilliance, and 4) seeking acceptance. If and when we have complaints about work over lunch or on our commute home, notice how many are the result of those four signs. We often chalk discontent up to poor communication, conflicting personality styles, or bad thinking. But underneath it all is ego, and the early warning signs of poorly managed ego won't disappear by merely trying to avoid them. Something has to take the space they occupy, or the signs quickly return.

The three principles of egonomics not only knock the early warnings signs out of their place, they occupy the vacancy. Those principles are humility, curiosity, and veracity. As we mentioned in the opening chapter, those three principles not only require us to do differently, they require us to *be* different. With the intent to lead and work better than we have, let's explore the first principle, humility.

Note: A free egonomics survey that measures the degree of humility, curiosity, and veracity in your team or company is available at www.egonomicsbook.com/teamsurvey.

6: seeking acceptance | key points

- When ego isn't managed well, we don't grow out of the junior high need for acceptance, we grow into it as "grown-ups."

- Whether we're on the receiving or giving end of acceptance, when we're too anxious for it, we are susceptible to insincere comments or artificial information. We're also prone to say whatever we think will get us the acceptance we need, which ironically increases the chances we'll get rejected.

- What value is someone adding, and what value is the company getting, if a leader is personally craving acceptance? If a person wants to be told only what makes him or her feel good, how close to reality could that person possibly be in making decisions?

- When we're reluctant to risk being candid rather than popular, conversations are artificial and reality goes under the table. That reluctance is a major reason "dumb" projects in companies don't get killed as early or often as they should.

- Most people think that when people have a problem with ego, they have too much. Seeking acceptance can be an early warning sign we have too *little* ego, which is equally ineffective.

- When others are in the driver's seat of our self-confidence, we shape our thoughts and actions to what we believe will be endorsed by others; we become pleasers and don't offer what's on our minds. People then get good ideas from us— but not our best.

7
humility

True humility is intelligent self-respect which keeps us from thinking too highly or too meanly of ourselves. It makes us modest by reminding us how far we have come short of what we can be.

RALPH SOCKMAN

In the first chapter we wrote that because of ego's economic impact, the first priority of business is managing the power of ego. If getting control of that power is our first priority, then humility is the first discipline for doing so. For each of us, there is a continuum of ego. At one end of the continuum, we have too little ego; at the other, too much. Humility is the equilibrium between the two extremes. Three unique properties of humility keep us at equilibrium:

1. we, then me (devotion to progress)
2. i'm brilliant, and i'm not (duality)
3. one more thing (constructive discontent)

When these three properties govern ego, we get positive results ego can't deliver by itself. To understand why, let's explore what humility is, what it's not, and how it works.

As we mentioned earlier, there was a host of questions our investigation of humility and ego set out to answer: What is it about ego that allows leaders to take their organizations to good but without humility never allows them to move to great? Why does it appear that ego is something we must have if we want to succeed, but having it often interferes with the success we pursue? Are there habits we can develop that manage the drive of ego? Should it be managed in the first place? If humility is so powerful, and a necessity for level-5 leadership, why don't more of us have it? Can we learn to be humble? If ego and humility can't coexist, what has to give, and what change is required? Our experience is that people are hungry for the answers; 83 percent of people we surveyed wish their organizations had more humility.

But despite the desire for it, humility has a mystery about it that's both appealing and unsettling at the same time. Traditionally, humility—or being humble—is known more for what it's not than for what it is; definitions of *humble* include "not arrogant or prideful," "not high in rank," or "not boastful." Most words associated with *humility* don't get clearer or more attractive. Among appealing words like *modest, polite, respectful, patient,* and *unpretentious,* the word *humility* is surrounded by unsettling negatives: *passive, apprehensive, content, cautious, fearful, hesitant, ordinary, quiet, self-conscious, meek, simple, submissive, soft-spoken, timid,* and *unambitious,* among others—words that don't exactly leave a favorable impression.

While leading our workshops, a question reveals what many

people believe deep down about humility: if two people were debating or competing, and one was egotistical and the other was
humble, who would win? The majority of people answer, "The egotistical person." Why? Because while humility is an admirable trait,
there's suspicion about its weaknesses: who wants anything to do
with humility if it's incompatible with winning? That question
wasn't easy at first to square in our own minds. In a relentlessly
competitive business environment where we're paid to aggressively
take market share from competitors, drive revenue and profit, and
compare and rank people internally for a limited supply of com-
pensation, where does humility fit in?

Even when humility gets a positive spin in the business press,
the apparent risks aren't far behind. For instance, in an article
for the *NewYork Post* titled "Iger's apparent humility seen as strength,"
the opening starts positive but ends with a warning. "You can say
this much for Disney CEO Bob Iger," wrote Peter Lauria, "he
doesn't seem to mind sharing the limelight. This time around, however, it could end up costing the 54-year-old executive his job.
While Iger's bold move to cede Steve Jobs both a Disney board
seat—and the largest individual stock stake in the company—
underscores precisely how far removed the Mouse House is from
Michael "Ego" Eisner's reign, it also places Jobs in a position to easily usurp Iger's authority." Praise of Iger's humility is quickly followed by the looming threat of unemployment.

If humility puts us at risk, it's no wonder we feel it belongs
more in a church than in a corporation. Not surprisingly, we don't
find many people in our leadership sessions—at least initially—
consciously focused on cultivating humility. Occasionally people in
our classes fold their arms and stare sternly as we begin the discussion on humility, as if to say, "Go ahead and try." After all, business is
anything but an altruistic endeavor, and at first glance, humility appears to be altruistic. A business leader at one of our workshops

raised his hand and said, "I've been taught my whole life to embrace ego. My parents drove it into me from the time I can remember. I've been taught—by just about everyone I know—that's how you succeed, that's how you lead, that's how you beat your competitors."

"Then why give it up?" someone asked. "You're young, the head of your own company, financially successful. What you've been taught seems to have worked for you." After a long silence, the CEO spoke. "Because in sitting here over the last three hours, I realize I've been out of balance with my ego," he said. "My mind's racing back to different situations I've been in, and it's killing me to think about the opportunities it has cost me. In spite of what I've achieved, my ego has hurt me as much as it's helped me. In fact, I think in some ways I've been my own nightmare competitor because of my lack of humility." What he realized is that despite his success, his ego was managing him, not the other way around. That left him unable to fully utilize its power. Humility would have given him the balance he was missing.

humility's equilibrium

What is humility? The quote that begins this chapter is the clearest definition, with slight modification: **humility is intelligent self-respect that keeps us from thinking too much or too little of ourselves. It reminds us how far we have come while *at the same time* helping us see how far short we are of what we can be.** With the definition of humility in mind, let's explore the relationship between ego and humility. For most people, tradition holds that the opposite of excessive ego is humility, when in fact having too little ego is just as dangerous and unproductive as having too much.

Since the three properties of humility exist only at the equilibrium, when we're on center, our talents stay true to form. But since

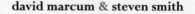

there's a natural tendency to deviate from the equilibrium, when we move just right or left of center, we begin to lose humility. As a result, our strengths morph into counterfeits—that is, into subtle weaknesses. Imagine that the spectrum of ego is magnetic, with the strongest pull coming from the two ends. At the center, the magnetic pull on either side has little effect on us. But the closer we move to the extremes, the more the magnetic pull affects us and the harder it is to make our way back. The longer we stay off-center, the more comfortable we become being off-center. If we don't quickly recover, we're more likely to develop egotistical habits.

Ego doesn't suddenly pull us to the extremes and twist us overnight into egomaniacs, or lead us to believe we're above the law. But once we're in the habit of being off-center, we do slowly start to believe we're above other things: reproach, being wrong, being questioned, the need to prove we're right, having a bad idea, following the lead of others, and so on. Being consistently off-center leads us gradually toward the extremes.

When an entire culture or team is off-center, it's rarely the responsibility of only one person, but the imbalance can't start without the permission of at least one person and the steady agreement of others. That's what makes the four early warning signs of ego so valuable: they let us know we're being pulled off-center, and therefore losing talent. But whether we're consistently or momentarily off-center, ego's drive is so strong, only humility can pull us back.

terminally unique

Jahn Prince is a charismatic, creative, and accomplished friend of ours. He was also pinned by ego at one end of the equilibrium. Early in his career, Jahn built a successful business and enjoyed everything that came with it: a beautiful home, a cabin, boats, cars, toys, and so on. "I was competitive and I was the center of the universe," he said. "I wasn't sure there was a God, but if there was one, I even saw him as a competitor." But regardless of his belief or disbelief, and in spite of his accomplishments, it seemed the deity had a plan for him. "One of the most difficult things for God to do, especially for those to whom he's given so much talent," said journalist Scoop Jackson, "is to take things away from them to keep them hungry—to shape their souls." Jahn's shaping began in 1979.

On December 30, 1979, Jahn's business burned to the ground. Forty days later, he lost his home to fire, nearly losing his two-year-old daughter before breaking through a window to rescue her. For every bolt of lightning life threw, Jahn stood resolute and rebuilt what he had lost. Working eighteen-hour days for months on end, Jahn personally rebuilt his home and his business. But that reconstruction was easy compared to the reconstruction he personally needed. For nearly two decades, Jahn was an alcoholic. In fact, even though he hasn't had a drink in eleven years, he would tell you he still is.

After drinking heavily one day, Jahn knew he had to make a choice: he was either going to let his disease kill him or call for help. He sought help. Today, Jahn counsels others suffering from addiction. Knowing humility to be a central step in the recovery process taught at Alcoholics Anonymous, we asked Jahn what role humility played for him. "You have to understand that the disease of alcoholism is cunning and powerful. But it's also patient," he said.

"It has nothing else to do but keep coming after you. One of the first steps you have to take to overcome alcoholism is to acquire enough humility to admit you're powerless over it on your own— you need help. But I was 'terminally unique.' I thought I was uniquely qualified to drink like I did and not have it affect me. I had a successful career and everything that comes with it. I wasn't a homeless guy living under the viaduct. I kept saying to myself, 'If I was an alcoholic, I wouldn't be this successful.' "

Jahn didn't reach for help earlier in his life because he didn't think he had a problem. "Even though I was successful, my real potential was being held hostage because I was looking at life through a Johnny Walker bottle," he said. "Alcoholism shuns detection. If you go to the doctor with a heart problem and she tells you that you need surgery, you don't say, 'No, I don't.' But with addiction, you ignore it. You think you have an argument against it when you really don't." After so many years without a drink, friends ask him why he still attends the AA meetings. "Alcoholism never goes away" is his answer. "Your ego keeps trying to tell you you're done—that you can do it on your own, that you're finished. Humility reminds you that you never are."

Vital lessons surfaced in our interview with Jahn that paralleled our study of the relationship between ego and humility, not the least of which is the idea of "terminal uniqueness." **Terminal uniqueness is thinking we're uniquely qualified to behave the way we do—that we wouldn't be as successful as we are if our behaviors or attitudes were destructive.** That belief blinds us to what is happening to us and around us. Consequently, we may not get worse, but we also don't get better. As we drift further from humility, ego delivers the misleading message that we're finished. Humility reminds us we never are. We can stay constantly aware that we're unfinished and therefore constantly improve if we embrace humility's three unique properties:

1. we, then me (devotion to progress)
2. i'm brilliant, and i'm not (duality)
3. one more thing (constructive discontent)

The deepest level of humility is at the intersection of those three properties. Because "we, then me" establishes the primary intent of everything we do in egonomics, let's explore it first.

1. we, then me

The core ambition of humility is a remarkable devotion to progress. In business, that devotion translates to the progress of our company: the project we're on, the client in front of us, the market we serve, and so on. That devotion requires a sequential focus: company first, me second. Devotion to progress doesn't exclude what we personally need, it just prioritizes the focus.

At first glance, devotion to progress could sound like a nice, but naive idea—naive because, according to most, that's not the way we currently do business. In a Rutgers and University of Connecticut poll, 58 percent of workers believe most top executives put their own self-interest ahead of the company's, while 67 percent don't believe their bosses have the firm's best interests at heart. The only realistic way to change that number is to believe that by putting the company's needs first, we will make both ourselves and the company better. And before anyone will buy a more selfless approach to business, we need to ask an ironic question: what's in it for me? **The truth is that the less we focus on our needs *first,* the more likely our needs will be met.** Let's explore the idea.

Imagine for a moment you're a salesperson for IBM (or any company). In a high-performance culture, the pressure is on. Like every salesperson, you have a monthly quota. Hitting your quota could mean many things: commission, promotion, reputation, college tuition, weddings, house payments, retirement, and so on. With that pressure, you have a sales presentation to make on a several-hundred-thousand-dollar proposal. If you walk into that meeting and begin making your presentation with your focus first and foremost on *your* needs—to hit your numbers and get your commission—are you more or less likely to make the sale? The answer is less likely. But why?

As soon as the clients sense a me-first intent from you, that intent taints the interaction on both sides. You may oversell product features, rush through a technical explanation, mistake understanding for agreement and enthusiasm, smooth over objections, or push too hard for the close. As the clients feel your intent, they grow suspicious of what you say, become guarded about what they say, and don't give you access to information or people they otherwise would. In turn, their trust in you goes down, you lose the sale, and your company loses the revenue. In fact, maybe you have a better product than your competitors, and the client loses the economic benefit of getting the best solution. Everybody loses.

In sales, the more important it is to meet your numbers, the more important it is to forget about *your* numbers and help clients meet *their* numbers. In other words, the more important it is for you and your company to progress, the more important it is for you to suspend the focus on that progress and devote yourself to the progress of your clients first. The irony is that in suspending your own needs, you are more likely to meet your clients' needs, which in turn advances the progress of your company, and you therefore become more likely to meet your needs.

when winning is losing

The same sequence of whose needs we focus on applies whether we're working to meet external or internal client needs. If progress is truly our primary motivation, we won't let individual passion and commitment to a project or idea drift into a me-first, company-second view. That doesn't mean we shouldn't fight fiercely for our individual team's needs, but we should be guided by what's best for the business, not just our own territory. Consider the email from a Fortune 100 general manager to his leadership team inviting a more "we, then me" focus:

To: Leadership team
Subject: Food for thought

As the planning process for [product name] unfolds, I'm seeing or hearing some behaviors that could be destructive to our long-term goals. Essentially, everyone is feeling the pinch of our budget reality, but most are also lobbying for their group to get a bigger piece of the work that we need to accomplish. Sometimes that lobbying is in the form of emails, sometimes it's in planning meetings, sometimes it's accomplished through prototypes, etc. My only conclusion is that somehow I've created an environment where people believe that the way to get more resources is to sign up for unrealistic deliverables.

Prototyping and dreaming are activities we need to encourage, so I don't want anyone to interpret my statement as not being in favor of that activity. As leaders, I expect you to guide the team through the tradeoffs it takes to make the transition from prototype or dream to funded project. Sometimes more than one good idea will exist in the same area and we'll be forced to choose. Sometimes even a great idea won't rise above the threshold that has us reprioritize other work in order to fit it in. Oftentimes, you will be asked to do more with less. In the end, *we have to do what's right for the business, even if the individual dreams of some of our best people can't be accommodated.*

I hope to hear statements from each of you like "Doing X is more important than Y. Even though I'm responsible for Y, I think we should cut it and move the resources to focus on X." Unfortunately today, I'm more likely to get "I understand Y better than anybody else . . . Y may not be the most important thing we could do, but it's really cool and it will motivate my team, so I should fight for it."

We all have work to do. Thanks.

What message is he trying to get across? The business comes first.

go ahead, be a survivalist

But let's say this manager's company is on the ropes and downsizing on the horizon. Is his business-first request unrealistic to people vying for a limited number of jobs? Should they ignore the email and take a "survival of the fittest" approach? Even though that's a typical response, it would be exactly the wrong approach. In good times, a company needs contribution from people, and people want to keep their jobs. But do company or employee needs change in difficult times? The answer is no.

The needs for *both* increase when times are hard: companies need more contribution and people need greater job security. **If "we, then me" is effective when times are good, it's no less effective when times are bad.** The irony of a survival-of-the-fittest mentality is that as pressure for survival increases, so does the temptation to abandon humility and adopt a "me, then we" attitude——to be defensive about our ideas, treat colleagues as competitors, occupy time showcasing our "you can't live without me" brilliance, and seek the acceptance of those who can send us to the unemployment line. As ego takes control, our performance decreases. By definition, that decline puts us one step closer to the exit. If ego minimizes our strengths, we won't be judged on what we're capable of contributing at our best, but on what ego's counterfeits allow us to contribute. The more we focus on self-survival, the less likely we are to survive. "We, then me" is the most direct strategy and incentive for survival——on both sides of the equation.

"Economists have long assumed that success boils down to personal incentives. We'll cooperate if it's in our self-interest, and we won't if it's not (sort of like lions)," said Jerry Useem of *Fortune*. "Then a team of researchers led by behavioral psychologist Linnda Caporael thought to ask: Would people cooperate without any incentives? The answer was——gasp!——yes, under the right conditions. Participants often cited 'group welfare' as motivation. To economists, shocking. To anyone who's been part of a successful team, not shocking at all. [The] boss who assumes that workers' interests are purely mercenary will end up with a group of mercenaries."

the economics of "we, then me"

It's important to remember that devotion to progress abides by an economic reality; since the company is investing for the return and living with the risk, its needs factor in accordingly. For instance, if an employee makes a mistake that costs the company money, the company eats the cost; it doesn't come out of the employee's pocket directly. As a result, the business comes first. But even with that reality, it doesn't make sense that a company would be interested only in its progress to the exclusion of the needs of its employees.

It's equally ineffective for an employee to pursue individual progress to the detriment of the company. A company shouldn't skew the balance to 90/10 in favor of its needs, and individual contributors should be clear the balance isn't 50/50 either. When either side miscalculates the ratio, they misjudge the consequences to a culture. When people perceive unfair disparity, they hold back, and devotion to progress evaporates in favor of "doing their job" and collecting a paycheck. Not all strikes from work are on picket lines with signs of grievances.

Devotion to progress doesn't mean you can *always* meet everyone's needs, but you can diligently consider them before you make a decision. Those considerations will be subjective, and only you can determine your motive behind them. The sequence of focus we're suggesting doesn't eliminate selfishness or guarantee selflessness, on either side. It does, at least, provide the opportunity to strike the right balance between "we" and "me."

the moment of truth

Devotion to progress sometimes requires sacrifice for causes greater than ourselves, with no immediate or apparent return to us. That devotion was displayed by one of the most courageous, devoted people we studied. Her name was Isabella Baumfree (which she later changed to Sojourner Truth). As an African American woman who escaped slavery, she became a powerful advocate for women's rights and freedom from slavery. In 1851, Truth went to the National Women's Rights Convention and requested to speak. She was such a powerful voice for freedom, her opponents made a move in an attempt to humiliate and disqualify her from speaking at the conference. It is reported that officials ordered her to go to the women's restroom and bare her breast to prove that she was a woman.

At that moment, Truth had a choice: she could walk away and allow injustice to subdue her voice, or agree to a demeaning test and liberate her voice. As she removed her clothing, she said, "It is to your shame, not mine, that I do this." To leaders full of humility, there is no humiliation—only purpose and progress. Humiliation is a feeling most often felt by those who lack humility. Upon getting dressed again, she delivered her "Ain't I a Woman?" speech. Here's an excerpt:

> *That man over there says that women need to be helped into carriages, and lifted over ditches, and to have the best place everywhere. Nobody ever helps me into carriages, or over mud-puddles, or gives me any best place! And ain't I a woman? Look at me! Look at my arm! I have ploughed and planted, and gathered into barns, and no man could head me! And ain't I a woman? I could work as much and eat as much as a man— when I could get it—and bear the lash as well! And ain't I a woman?*
>
> *I have borne thirteen children, and seen most all sold off to slavery, and when I cried out with my mother's grief, none but Jesus heard me! And ain't I a woman? Then they talk about this thing in the head; what's this they call it? [a member of the audience whispers, "Intellect."] That's it, honey. What's that got to do with women's rights or negroes' rights? If my cup won't hold but a pint, and yours holds a quart, wouldn't you be mean not to let me have my little half measure full?*

Truth's message was a revolution for the times, and her humility was the delicate balance between the arrogance that wouldn't have allowed her to walk into that bathroom, and the lack of ego that would have prevented her from asking to speak at all. In spite of her feelings of inadequacy about her ability to speak to a large audience, she had the conviction that what she had to say from center stage was worth hearing and would make a difference. She stayed at the center of humility's equilibrium, and that made it possible for her to have a profound impact on the women's movement.

2. i'm brilliant, and i'm not (duality)

Because of the genuine confidence humility produces, we can be both bold and meek at the same time. We can be as comfortable passionately making a point as listening to another's opposing point. Humility can follow the lead of someone else one moment and just as easily be the leader the next. That duality is the second unique property of humility.

Duality fuses traits that otherwise appear to be in conflict, adding complements to our strengths so they don't become one-dimensional. Take, for example, someone with the strengths of intense passion and fierce determination. At first glance, those characteristics seem incompatible with traits like meekness and flexibility. That perceived incompatibility is a false dichotomy.

Many leaders believe that some traits they have are incompatible with others they would like to acquire. During a workshop on power and leadership taught by Dr. Roderick Kramer of Stanford University, he asked participants which leadership qualities they wished they possessed more of. "Despite their proven success," said Kramer, "these leaders felt they were still too nice and too concerned about what their employees thought of them." In other words, they wished they were tougher. One executive said, "I would love to have Carly Fiorina's ability to stare down her opponents." When we're unaware of duality, we believe it's either this or that—either we have to be tough (and stare people down) or we have to be nice (and too soft).

But humility isn't a dichotomy, it's a duality. As such, humility has the capacity to say I am something and I am nothing—at the same time. I am accomplished and, at the same time, unfinished; talented and average; special, and better than no one; extraordinary and ordinary; popular and unknown; deserving of respect, and no more deserving than another. "The test of a first-rate intelligence," said F. Scott Fitzgerald, "is the ability to hold two opposing ideas in the mind at the same time and still retain the ability to function."

When we embrace humility's confident, dual nature, the early warning signs of ego are eradicated. Comparison weakens because while we can strive to be something significant, we don't suffer from the delusion that we can be everything. Seeking acceptance is uneasy next to humility because we're at ease being both loved and disliked. Showcasing can't occupy the thoughts of a person who acknowledges his brilliance and yet understands that it's not the only brilliance on the planet, or even in the room. Defensiveness can't penetrate our management style when we're willing to admit that, although we're often right, we're also often wrong.

Duality doesn't erase our identity but simply balances and elevates the traits we already have. Duality doesn't force us to become something we're not. **Humility isn't the architect of plain personalities. It is the engineer of stronger ones.**

what color is humility?

On February 14, 1986, Dr. Taylor Hartman, who wrote *The Color Code* on personality traits and characteristics, was nearly prevented from completing his work. As he was driving home from a Valentine's Day dinner with his wife, Jean, they were involved in a head-on collision. As a result of the crash, he suffered severe memory loss. He couldn't remember patients from his practice. He temporarily lost his own identity, causing him to feel like a stranger to his wife and family. "For the first time in my life," said Hartman, "I recognized how enviable it is to be somebody—to feel truly unique and alive. I desperately needed my sense of identity. I felt desperate and lost without my personality." As time passed, Hartman regained his personality, his memory, and his identity. During his recovery, he began to appreciate more deeply the differences in personality among his family and friends, each of whom brought unique value and perspective to his life.

His suffering and return to health reignited his commitment to his innovative work on personality theory. Hartman's work is groundbreaking. Not only does his research suggest that we're born with a certain personality type as unique and genetic as a fingerprint, but he asserts that our core motive drives our behaviors. And while personality and typical behaviors associated with each personality type can change dimensions, who we are and our core motivation never changes. "Your personality watches over you like a parent," says Hartman. "Without clear-cut personality traits to mark our paths through life, we would become lost." He labels his four categories of personality red, blue, yellow, and white. The chart below shows the core motives and gives very brief descriptions for each.

Red–power values productivity, wants to be respected	**Blue–intimacy** values relationships, wants to be good
Yellow–fun values being fully engaged in life, wants to look good	**White–peace** values independence, wants to feel good and be respected

So if you were to vote, what personality do you think would have the easiest time acquiring humility? When we ask that question during our leadership sessions, whites are the first voted in. Blues are easily voted into second place, while yellows are hardly mentioned, and reds are a complete shutout. After the initial vote we sit silent, and within seconds the debate among participants begins. Eventually, the class gravitates to general consensus: "No one has the easiest time acquiring humility." They're right. In our experience, there is little or no correlation between personality type and the capacity for humility. Duality isn't about blues switching their core personality over to white, yellows turning blue, or reds losing their color. Humility is not homogeneity.

What is true about personality is that the early warning signs can be linked to specific personality types: reds with showcasing, blues with defensiveness, yellows with comparison, and whites with seeking acceptance. But in terms of personality and the development of humility, nobody has an easy road. Duality doesn't require abandonment of who we are, but it does require adaptation.

balancing act

Without sacrificing our personality, duality allows "opposing" traits to coexist. That's why we need duality: it frees us from a one-sided development of our strengths. By coexisting, our talents stay true to form: we neither overdo nor underuse each trait.

strength	duality's balance
ambitious	selfless
certain	open-minded
charismatic	down-to-earth
competitive	collaborative
decisive	receptive
determined	flexible
direct	diplomatic
fearless	discreet
independent	inclusive
intense	easygoing
motivated	patient

If either trait excludes the other, that particular trait weakens in the other's absence. For example, let's use the first two traits listed in the chart above: *ambitious* and *selfless*. If we overrely on ambition in a debate, we crowd out other ideas or people to make our point. We use over-the-top words like "always," "never," "everyone," or "nobody" to convey the passion of our argument, which sends a message to colleagues: this is oration, not conversation. On the other hand, if we lean too heavily on being selfless, we choose words so carefully, hoping not to rock the boat, that our point gets steamrolled in the process. Our passion is lost in politeness, and confidence loses out to deference and courtesy.

unfinished business

Since everyone is unfinished and missing at least one balancing trait, we each have work to do. For some the work may be minor remodeling, for others it may look more like demolition. In either case, the scope of work to be done depends on the role we allow duality to play. "Many of the more conventional books on leadership show leaders as mythic and heroic figures," says Dr. Kramer of Stanford University. "Students want their leaders to be perfect and without any personal blemishes. What they fail to realize is that sometimes the very qualities that make someone imperfect also help explain their tremendous drive to succeed and energy to focus on one narrow realm of achievement. [Steve] Jobs is a great example. He is a creative genius and yet he has an amazing ability to alienate some people and drive them away from his organization."

But what is it about creative genius that alienates people and drives them away? It isn't creative genius that's the problem, it's what's *missing* from genius that's the trouble. Early in his career, Jobs was described as someone who ruled "by force of personality, making numerous enemies with his ridiculing of the ideas of others, his unwillingness to hear views contrary to his own, and his outbursts of bad temper." But why argue for Jobs to add to his genius traits like inclusion or mutual respect when he's responsible for starting Apple in his parents' garage and growing his company within ten years to a $2 billion organization by the time he was thirty? Why would "balance" even matter? Because what he accomplished to that point is a narrow view of what he was capable of achieving. When we're too narrow in our development of traits, we limit what we accomplish. As it turns out, humility had a lesson in store for Jobs that would balance his creative genius and as a result widen what he achieved. In his commencement speech to the graduating class of 2005 at Stanford University, Jobs shared his lesson in humility:

> *And then I got fired [from Apple in 1985]. How can you get fired from a company you started? Well, as Apple grew, we hired someone who I thought was very talented to run the company with me, and for the first year or so things went well. But then our visions of the future began to diverge and eventually we had a falling out. When we did, our Board of Directors sided with him. So at thirty I was out. And very publicly out. What had been the focus of my entire adult life was gone, and it was devastating. I really didn't know what to do for a few months. I felt that I had let the previous generation of entrepreneurs down—that I had dropped the baton as it was being passed to me. I met with David Packard [cofounder of Hewlett-Packard] and Bob Noyce [cofounder of Fairchild Semiconductor and Intel, and known as the Mayor of Silicon Valley] and tried to apologize for screwing up so badly. I was a very public failure, and I even thought about running away from the valley.*

If we don't let humility teach us first, circumstance—like a stock market "correction"—will usually do the job. Stunned at the turn of events in his career and unable to explain why, Jobs said, "Sometimes life hits you in the head with a brick."

Ejected from Apple, Jobs started his next venture, a computer company appropriately named NeXT. But NeXT didn't come close to producing the success of Apple. Seven years later, Jobs closed the factory, laid off half the employees, and shifted the company's direction to software development. Not until 1995 did NeXT turn a profit. In December of that same year, Apple bought the company for $400 million. The same year Jobs started NeXT, he also bought a struggling computer animation studio named Pixar from movie mogul George Lucas. The Pixar story was a little brighter; in 1988 it won an Oscar for its computer-animated short film *Tin Toy*. In 1991 Pixar secured a deal with Walt Disney for three animated films and started work on the blockbuster movie *Toy Story*.

But none of these events represents the most interesting part of Jobs's story. In 1997 it must have felt like déjà vu when Jobs was named "interim" CEO of Apple, which was in a near free fall. One of his first moves was to drop the very operating system that he had developed at NeXT and that Apple had purchased from him two years earlier. That move wasn't the Steve Jobs of old. "Every year he's mellowed and matured," said Susan Kelly Barnes, NeXT's former chief financial officer. She's not the only one who noticed changes in Jobs. A biography by Kirk Beetz reveals what can only be described as a metamorphosis of Steve Jobs:

> *Although he was still certain that his vision for Apple was the only right one, Jobs' management style had radically changed from what it had been in 1985; he seemed more relaxed and open to ideas. In fact, he seemed to relish other people's ideas; perhaps his work at Pixar had improved his ability to work with the creative people at Apple. He wisely surrounded himself with top-notch executives in all the key corporate positions, and he held on to them rather than driving them away. Almost by willing it, he transformed the corporate culture into one in which employees wanted to come to work and where they saw themselves as part of a great company that had a mission to change the world for the better. Moreover, Jobs, the hobbyist of old, brought the fun back into tinkering with electronics.*

The irony of duality is that when we acknowledge we're unfinished, we become stronger. Jobs seems to agree. "I'm pretty sure none of this [NeXT, Pixar, his return to Apple, the iPod, and iTunes] would have happened if I hadn't been fired from Apple," says Jobs. "It was awful-tasting medicine, but I guess the patient needed it."

Duality is the admission that we are knowledgeable *and* ignorant, strong *and* weak, right *and* wrong, capable *and* at the same time incomplete. Let's now return to some of the less than attractive traits we mentioned earlier that surround the word *humility*: *submissive, meek, quiet, simple, cautious, soft-spoken, self-effacing,* and *passive*. With duality, most of these traits now appear to have strengths when not isolated. Sometimes it requires more inner strength to be submissive than it does to be independent. Duality exists in all of those characteristics—meekness and boldness, modesty and brilliance, self-effacement and self-confidence. Duality, as a unique property of humility, leads us to an appropriate sense that we're unfinished, and thereby puts us on the doorstep to the final property of humility: one more thing (constructive discontent).

3. one more thing (constructive discontent)

In addition to "we, then me" (devotion to progress) and "i'm brilliant, and i'm not" (duality), the last unique property of humility is "one more thing" (constructive discontent). U2 band members Bono and Larry Mullen epitomize the essence of "one more thing." As the lead singer of U2, Bono has won fourteen Grammys and produced fifteen albums that have sold 130 million copies. When asked what his favorite song or album is, Bono answered, "We haven't written it yet." Larry Mullen, U2 founder and drummer, added, "We're constantly unsatisfied as a band. We've got all this stuff, but maybe we haven't earned it. There are contemporaries who have worked equally as hard as U2 and don't have as much success. We're uncomfortable with it; we need to prove ourselves." That pursuit of perfection and proving oneself is the power of "one more thing."

Constructive discontent works hand in hand with humility's devotion to progress. In fact, humility is wholly dedicated to progress. And when it comes to progress, Toyota is a model citizen of constructive discontent. In reality, it's not "Toyota," but the people at Toyota, who are currently on track to make their company the world's largest automobile manufacturer. In fact, by the time you're reading this, projections suggest they already will be. For the third year in a row, Toyota was awarded International Engine of the Year for the revolutionary hybrid Prius. If you added the J. D. Power 5 Stars and Motor Trend Cars of the Year awards, you would need an endless inventory of stars and trophies. In a *Fast Company* article on Toyota's dissatisfaction with satisfaction, Charles Fishman writes of a recent improvement the Georgetown, Kentucky, Toyota plant made in how it paints cars. While their process wasn't "broken" by competitive standards, it wasn't perfect. That imperfection was incentive enough.

Fishman goes on to describe how they improved the painting: nozzles, paint cartridges, paint flush changes, processes, etc. "Cars now spend eight hours in paint, instead of ten," writes Fishman. "The paint shop at any moment holds 25 percent fewer cars than it used to. Wasted paint? Practically zero. What used to require one hundred gallons now takes seventy." But the details of the specific improvements aren't really the point. "[Improvement] is rooted in an institutional obsession with improvement that Toyota manages to instill in each one of its workers, a pervasive lack of complacency with whatever was accomplished yesterday. [What's] interesting is to compare how they think about work at Georgetown with every-where else. How come the checkout lines at Wal-Mart never get shorter? How come the customer service of your cell phone com-pany never improves, year after year? How come my PC gets harder to operate with each software upgrade? It's almost as if Toyota people see the world with special four-dimensional glasses; the rest of us are stuck in 2-D."

When driven by constructive discontent, we aren't looking for a final destination thinking we're "finished." Instead, we value the movement along the way as much as, or more than, the end result. "We're all incredibly proud of what we've accomplished," said Chad Buckner, an engineering manager of Toyota's paint division. "But you don't stop. You don't stop. There's no reason to be satisfied." His colleague John Shook added, "Once you realize that it's the process itself—that you're not seeking a plateau—you can relax. Doing the task and doing the task better become one and the same thing." What Toyota has realized is the difference between merely having a process for kaizen (a Japanese word for "improvement"), and a culture with a kaizen attitude.

The Toyota story is an example of small changes made inside a very large corporate machine. Important changes aren't always a vision that descends upon us, seizes us, and galvanizes everyone. If you just consider the paint change improvement as a snapshot, it wouldn't seem revolutionary. But small, incremental changes ac-cumulated over time make the bigger difference. That doesn't mean that constructive discontent is only about small, nearly indiscernible differences. Sometimes changes *are* revolutions, but most of the time they're not. Besides, whether the changes are big or small misses the point—it's the attitude and drive that analyze opportunities and pursue change that matters. To explore why, let's return momentarily to the work of Jim Collins in *Good to Great*. There was something about Collins's research that was different from any other in our study of the last fifty years of management writing. His work wasn't an investigation of companies that were great from the day they were born. It was a study of transformation: decades of good performance, marked by a transition period to great. In that transition, most of the good-to-great companies weren't forced by any urgent dilemma to change.

Market conditions didn't transform these companies; in fact, Collins created criteria to ensure it wasn't the market's "fault" they made the leap. Each company had to move itself. In essence, these cultures appeared dependent on humility because they *wanted* to change, not because they *needed* to change—in other words, because of constructive discontent. To a certain degree, Intel cofounder Andrew Grove's statement that "only the paranoid survive" is an extreme version of that very idea. That's why the acute awareness of the *early* warning signs is so important. They're signs that let us know progress has stalled. In the pursuit of progress, constructive discontent makes us less comfortable where we are, and less stubborn in making a change.

But when you carefully inspect the tasks required for that change, it becomes more apparent why humility surfaces so prominently. Collins first observed what he came to call the "first who, then what" strategy. That meant companies had to get the "right people on the bus" and the wrong people off, even before they decided what they were going to be or do as an organization. Once the seats on the bus were taken, each company had to discover what they *could* be best in the world at, regardless of what they were currently doing or *wished* they could be best at. But it wasn't the "company" that had to make those admissions. It was people; it was the leaders. In other words, human beings had to discern the difference between what they *wanted* to be best in the world at and what they really *could* be best in the world at—a critical distinction not easily recognized with too much or too little ego. In their pursuit of great, every task that lay ahead of these leaders required uncommon dialogue.

humility's traction

As we mentioned earlier, egonomics is a study of great moments, not great leaders. But over time crucial moments build reflexes in us that keep us closer to the center of humility's equilibrium or push us farther away. Of the interviews we conducted for the study of egonomics, one of the more remarkable set of reflexes we observed was that of Jim Thyen.

Thyen is CEO of Kimball International, a $1.2 billion furniture and electronics company. Given our emphasis on economic performance and ego's role in that performance, some might be surprised that we're writing about a company whose sales have been flat for five years. To an outsider, Kimball certainly wouldn't seem to qualify as a good-to-great company. But the numbers on the outside don't always reveal the story on the inside. The transformation to greatness is usually reported at the end of the road, when remarkable results sing the company's praises and the glamour of a goal reached conceals the labor and sweat it took to get there. This is a story of sweat.

Kimball International began in contract furniture in 1949. From there it expanded and diversified. Television cabinetry in the 1950s, pianos in the '60s (at its peak, Kimball made over 250 pianos and 150 organs every day), commercial office furniture in the '70s, and residential and hospitality furniture and electronics in the 1980s spurred the company's growth to $1.2 billion with over nine thousand employees by 2000. Named to the Fortune 500 in 1988 for the first time, Kimball was twice included as one of "America's Most Admired Companies."

But that was about to change.

Kimball's consistent performance over decades caused everyone to feel good about the business. During the good times, Kimball lived by the "might as well" strategy. They expanded horizontally and vertically, continued to invest in pianos simply because it was their legacy, and moved into markets when customer demands in those markets was changing rapidly. Despite the changes, they told themselves they could do it all. But when they did it all, the diversification masked the rapid changes coming. Markets started to shift, the effects of a recession began, and revenue in certain business units dropped suddenly, accelerated by September 11, 2001. Kimball's overall market declined from $12 billion to $8 billion.

Over the years, Kimball slowly insulated itself. "We weren't recognizing that the 'water in the pan' was getting warmer one degree at a time," said Thyen. "Our headquarters was located in a community where most people shared similar experiences and mind-sets. For instance, self-reliance was ingrained into the company culture, and that self-reliance naturally comes with a strong sense of pride, which gradually led to isolationism. The similarities among us were so strong that changes in the market didn't send alarm signals. I feared we were headed down the slippery slope of entitlement. We believed the world should come to us."

While Kimball waited for the world, the world didn't budge. Globalization and the Internet changed the customer relationship with manufacturers. Reading customer expectations was no longer simple. As with many companies, the retail economic buying power had shifted heavily to informed, sophisticated women buyers, and the typical buyer had scores of choices and knew what she wanted, when she wanted it, and what price she wanted to pay. Brand value shifted from product to experience.

Meanwhile, Kimball's residential and hospitality market supply was aggressively moving offshore. The entertainment (TV) cabinet market was declining rapidly. The hardwood lumber market shifted from domestic to international. Horizontal market segments quickly became more focused and demanding. Vertical markets were evolving with different rhythms and demands. With all the change, Kimball was trying to serve those markets with a single business model, which caused conflict in performance and capital needs.

In the midst of those changes, Thyen was asked to become the company's president, the first non-family member in forty-five years to take the helm of Kimball International. Before he took the position, Thyen spoke with individual members of the board. Because the company was managed, controlled, and owned by a family, Thyen knew the next forty-five years would look much different from the previous forty-five years—depending on what the founding Habig family decided to do. Looking ahead, Thyen asked a pivotal, strategic question: "The good Lord seems to be driving me to ask a critical question before I can make a decision whether to accept your invitation to be president. Are we going to run this company for the family or for our customers?"

As you might guess, the reaction was one of surprise. But Thyen trusted his colleagues and knew his question would be seen as one for debate, not one of a disbeliever. Our experience as consultants is that average leaders don't ask questions of constructive discontent often enough, never mind when the question might jeopardize a promotion. But Thyen isn't typical. "Why would you even ask a question like that?" replied one board member. "We've always run our business for customers."

If that was the answer, then Thyen wanted to know exactly who those customers were, how they felt, and what they wanted. "We couldn't expect the world to come to us anymore," said Thyen. "We had to humble ourselves and go out to the world." Because he was determined to guide his tenure as president by the company's guiding principles, the next eighteen months found Thyen flying around the world talking face to face with customers, employees, and suppliers.

As the former CFO of Kimball, he knew the numbers inside and out. What he didn't know was how customers really felt. "The brutal reality was that our business model was dying," he said. "It wasn't dead on paper (which is where we tended to focus), but as a result of my conversations with our clients and suppliers, I came to realize it was dead." But "dead" wasn't apparent to everyone. Despite the market alarms going off, performance was still good *enough* at Kimball: they were profitable, had no debt, continued with solid cash flow, and still had dominant market share in automotive electronics.

Upon each return from the market, where he had listened to customers firsthand, Thyen shared what he had found and what he believed it would take to move the company in the right direction. That meant change—in fact, serious change for some family members in key executive positions. In response to Thyen's proposed changes, one responded, "I believe that's the right direction for the company, but I don't want to make the journey. I don't want to put in the energy. Let's find a way to transition me into a different role and find someone that can do what needs to be done."

It was a remarkable commitment to "we, then me," taking hold in a courageous, honest moment from someone who had helped make Kimball what it was—someone who had the influence and ability to easily resist. Thyen deeply admired the response. "Can you imagine what it takes to sit there and listen to the changes

that need to be made,"Thyen said, "and not take it as a personal attack on legacy, given they had been at the helm for over thirty
years?"

But like any real effort for change, it had to start at the top.
Thyen took the position, working to keep himself within the equilibrium of humility. Genuinely confident he could do the job, in the
spirit of duality he acknowledged that he was "part of the problem.
I took the position, but it was with some apprehension and self-
doubt. Ego gives you a set of filters that you don't even know you
have, and I didn't know what mine were." And breaking with tradition wasn't easy, for Thyen in particular. "When other CEOs are
asked to help change a company, they often come in from the outside," said Thyen. "They get to pack, change wardrobes, and move
across the country. I didn't get that opportunity. I've been here
since 1966. Everybody knew me."

In assuming the role of president, Jim demanded two things
of colleagues: 1) to not assume they knew what he was thinking,
or what he was going to say, and 2) to help him change. Devoted
to the organization's progress first and not his image as president,
he was candidly and consistently transparent, conversation by conversation, meeting by meeting. "You know me. You probably know
what I'm going to do or say before I do," he admitted. "But if I
take this position, I have to change. I won't be perfect. I'm going to
slip and I'll need your help. We've been in the same town, driving
the same roads, shopping at the same stores for thirty years.
We need to respect the past. But we can't afford to be tied to it, or
by it."

In the spirit of diversity, the mix of the board of directors needed
adjustment: it was too homogeneous. The board had been domi-
nated by owners, controllers, and managers. "We only had one independent," said Thyen, "but frankly we had never really brought
him *into* the board." Additionally, there were no women on the

board. That needed to change. "We needed people who could complement the talent we had, but who couldn't finish our sentences," Thyen continued. "We needed board members with skills for where the company was heading, not where we had been."

Over the next few years, Kimball executives filled the board with a diverse group of talented, senior executives and CEOs from FedEx, Cummins Engine, Quaker Oats, and Pepsi, among others. Another change in the board required some family board members to agree to a different role. They were asked to sit on committees and provide insight on direction that only their unique history could provide, but at the same time they agreed not to vote; they would "preserve history and legacy without sacrificing the future by being tied to it." They serve voluntarily and without fees, revealing their own humility and deep devotion to the company's progress first, themselves second. In making the hard changes, there were never fights—but there were strong words. With humility you're less likely to make conflict personal, or take it personally. Animosity showed up from time to time, but humility prevented it from lingering.

With a diverse, committed board in place, Kimball made steady but bold changes over time. In 2001, the company employed 9,000 people, most in the United States. Today, Kimball has 8,200 employees, but less than half are in the United States. Kimball executives had to manage with humility, not arrogance, to make the transition successful. "If a manager didn't know their employee's first names and something about their families," said Thyen, "it was an indication to us they were too far removed from their people. We encouraged them to really know their people. There are no 'Mr.' and 'Ms.' here. You can't afford that formality in a real transformation effort. It creates too much distance." An unwritten rule at Kimball is that if people need a third-party advocate, that is, a union, to communicate with management, management isn't doing their job.

That philosophy contributes to openness between employees and management. In the course of closing sixteen plants in small towns, exiting nine markets, and laying off nearly 5,000 employees, there were no lawsuits and no union campaigns. As hard as the layoffs and restructuring were, even people no longer employed by Kimball recommend others to the company, and most talk highly of their experience. Internationally, Kimball exited France and Austria, keeping its reputation intact with those governments. In the process, not a single client fired them. The company entered other countries, with manufacturing in Poland, China, Thailand, and expanded their presence in Mexico.

Meanwhile, in an attempt to not abandon any community they needed to exit, company executives met with local government leaders. In one case, they pledged cash to fund an economic development council to diversify the city's economic base. The aim was to help restore the employment and tax revenue Kimball had provided over the years, and increase employment opportunities and per capita income. While that might not sound remarkable, Kimball made that cash donation on the condition the city would solicit competitors of Kimball. This strategy caught us off guard during our interview. When we asked why, Thyen used an analogy. "We did it," he said, "because the community needed it (they were too dependent on us) and we needed it (competition makes you better). In basketball, you don't get better playing your little brother. You only get better playing your bigger brother, and we needed more big brothers." Humility isn't afraid of competition.

During the massive and rapid transitions, Kimball stayed profitable. Over the last three years with Thyen as president and CEO, Kimball is not only still in business, they're back on track. Their cash balance is the highest it's ever been, and they have no debt. Kimball has exited almost a dozen businesses, sixteen cities, and two countries without ever losing profitability. Meanwhile they're producing organic growth in their furniture business at nearly twice the industry's growth rate. Kimball International is on a $2 billion pace over the next three years, with acquisitions in electronics that will add another $250 million.

According to Thyen, the recovery isn't about him. "I'm not the only one responsible for our success. I never have been. Everyone deserves credit for what we've achieved and what we have yet to accomplish. I'm also not only a 'leader' because I'm now the CEO," Thyen said. "I'm also a follower. We're all followers. We've been followers since the time we were born. You need humility to lead, but you also need humility to follow. Leaders need followers— there is no leader without followers. And in leading, you need to hire people who have different viewpoints and experiences—a group around you to keep you humble, because in leadership, it's so easy to be egotistical."

We asked managers at Kimball what they thought of Thyen. Observations of his leadership were as strong as our own impressions. What equally impressed us was how congruent these managers were with the Kimball values they helped create with the Habig family and Thyen. His leadership style is best framed by a comment his wife, Pat, offered him before he took the position. "In the end," she said, "all you are is a voice and a memory. Use your voice well to create the proper memory." Kimball International isn't perfect. But despite its imperfections, people there exemplify what's possible when leaders and followers alike commit to progress and pursue it with humility.

In Kimball's pursuit of progress, the most difficult tasks required uncommon dialogue and intense debate. Humility was the catalyst in every conversation that counted.

But how do we apply the three properties of humility in day-to-day conversations so the pressure those conversations always bring moves a company forward, rather than idling it or sending it five steps backward? In the next chapter, we move decidedly toward application, paying particular attention to two key elements: 1) the *intensity* of our dialogue, and 2) the *intent* driving our debates. Let's explore how intensity and intent work together.

7: humility

- For each of us, there is a continuum of ego. At one end of the continuum, we have too little ego; at the other, too much. Humility is at the equilibrium and keeps ego balanced between the two extremes.

- Humility is intelligent self-respect that keeps us from thinking too highly or too meanly of ourselves. It makes us modest by reminding us how far we have come *and* how far short we are of what we can be.

- For most people, tradition holds that the opposite of excessive ego is humility, when in fact having too little ego is just as dangerous and unproductive as having too much.

- The three properties of humility exist only at the equilibrium. When we're on center, our talents stay true to form and we make our greatest contributions. But since there's a natural tendency to deviate from the equilibrium, when we move just right or left of center, we begin to lose the power of humility. As a result, our strengths morph into weaknesses that parade as strengths.

- The closer we move to the extremes on humility's equilibrium, the harder it is to make our way back to the center. The longer we stay off-center, the more comfortable we become being off-center. If we don't quickly recover, we're more likely to develop an egotistical reflex in the way we work.

- When humility doesn't manage the power of ego, comparison, defensiveness, showcasing, and seeking acceptance paint us into a corner of contentment—the feeling that we're finished, that we're complete. While pure ego fights to tell us we're finished, humility reminds us we never are. The realization we're unfinished comes from humility's three unique properties: 1) we, then me (devotion to progress), 2) i'm brilliant, and i'm not (duality), and 3) one more thing (constructive discontent). The intersection of the three properties is humility.

8
humility, part II: intensity and intent

What the eye is to the body, the intention is to the soul.

JOHN WESLEY

Because humility has the undeserved reputation of being quiet, people mistake humility for perpetual harmony. But harmony rarely comes without a little bit of turbulence first. "Unless one considers alternatives, one has a closed mind. This, above all, explains why effective decision makers deliberately disregard the major command of the textbooks on decision-making and create dissension and disagreement rather than consensus," said Peter Drucker. "Decisions of the kind the executive has to make are not made well by acclamation. They are made well only if based on the clash of conflicting views, the dialogue between different points of view, the choice between different judgments. The first rule in decision-making is that one does not make a decision unless there is disagreement."

In the pursuit of progress, there will be intensity. We can't accelerate progress without "clash," "differing points of view," and "conflicting judgments." But if we can't handle intensity, we won't get diversity of thought. When diversity goes down, research shows that so do the odds of success. **If we mislabel intensity as being egotistical, we trade progress for soft conversation and swift consensus.** Our intent shapes the intensity of debate, and humility shapes our intent. As it does, humility generates genuine confidence that doesn't allow us to confuse our identity with our ideas. The clear distinction between the two frees us to raise the level of intensity in the exchange of ideas without crossing the line into the early warning signs. In others words, humility makes intensity constructive, not destructive.

Let's first clarify what we mean by *intensity*. "You need executives . . . who argue and debate—sometimes *violently*—," said Jim Collins, "in pursuit of the best answers." The words Collins and Drucker use are interesting choices in describing what it takes to make good decisions: *clash, conflict, disagreement, dissent*.

But . . . *violent*?

When's the last time any of us read a book on communication with the opening line "The first rule of effective communication is to embrace violence"? If there is a place for violence in communication, then effective debate depends on what kind of violence you're talking about. The first words that surface in connection with the word *violence* are *aggression, fighting, hostility, brutal, cruel,* and *vicious*—definitely not words that smooth the exchange of ideas. The worst of these traits cause many people to avoid debates altogether because of the emotional hangover they leave.

For example, a client told us a story about a friend who was appointed the lead negotiator for management in a labor dispute with union leaders in California. As the negotiation began, it became apparent that her counterpart intended to be her opponent. His approach was aggressive; he frequently interrupted her, made un-reasonable demands, and hurled personal attacks. She fought back the temptation to spar with him and remained committed to a de-bate of the issues and understanding his views. But it wasn't easy. The first fifteen minutes seemed like hours. The second fifteen minutes were even worse, followed by another fifteen that showed no signs of letup.

Finally, realizing his attacks were going nowhere, he slammed his fist on the table and demanded, "What are you doing?" She asked, "What do you mean, 'What am I doing?' " "Well," he said, "aren't you going to come back with something?" "No, I'm not. Before we started, I committed to myself that I would understand your point of view," she replied. "I'm trying to do the best I can, even though it's difficult with some of the things you're saying." "Well," he responded, now more calmly, "I guess we'll need to talk then." That's the point—talk.

"violent" talk

In producing talk—especially intense debate—don't make it per-sonal, and don't take it personally. "Foolish is the person that takes offense when none was intended," someone once said. "More fool-ish is the person that takes offense when it *was* intended." In the pursuit of intense debate, we need to be the opposite of violent—for instance, peaceful, gentle, and tranquil—but these qualities are not enough by themselves to produce *real* talk. Upon further inves-tigation of the word *violence*, a second set of words describes a pro-ductive violence: *fierce, passionate, hard, powerful, strong,* and *intense.* To distinguish the two kinds of violence, we'll refer to good vio-lence as *vigorous*—as in "vigorous debate." Not *every* debate needs vigor, but when it is needed, the words just listed should character-ize those debates. Vigorous debates require a heavy investment of humility to keep intensity productive, to keep vigor from becoming violence, and, when necessary, to keep us from being lulled into courteous but meaningless exchanges that *continue* discussions, but don't *advance* them.

when nice isn't

If you're not used to it, it's easy to mistake vigorous debate for animosity. While we were facilitating a discussion with a product development team, one person abruptly halted the meeting. "Time out," he pleaded, pointing to two of his colleagues. "Do you guys even like each other?"They were surprised. For years they had been successful collaborators and friends. Curious, we asked why he would ask that question. "Because," he said, turning to them, "you argue with each other's point. Then you make a point, and the next moment you turn around and disagree with the very point you just made. This isn't productive at all."Then he asked for a break, saying, "I need a reprieve from the intensity."

After the meeting he changed his mind about what he said; the debate *was* productive. In looking back on the meeting, we realized how much sense his reaction made considering the culture he came from before working with this team. Disagreement and disloyalty were one and the same. Position equaled authority and omniscience. He had acclimated to a culture of safety where silence was confused with agreement. Too many trade debate for what they perceive to be harmony in the name of misdefined humility. We watch people attempt debate, but instead they end up spending energy in deferential diplomacy or political tiptoeing, losing real argument for the sake of niceness.

In too many companies, the pendulum of argument swings to one side (violence) or the other (niceness)— either of which trades intellectual diversity for isolating, egotistical clashes or tranquil, pseudoharmonious agreement. We're not recommending less civility or understanding. We are encouraging the right kind of argument. The willingness and ability to listen has its place, and a crucial one at that. But progress requires more than listening. It requires us to passionately push ourselves to explore every angle and go to intellectual extremes that test our assumptions before we make a decision.

Consider Alfred Sloan, the former chairman of General Motors from 1937 to 1956. In a meeting, Sloan shared his ideas with his top executives. Then he asked what everyone at the table thought. They nodded in universal agreement. In response to what he felt was premature agreement, he said, "Then I propose we postpone further discussion of this matter until our next meeting to give ourselves time to develop disagreement and perhaps gain some understanding of what the decision is all about." To keep vigorous debate from turning violent requires an understanding of 1) how intensity works, and 2) how it's managed with humility—in us and others. Let's break down an actual conversation from 1969 that reveals both.

managing intensity in the moment

In 1968, Richard Nixon was elected president of the United States. After his taking the oath of office, his administration proposed a package that would cut government funding for National Educational Television by more than half—a cut that would cripple what we know today as the Public Broadcasting System (PBS). On May 1, 1969, at the invitation of PBS executives, Fred Rogers (aka children's television host "Mr. Rogers") was invited to speak and submit a paper at a hearing chaired by Senator John Pastore from Rhode Island.

Rogers and his colleagues had approximately fifteen minutes to make their case to a committee that had, for all intents and purposes, made the decision to cut their funding. With the future of PBS hanging in the balance, imagine the pressure Rogers and the PBS executives felt. For Rogers, his show and the lives of the children he touched every day were at stake. For PBS, their future was on the line. If you think back to the climate of the United States at the time, it wasn't such "a beautiful day in the neighborhood."Within the previous year and a half, the following events had occurred:

- Thirty-four thousand soldiers had died in the Vietnam War. Over 250,000 people protested against the war in Washington, D.C.

- Three hundred forty Harvard students took over the university's administration building. Four hundred state troopers and police officers cleared them out with tear gas and nightsticks.

- At Cornell University, a thirty-six-hour sit-in was held in the student union building by black students with automatic weapons in fear that white students would attack the building.

- At Berkeley, a National Guard helicopter dropped chemicals on protesters. Nineteen University of California faculty were among those burned by the substance.

- Charles Manson and others committed the "Helter Skelter" murders.

- The Civil Rights movement was in full swing.

- The Supreme Court ordered an end to all school desegregation "at once."

- Dr. Martin Luther King, Jr., and Robert Kennedy had both been assassinated one year earlier.

These were turbulent times. Money was tight. Emotions were high. Upon concluding his introductory comments, the PBS executive slid the microphone over to Mr. Rogers, seated on his right.

SENATOR PASTORE: *(challenging)* All right, Rogers, you've got the
    floor.

MR. ROGERS: *(holding a document he was asked to submit)* Senator
    Pastore, this is a philosophical statement and would take

about ten minutes to read, so I'll not do that. One of the first things that a child learns in a healthy family is trust, and I trust what you've said, that you will read this. It's very important to me. I care deeply about children. My first—

SENATOR PASTORE: *(interrupting)* Will it make you happier if you read it? *(said sarcastically and with a condescending tone, to which the audience and members of the press nervously laugh)*

If tension wasn't high in the room before, it was now. Pastore's early message was clear: the answer is no, and you're wasting my time. Rogers was visibly stunned by the interruption and sarcasm. That interruption was the perfect opportunity for the early warning signs of ego to undermine progress. We'll return to the rest of the interaction between Pastore and Rogers later, and we'll show you how the conversation ends. For now, let's look at dynamics that affect our interactions.

At that moment, Rogers had two things working against him: 1) the surge of power of his own ego working to "protect" him, and 2) someone else's closed mind. Let's start with the first: managing the power surge of our own ego. To understand how ego affects our intensity and intent behind a discussion, let's look at what would likely be going on inside our head and heart if we were in Rogers's shoes.

in a heartbeat

When we feel threatened, in the space between two normal beats of our heart, our response to a threat becomes physiological. Dr. John Gottman calls this escalation of emotion "diffuse physiological arousal (DPA)." Dr. Daniel Goleman calls it the "neural tripwire." Whatever it's called, here's what happens: we start secreting adrenaline, chemicals cause our heart to race (up to thirty beats per minute faster), our heart contracts harder, arteries constrict, blood is drawn away from the periphery into the center of our body, blood supply shuts down to our gut and kidneys, and perspiration increases. None of this would be a problem if we were trying to run away from a predator. But we're not. We're in a conversation. But that's not what our brain is telling us.

When we're in DPA on the inside—and acting like we're not on the outside—things happen in the brain that create tunnel vision, and we can't hear all of what's being said. This isn't just figurative deafness; at its peak, DPA literally interrupts our hearing. At that moment, as much as we would wish otherwise, we can't think as clearly as we normally do. For example, have you been in an argument and much later, perhaps on the drive home, thought of the perfect comeback to something someone said? That's because you've had a chance to calm down and your brain is working again. But in those fight-or-flight moments, we don't have access to our best thinking. Dr. Gottman's research confirms that idea.

One of his experiments involved observing couples arguing. When the intensity pushed one of them into DPA, Gottman walked into the room and told the couple that his recording equipment had broken. He asked them to put their discussion on hold for a few minutes until the equipment was fixed. Nothing was *really* wrong with the equipment; as researchers, he and his team wanted to see what would happen if the couple were given a chance to "cool down." As soon as their heart rates dropped closer to a resting heart rate, Gottman walked back into the room, told them the equipment was "fixed," and asked them to pick up their discussion where they left off. The result?

In his words, "It was as if the couple had a brain transplant." The tone of the conversation was different. They were more authentic and less guarded—no longer making their conflict personal or taking it so personally. They were more open and, as a result, became rational and level-headed. They were still arguing, but their argument wasn't affected by DPA.

The early warning signs of ego in a conversation indicate we're in DPA. Ironically, if we feel we're under attack and need to defend, DPA does very little to keep us "safe." That begs the question, what are comparison, seeking acceptance, showcasing and defensiveness trying to protect? The answer is inside each of us.

the power station

Inside each of us we have what we call a "power station" that represents, among other things, our identity—who we are. Literally, *ego* means "me"—at least the "me" we're conscious of. If we perceive that our identity is under attack, the intensity of our response to protect "who we are" increases. Look at the figure shown here. Most of us feel the need to protect ourselves, with increasing intensity, when challenged in the following areas (working from the outside circle toward the center):

ideas

- **execution:** challenges to the tactics or details of how we think we should execute our strategy.

- **strategy:** challenges to what we think we ought to do—our plans based on our viewpoints.

- **viewpoint:** challenges to what we believe to be true or false, right or wrong, good or bad, and so on. Our viewpoints come from our synthesis of information, either in a given situation or over time. This synthesis leads to our assumptions, which may show up in differences of opinion about the meaning of data, an idea's relevance, or the significance or outcome of a situation.

identity

- **values:** challenges to the values we deem important, such as fairness, respect, integrity, honesty, kindness, and loyalty.

- **character:** challenges to who we think we are—personally and professionally. A challenge could be anything from misperception (such as, "If you're *only* a project manager, why do you need to be involved in a strategy discussion?") to outright, if unspoken, prejudice (based on race, religion, gender, age, appearance, credentials, and so on).

To illustrate how our internal reactions are triggered in a conversation, consider how a typical power station works.

warning: do not enter

There is a power station near our offices. It's like any other building, fire hydrant, or mailbox in the backdrop of our daily surroundings: for the most part it's unnoticed. One day it caught our attention, and so out of curiosity we decided to get a closer look. As we neared the gate, we were quickly alerted that this would be a restricted visit: heavy-duty locks, an eight-foot chain-link fence laced with razor-sharp barbed wire, and a dozen high-voltage warning signs guaranteed it. As we walked toward the fence, the steady hum of roughly 69,000 volts surging through the lines and transformers was unmistakable.

That hum represents enough power to light up the entire city. At home, our families were using it to play video games, cook, clean, listen to music, and watch television. At our offices, people were using that power to run air conditioners, lights, laptops, printers, and phones. One block away from the power station there were no chain-link fences, warning signs, or locked gates; the intensity of the electrical current was low and usable. But from two yards away we were warned to stay out. The difference was the sheer intensity of electrical power, and how it was managed.

While walking around the chain-link fence, we were more than happy to keep our distance. There's a certain amount of awe (and fear) associated with the power of electricity—for us. But in fact, electrical power is extremely predictable—*if* you understand how it works. If you violate the principles by which electricity operates, it quickly switches from productive to fatal. Our lack of knowledge about how electricity is controlled is what's dangerous, not the power itself. But knowing power's potential—for both good and bad—elevates our respect for it.

Our identity is like a power station; it powers everything we say, think, and do. When we confuse challenges to our ideas with challenges to our identity, the early warning signs appear as a way of saying, "Stay out." Like electricity, the power of our identity is also extremely predictable *if* we understand how it works and what we can do to manage it.

Considering our personal power stations of identity, think back to the conversation between Senator Pastore and Fred Rogers. Consider the timing of Pastore's sarcastic remark to Rogers. Not only was it condescending and filled with excessive ego, it was delivered at the very moment Rogers shared what meant most to him: children. Rogers was revealing who he was (his identity) and what he prized most (his values)—the center of his power station. At that moment Pastore attempted to trip Rogers's wires with a condescending comment that went straight to Rogers's identity. It may not have been conscious on Pastore's part, but conscious or not, it had the same effect. How we manage and channel the intensity of our own internal power station, and influence others' as well, determines whether ego works for or against us.

In managing that power, our response is determined by our perception of what we believe is being questioned or threatened. **The weld between our *identity* and our *ideas* is sometimes so tight that we don't separate the two, or we can't separate them easily when questions or perceived threats present themselves.** But why is it so hard to separate the two and see another point of view, particularly when two people's viewpoints are opposed to each other? Who better to answer that question than a trial attorney who argues opposing points of view every day. We asked Gerry Spence, one of the most distinguished trial lawyers in the United States. "We all have a personal image that we must protect," he said. "For example, I do not want to be seen by others, and particularly by myself, as weak, as ill advised, as less than worthy, as stupid, as someone who cannot be respected. I will do whatever is necessary to preserve my personal image of myself. The more fragile my self-image, the harder I will struggle to preserve it."

One morning on the way to work we listened to an example of the confusion between who we are and what we do or have accomplished. Colin Cowherd on ESPN Radio was talking about athletes who are past their prime but having a difficult time seeing it themselves.

It's tough for guys like Brett Favre, Shaq, and Randy Johnson. If you listen to their quotes, they still think they're an A-plus. Brett Favre: "We just need one more guy." Brett . . . you're just not good enough to be one more guy to get to the Super Bowl. Shaq: "It's the refs. The refs are after me." No, they're not. You're just heavier, slower, and thirty-six years old. Randy Johnson: "It's a cycle [bad games, good games]." No, it's not. You're forty-two with thirty-seven hundred innings, not counting spring training. It's who you are now. Sports are their identity. For athletes their bodies are their careers—are their identities. For most of us, when youth leaves us, we still have our identity. For pro athletes, they lose theirs.

Cowherd's point is an important lesson. If we can't distinguish who we are from what we do, what we have, or who we do it with, we won't see past our titles or tenure in a discussion. If we say to ourselves or others, "I'm the vice president," "I'm the CEO," "I'm the director of public relations," or even "I'm the creative one" or "I'm the advocate for diversity here," then we're parading our identity, and take the conversation personally. In response, others walk away (maybe not physically, but certainly mentally and emotionally). In our devotion to progress, we must be able to vigorously debate ideas and not let identity get in the way.

Now let's return to the 1969 PBS Senate hearings to see how Mr. Rogers kept his identity separate from his ideas, and how the testimony turned out. After absorbing the initial blow from Senator Pastore, Fred Rogers stayed anchored at the equilibrium of humility.

ROGERS: I'd just like to talk about it, if it's all right—
PASTORE: *(interrupting again)* All right, sir. Okay.

Rogers began to discuss the state of television, the role violence plays in television, and how it undermines the emotional development and mental health of children. At first, Pastore appears to patronize, acting as if he's listening, but his body language sends a different message. But the transformation that occurs is visible. Within minutes, Pastore turns increasingly sincere, asking questions about Rogers's program. Rogers continues:

ROGERS: This is what I give. I give an expression of care every day to each child, to help him realize that he is unique. I end the program by saying, "You've made this day a special day by just your being you. There's no person in the whole world like you, and I like you just the way you are." And I feel that if we in public television can only make it clear that feelings are mentionable and manageable, we will have done a great service for mental health. I think it's much more dramatic to see that two men could be working out their feelings of anger—much more dramatic—than showing something of gunfire. I'm constantly concerned about what our children are seeing. And for fifteen years I have tried in this country and Canada to provide what I feel is a meaningful expression of care.

PASTORE: Do you narrate it?

ROGERS: I'm the host, yes. And I do all the puppets, and I write all the music and I write all the scripts—

PASTORE: *(interrupting)* Well, I'm supposed to be a pretty tough guy and this is the first time I've had goose bumps for the last two days.

ROGERS: Well, I'm grateful, not only for your goose bumps, but for your interest in our kind of communication. Could I tell you the words to one of the songs I feel is very important?

PASTORE: *(with sincerity)* Yes.

ROGERS: This has to do with that good feeling of control which I feel children need to know is there. And it starts out, "What do you do with the mad that you feel?" and that first line came straight from a child. I work with children doing puppets in very personal communication with small groups.

Rogers then read lyrics teaching children to know "that there's something deep inside" each of us "that helps us become what we can."

PASTORE: *(visibly moved)* I think it's wonderful. I think it's wonderful. *(pauses, as he looks down the line at his fellow senators)* Looks like you just earned the twenty million dollars.

Applause erupted.

Good leaders keep their minds open. Great leaders open the minds of others in the most intense circumstances, even against the odds of prejudice, politics, and habit. Despite Pastore's early contempt, Rogers remained devoted to progress. In the intensity of debate, humility is like a two-way surge protector; it keeps us from making the debate personal or taking it personally. That keeps the energy of our personal power stations focused on the debate and exchange of ideas instead of on protecting personal identities.

lego la-la land

Confusing identity with ideas can create problems for a company culture as well. When Jorgen Vig Knudstorp took over as CEO of Lego, the company was losing hundreds of millions of dollars each year. Tasked with turning Lego around, Knudstorp ran into a culture where the weld between identity and ideas was unexpectedly strong. Previously, the company refused to create toys with any hint of violence or fighting, despite the fact that their primary target market was boys. While that principle might sound noble (and maybe it was), it went too far and got in the way of the company's progress. "When Lego decided in 1999 to launch a Star Wars series," said Niels Sandal Jakobsen, a Lego executive, "getting the license from Lucas was nothing compared to the internal struggle over having the word *war* appear under the Lego brand." In other words, the word *war* was a violation of their identity or "who they were."

In an article by Nelson Schwartz for *Fortune*, a senior toy designer told Schwartz, "People had personal relationships with elements [certain Lego pieces]" and fought to keep them alive. But the focus on their favorite Lego pieces kept them from realizing what the company needed to turn around. "The company was very focused on doing good—that's fine," said Knudstorp, "but the attitude was 'We're doing great stuff for kids—don't bother us with financial goals.' "When the line between identity and ideas isn't clearly drawn, our focus stays riveted to the wrong area (such as keeping an element alive versus keeping the company alive) and increases resistance to change, making progress painfully slow and unlikely. To the credit of the Lego team who challenged themselves to separate identity from ideas, Lego is now turning the corner profitably.

Confusing our identity with ideas explains why we can be five feet from each other in a meeting but still feel like we're five miles apart. Humility closes that distance and keeps debates vigorous by applying two key ideas to communication:

1. Maintain unconditional positive regard.
2. Channel intensity from identity to ideas.

1. maintain unconditional positive regard

Regardless of what others say or how they act, a genuine exchange of ideas isn't possible until people are sure that what is being questioned is their ideas, not their identity. If that security is missing or in question, progress stalls because minds close to questions, challenges, new ideas, differences, and so on. Our ability to create open minds is driven largely by what others feel our regard is for them.

Carl Rogers was one of the most influential psychologists in American history. Along with Abraham Maslow, Rogers deserves much of the credit for the move away from early psychology that too often held the human race in disregard. Instead, his theories hold that normally, people are mentally healthy. Mental illness and other human problems are seen as distortions or exceptions to that natural state. In a brief biography written by his daughter Natalie, the last ten years of Rogers's life were devoted to applying his theories in areas of national social conflict, and he traveled worldwide in that effort. In Ireland, he brought together influential Protestants and Catholics; in South Africa, blacks and whites; in the United States, consumers and providers in health care. Which brings us to one of Carl Rogers's most important practical approaches, and a deeply effective way to vigorously debate with humility—unconditional positive regard (UPR).

In Rogers's work, UPR meant that everyone is worthy of respect and capable of contribution, even when they don't particularly act that way or even feel that way about themselves. Rogers used UPR effectively with clients, and it's equally valuable in our business relationships. UPR assures people we're not interested in changing their identity, even if we are inviting them to change their mind. If people don't feel it necessary to protect their identity, they're able to focus on debating ideas.

But as the word *unconditional* suggests, this isn't a temporary state of mind that ends the moment we judge someone isn't "wor-thy" of our respect. It is categorical. We also can't artificially put a time limit on UPR and say to ourselves, "Okay, I'll do this for ten minutes, but then it's over." We don't know when the other person will say, "Well, I guess we'll need to talk then." But when people's history is working against them, viewing them with UPR can be hard to do. Maybe they've violated expectations more than once. Maybe they've lost our trust. Maybe there is no reason to hope they'll change. Whatever the reason, however legitimate, we still try.

When we hold a person's identity in UPR, it doesn't mean we're naive. We should enter every discussion with our eyes wide open, mindful of what we perceive is actually happening now or has happened in the past. We may not agree with others' values, views, strategies, or ideas about execution. But they still deserve our respect as human beings. Although intellectually simple to grasp, UPR is not easy to apply in practice. Of all his contributions to psychology, Carl Rogers pointed to UPR as the one most capable of shifting the momentum of human dynamics.

a flight to UPR

While waiting for a flight from Houston to Phoenix, I (Steve) learned an important, unexpected lesson on the power of UPR. Personally, I struggle with this concept despite knowing its power. While talking with a colleague on my cell phone, out of the corner of my eye I noticed someone walking down the concourse. It wasn't hard to get a sense of who he was by his appearance. This was one guy you didn't want to mess with. He had tattoos up and down both arms and on his neck. He had his hat on backward, two pierced ears, and two teardrop tattoos below both eyes. I've never been in a gang, but I knew enough about gangs to know that the teardrops meant he had lost a family member or fellow gang member, most likely to murder. The teardrops were his way of honoring those he had lost. In addition to his outward appearance, there was something about him that didn't feel particularly friendly. When I looked up again, he had passed by.

As I made my way to the gate, he was standing in the middle of the aisle leading to the Jetway, popping his gum. With each pop, someone would look up and then away to avoid eye contact. I watched people go out of their way to avoid interacting with him or drawing his attention. I could relate. A moment later I received another phone call and was consumed in the conversation. While I was talking, I unconsciously made my way toward the luggage carts and leaned against them. When I finished my call, I looked around to reorient myself and noticed he was standing next to me.

As the pilots checked in, grabbed their paperwork, and walked down the Jetway, he anxiously asked out loud, "Are we supposed to get on the airplane?" I told him we still had about fifteen minutes before we would board. "Oh," he said with visible relief, "I'm just a little uptight. This is my first time flying." I could have easily ignored him, walked to the gate, and been about my business. Candidly, I thought about it. Instead, I asked him for his ticket and explained the boarding process. At that moment, with no real reason, I had unconditional positive regard for him—regard that wasn't justified by his appearance or by how well I knew him. I wasn't trying to practice anything. More than anything, I started out trying to be helpful and then grew more curious. I asked him where he was going. "Home," he said, "after sixteen years in prison . . . Just got out a few hours ago."

He told me what gang he was in and that he had been in prison for drug trafficking, stolen cars, and other crimes. He described his life, his crimes, his regrets, his experience in prison, and the changes he saw in himself. Much of his time in prison was spent in solitary confinement. We talked about other things. There was a free flow of conversation and openness. As others watched us talk, they seemed curious and surprised that we—two apparent opposites—would be talking like we were. As I boarded the plane, we put our arms on each other's shoulders, the closest thing to an embrace I could imagine he'd had for a long time.

I take no credit for being special here. For my friend, his track record was carved on his face and hard to ignore. UPR isn't about ignorance. I was aware of his past, but it wasn't relevant for the quality of our present conversation. UPR suspends judgment of race, religion, age, title, tenure, position, and politics to allow us something as simple and basic as an open, honest discussion, one that's appropriate for the context. As I look back on this experience, the great irony is that he was just released from prison, and what I discovered is that as I held him in UPR, I was released from my own version of a prison.

In the same way we're tempted to label people we don't know, we label people we _do_ know. We decide we don't like them, what they do, how they look, how they talk, what they stand for, and so on. We "know" how they'll respond and what their motives are. We think we know whether they'll be open, critical, creative, judgmental, or hard to work with. We justify our prejudices. But bias affects our regard and, consequently, our openness with each other.

It's not easy to hold people in UPR when they have a history with us, we have baggage about them, or the debate is hitting close to home. If that's the case, we have to work harder to suspend judgment about the intent behind what they say or do. But the more intimately we know someone, the more the line between identity and ideas blurs: they seem identical. We have to work diligently to keep them separate. We'll never maintain UPR in every circumstance with every person. But one more moment is all we're looking for. If enough moments add up, the momentum of our collective conversations and debates in an organization will shift.

2. channel intensity from identity to ideas

Intensity in a discussion or debate can cause us to do one of two things: 1) turn *away* from people and *against* their ideas, or 2) turn *toward* people and open our minds to their ideas in pursuit of progress. How we turn, and what level of humility we turn with, determines the fate of everything from a conversation to a career to a company's success. Disney CEO Bob Iger used the principle of turning *toward* people to ensure the success of the Disney-Pixar merger.

"Here's the scene: It's 3 p.m., Wednesday, Jan. 25, in Sound Stage 7 on the studio lot of Walt Disney Co. in Burbank," wrote Brent Schlender of *Fortune*. "Five hundred cartoon people—artists, producers, voice artists, etc.—are jammed into the warehouselike building, murmuring and fidgeting in anticipation. The deal is surprising because Pixar's longtime distribution pact with Disney fell apart in acrimony and is due to expire after the release in June of *Cars*, a kaleidoscopic celebration of racing, Route 66, and life in the slow lane. But in a startling twist, not only is Pixar becoming part of Disney, but the upstart studio is also *taking over* the creative direction of Disney's own flailing animation operations—the people in this very room! [It's] as if Nemo swallowed the whale." When John Lasseter, Pixar's immensely talented version of Walt Disney himself, entered the room to meet this crowd, applause exploded and went "on and on."

What most interested us as we read Schlender's story wasn't the eruption of applause for Lasseter but how the Pixar-Disney deal finally happened in the first place. After months of frustrating negotiations and murky intentions between Michael Eisner and Steve Jobs, rumor had it that Eisner was finally on his way out as CEO of

Disney. Lasseter was nervous about the deal with Disney because the way the deal was currently structured, Disney would own Pixar's characters—or in Lasseter's words, "our children." After years of developing at Pixar wonderful characters (including Woody, Buzz Lightyear, the Incredibles, Nemo) that had the same warmth and charm of Disney's early characters, he wondered if the deal would wipe out years of passionate work and sacrifice. "We have this precious entity that is Pixar," said Lasseter. "It's like a living organism, like we had found out a way to grow life on a planet that had never supported it before. We wondered if a deal like this would ruin it all. But Steve [Jobs] said to Ed [Catmull, Pixar's founder and president] and me, 'Get to know Bob Iger. That's all I can say. He's a good man.' "

As you can imagine, the intensity was high. The day it was announced that Bob Iger would replace Eisner, Iger called Lasseter to arrange a meeting. Notice how Iger uses humility to turn *toward* Lasseter and the effect it had on both of them (in Lasseter's own words):

> *Bob [Iger] came up to my home, had dinner with me and my wife, and met my kids. And right away I realized this guy is different. It's not that he was just saying the right things. You could feel that he meant it. I think the simplest thing was that he readily admitted what he didn't know and was comfortable with that. But he said he did know one thing: that animation is the heart, soul, and engine that drives this train called Disney, and that it was broken, and that it needs to be fixed. [I] was still nervous about how Pixar was going to change if it became a part of Disney. And Bob simply said, "[Buying Pixar] is going to be very expensive, so it's in my best interest to do everything I can to keep it the same." He was so calm and logical. No politics, no hidden meaning. And what I real-*

ized is that Steve [Jobs] was right about this guy. [emphasis added]

The more something means to us or the closer it is to our identity, the greater the chances we turn *away* from people, or *against* their ideas. In this case, Iger's humility to admit what he didn't know and Lasseter's willingness to stay open and listen created an atmosphere where there was no room for ego to interfere—this despite Iger's being the CEO of a company with the tradition and fame of Disney, and Lasseter's deep concern that his life's work might be at risk. With no interference, they created a "neutral zone" that clarified intent and established mutual devotion to progress. That neutral zone gives everyone a chance to breathe, making it easier to channel intensity away from identity and toward ideas. But how do you create a neutral zone? By preventing DPA (diffuse physiological arousal) from interfering, or by exiting it once it's triggered.

shifting from identities to ideas

The four early warning signs of ego indicate we've entered DPA territory. To escape that territory, we need to deepen understanding before we continue any discussion at all. We can't have a meaningful discussion or debate in DPA; its push for us to fight or close down is too powerful. But as much of a relief as it is to escape DPA, escape by itself isn't enough. Once we're free, advancing a discussion—not merely continuing it—requires the right level of intensity.

In a debate of ideas, there is an optimal level of intensity we call elevated physiological arousal (EPA). Words that start with the letter *e* best describe EPA: *engaged, enthusiastic, eager, energetic, effective, excited,* and *encouraged*. We shift intensity to EPA by the questions we ask. For the balance of the chapter, we give practical ways to exit DPA and create a neutral zone so that we can raise EPA. The goal of learning these skills is to embrace intensity, not avoid it.

language for exiting DPA

When people are in DPA, consider using an "opening statement." The opening statement got its name for two reasons: 1) its aim is to open minds which have started to close, and 2) it's the first thing we say before we ask questions. Opening statements sound like

- "You might be right . . ."
- "Even though that's hard to hear, I'm glad you're saying something . . ."
- "Okay. Let's talk that one through."
- "Say a little more about that."

An opening statement doesn't equal agreement. In one of our leadership sessions, a manager was practicing an opening statement in a conversation. The line from the scenario she read started with the phrase, "You might be right." She stopped and said to her colleagues with whom she was practicing, "I couldn't use this as an opening statement. What if I don't agree the other person is right?" She interpreted "You might be right" as "You *are* right." She didn't even hear "might." We're afraid understanding equals agreement, and so we miss an opportunity to signal our intent and open minds.

On the other hand, we were coaching a person who said, "I love this [opening statement]. It disarms the other person by agreeing with them right up front." Opening statements aren't intended to agree *or* disagree. They are intended to *open minds* for either debate or understanding, depending on the need. And they're as much a reminder to keep our own minds open as they are a way of opening the minds of others. For example, let's say you're having an outsourcing/operations streamlining discussion and someone says, "There's nothing an outside firm has that we don't have in my department. Besides, consolidating our vendors, and even eliminating some, is way too complicated. We can't do it. That's why I suggested we don't consolidate in the first place. Is no one listening to me on this?"

To decide if understanding or debate is needed, ask yourself what the message is between the words. In his own mind, this person may have gone straight to the unemployment line; in less than a second he shifted from the neutral zone to DPA, and the discussion switched from *we* to *me*. At that moment, it's probably not passionate debate that's needed, but deepened understanding. What would you say?

  a. Why can't we do it? Give me some justification.
  b. You seem really upset about the decision, and not listened to. Is that right?
  c. Maybe no one's listening because you're being defensive.
  d. I don't want anyone feeling like they're not listened to. Let's start with why it doesn't make sense to consolidate, and let's look at it from every angle. I'd like to hear your thoughts first.
  e. If it's too complicated, we definitely shouldn't move forward. What are you seeing that doesn't make sense?

Which one would be the best choice? That depends on your relationship with this person and if you think they're in DPA or EPA. They have an opinion and now—with unconditional positive regard and devotion to progress—you have choices.

In this situation, the early warning sign of defensiveness indicates we're in DPA territory. That means we need understanding. As a result, options *d* and *e* are the most effective. Debate can follow understanding, but if we move directly to debate at this point, we make the situation worse. It's also possible that *a* or *c* might work, but only with the right relationship and intent. Nearly every time we show option *b* in our workshops, there's a collective "Yuck!" Even though the choice shows empathy, it feels like a touchy-feely technique.

language for engaging EPA

After we exit DPA and reestablish the neutral zone, we often need to raise the intensity of a debate to explore the best route toward progress. Raising the intensity of a discussion with EPA wakes us from routines and contentment. That invitation might start with statements like

- "I like a lot of what you're saying. The fact that I like it so much, combined with the fact that we're all in agreement, is what makes me nervous. As I think about it, here's what's missing for me . . ."
- "To get a different point of view, I'm going to argue the opposite and take it to an extreme just to see if there's any validity to it. I'm not even totally sure I believe this myself, but I want to make sure we're not falling in love too fast with what sounds like a great idea."
- "I like some of what you're saying. They're good points and I think we'd be making a big mistake if we threw them out. There are also some things that don't work at all for me, so you'll have to help me see my way clear on them. For instance . . ."

These statements assume that you're doing the inviting. But what if you're not in control and debate isn't "invited"? One of our clients was faced with a tough situation. Her boss said, "We need to

lay off half your sales team. I need the list from you by Friday."
While there's not always room for debate, options might include

a. "What? Where did this come from? Is laying people off
the only way we can compensate for sales being down?"
(defensive)

b. "I can have a list to you by Friday. Just out of curiosity, could
I ask a question? Cutting our sales staff in half will definitely
cut some short-term costs, but that's also going to have an
impact on revenue, and I'm unclear about the trade-offs.
I'd like to talk this one through from different angles, and if
firing salespeople is the best option, then as difficult as it is,
I'll be the first to vote for it (and I understand you don't
necessarily need my vote). Does that sound reasonable?"
(debate)

c. It seems like our first response to any financial pressure is
to hire or fire. We may be getting sucked into a habit here
that prevents us from achieving the kind of growth we're
looking for. Is a layoff the best approach? (debate)

d. I know it's not easy for any of us to fire people. I guess
there could be a lot of different reasons driving that strategy. Can we go down a couple of different roads and talk
about what's leading us to believe that's the answer? (understanding)

Imagine the pressure and anxiety that comes from having to deliver bad news and fire people. Losing half your sales force could
jeopardize hitting your numbers and eventually put *your* job at risk.
That could push you immediately out of the neutral zone and into
DPA, and then good questions won't occur to you. You might disagree with the decision, but your best arguments will escape you if
you slip into DPA.

Again, any choice depends on the relationship you have with the person and the context of the situation, including the topic, the timing, or what's at stake.

humility + curiosity

Debate in a company is as critical as financial capital, but certain human dynamics interrupt debate and cost money. There are two types of intensity; one is productive, the other destructive. When destructive intensity shows up, so do ego's early warning signs. If we don't do something about those warning signs, people go into DPA and debate stalls. So does progress. The guidelines in this chapter keep debates productive. If we apply UPR, use opening statements, and make our intent clear, we can shift intensity from identity to ideas. That shift keeps minds open, keeps communication clear, and accelerates the exchange of ideas.

Finally, in the spirit of vigorous debate and deepened understanding, humility prompts us to ask, "Who cares if *I'm* right at this instant, as long as *we* get it right eventually?" **If we're devoted to progress, it doesn't matter *who* has the answer, only that the answers are found.** Finding those answers begins with humility but doesn't end there. Shifting conversations from statements and judgments to exploration requires a relentless, focused application of the second principle of egonomics—curiosity. What type of curiosity we need most, and how to get it and use it, is where we're headed next.

8: intensity and intent $\boxed{\textbf{key points}}$

- Because humility has the undeserved reputation of being quiet, people often mistake humility for perpetual harmony. But harmony rarely comes without a little bit of turbulence first.

- In the pursuit of progress, there will be intensity. We can't accelerate progress without clashes, differing points of view, and conflicting judgments. But if we can't handle intensity, we don't get diversity of thought.

- Vigorous debates require a heavy investment of humility to keep intensity productive, keep vigor from becoming violence, and, when necessary, keep us from being lulled into courteous but meaningless exchange.

- In too many companies, the pendulum of argument swings to one side (violence) or the other (niceness)—either of which trades intellectual diversity for isolating, egotistical clashes or tranquil, pseudoharmonious agreement.

- Progress requires more than listening. It requires us to passionately push ourselves to explore every angle and go to intellectual extremes that test our assumptions before we make a decision.

- When we're in DPA on the inside—and acting like we're not on the outside—things happen in the brain that create tunnel vision, and we can't hear all of what's being said. This isn't just figurative deafness; at its peak, DPA literally interrupts our hearing. At that moment, as much as we would wish otherwise, we can't think as clearly as we normally do.

- The early warning signs of ego in a conversation indicate we're in DPA. Ironically, if we feel we're under attack and need to defend, DPA does very little to keep us "safe."

- Inside each of us we have what we call a "power station" that represents, among other things, our identity—who we are. If we perceive that our identity is under attack, the intensity of our response to protect who we are increases.

- The power station includes our identity and our ideas. Ideas include execution, strategy, and viewpoints. Identity includes values and character. In managing that power, our response is determined by our perception of what we believe is being questioned or threatened.

- Humility keeps debates vigorous without letting them become violent by applying two key ideas to communication: 1) unconditional positive regard (UPR), and 2) the separation of identity from ideas.

- Regardless of what others say or how they act, a genuine exchange of ideas isn't possible until people are sure what's being questioned is ideas, not identity.

- UPR assures people we're not interested in changing their identity, even if we are inviting them to change their mind. If people don't feel it necessary to protect their identity, they focus on debating ideas.

- When we hold a person's *identity* in UPR, it doesn't mean we're naive. We should enter every discussion with our eyes wide open, mindful of what we perceive is actually happening or has happened in the past.

- It's not easy to hold people in UPR when they have a history with us, we have baggage about them, or the debate is hitting close to home. If that's the case, we have to work harder to suspend judgment of the intent behind what they say or do. But often the more intimately we know someone, the more the line between identity and ideas blurs.

- Intensity in a discussion or debate can cause us to 1) turn *away* from people and *against* their ideas, or 2) turn *toward* people and their ideas in the pursuit of progress.

- The four early warning signs of ego indicate we've entered DPA territory. To escape that territory, we need to deepen understanding before we continue any discussion at all, let alone engage in vigorous debate. We can't debate in DPA.
- There is an optimal level of intensity in a debate we call elevated physiological arousal (EPA). A person in EPA is engaged, enthusiastic, eager, energetic, effective, excited, and encouraged.

9
curiosity

Genuine ignorance is profitable because it is likely to be accompanied by humility, curiosity, and open mindedness; whereas ability to repeat catch-phrases, cant terms, familiar propositions, gives the conceit of learning and coats the mind with varnish, waterproof to new ideas.

JOHN DEWEY

Ego's four early warning signs lock the gate to learning and prevent access to the minds of others. Humility unlocks that gate through "we, then me" (devotion to progress), "i'm brilliant, and i'm not" (duality), and "one more thing" (constructive discontent). Curiosity is the catalyst that freely explores the territory of ideas, perceptions, biases, and beliefs behind that unlocked gate.

Curiosity works with humility to extinguish the four early warning signs of ego by 1) placing the pressure of comparison squarely on ideas, not people, 2) unbolting defensive positions, 3) reopening the box of knowledge that closes when brilliance is showcased, and 4) inviting someone seeking acceptance to ask questions rather than go along. The good news is that most everyone is curious, so we have a head start. But to what degree we're curious is another question, and the answer is vital in determining the value we create.

sparked or sparking?

There are two types of curiosity: *state* and *trait*. *State curiosity*—the kind most people have—waits on something to spark it. Whether it's the technical ease and simplicity of a Segway, the majesty of the Taj Mahal, Michelangelo's breathtaking art in Saint Peter's Basilica, Stephen Hawking explaining the universe in laymen's terms, a magician's trick, or how Google searches the world for just the information we need in 0.17 seconds, our curiosity is sparked. But state curiosity is temporary. Quickly after we're removed from the state that sparked our curiosity (the question, the experience, the perplexity), our curiosity fades; it lies dormant until the next time it's sparked. *Trait curiosity*, on the other hand, doesn't wait to be sparked. It does the sparking. The central difference between the two is illustrated by Sir Richard Branson.

Branson—knighted by the queen of England in 1999 for "services to entrepreneurship"—is the handsome, adventurous entrepreneur of the Virgin Group. As outsiders, most of us wonder what people like Branson are *really* like when they're off camera and away from the microphone. Here's one firsthand story. An associate of ours was boarding a Virgin flight from London to L.A. when he noticed Branson on the same flight. Upon reaching 10,000 feet— when the ping revealed it was "safe to move about the cabin"— Branson popped out of his seat and walked straight to the back of the plane. He chatted with every kind of passenger—parents, children, teenagers, adults, businesspeople, and so on. He didn't ask people about the fare they paid—*never* about price. Instead, Branson asked how they *felt* about their seats, food, movies, games, service, and the children's goodie bag. He was curious not necessarily about technical travel facts but about what they were *experiencing*.

No one prompted the multibillionaire to get out of his comfortable seat and spend his flight time talking with guests. His dash to the back of the plane didn't appear at all sparked by a superficial or egotistical motive to be noticed. In fact, the person we talked to said he was doing it as discreetly as someone with Branson's fame could. He was incredibly, insatiably curious. He still is. Branson flies Virgin at least once a month to stay in touch with the experience. And Branson's brand of curiosity is contagious. As a tentacle of Virgin's curiosity, a page on the company's website under "Got a big idea?" invites anyone to share an idea. Here's the condensed version of the first few steps:

1. So, you're onto a winner?

We're always looking for the next BIG thing. If you have a fantastic idea for us, then *we're all ears*. We're *always on the lookout for fresh ideas* to improve our current companies and to create brand-new ones. Especially if it builds on our exciting businesses or creates brand-new ones. All our Virgin companies *live and breathe our core brand values* and all new proposals or ideas need to reflect these values. [Those core values are then listed.] So if you think you've an idea that fits the bill and has the potential to become a major global business, *we would love to hear from you.*

2. So where are we looking for those winners?

We've got many different businesses across the world. *To make it all easier and clearer* we like to group them into areas. [Those areas are then listed.] These are the areas that we are keen to develop in the future and where *we believe our winning ideas are currently hiding.*

3. Getting your message across

Click here for a contact list. If your idea does not fit with our current companies but it is fantastic in its own right, you can send it to Corporate Development at Virgin Management to the address in Section 6 and we'll be happy to review it. *(We should have it back to you in 3 weeks.)*

We cruised hundreds of websites, including Virgin's competitors', and found nothing like it. Not only does Virgin make it easy for you to get access to share your idea, the company's curiosity and warmth radiate throughout the invitation. Even strangers, with perhaps even stranger ideas, are treated like invited guests. But the question might be, "So what? What's the payoff with that level of curiosity?"

Over the last thirty-five years, Virgin has created businesses in music megastores, air travel, mobile, financial, retail, entertainment, Internet, drinks, rail, hotels, and leisure, with around two hundred companies in over thirty countries. According to national surveys, Branson is the most admired businessman in the UK, along with being numero uno as a role model for students, as the choice for London mayor, as a father, and he's the number two choice for prime minister among youth, after Tony Blair. In business, the market always gets the final vote. Here's how the market votes about the "professional, but uncorporate" Virgin Enterprises:

- 100 percent brand awareness in UK, 96 percent in Australia, 56 percent in USA
- number one brand to represent Britain in the future
- number one most respected brand among men

- second most "responsible" brand (after Body Shop)
- Forbes's fourth best marketed brand in the world
- more trusted than the Bank of England

The name Virgin came from a female friend who, in starting the company with Branson, commented, "We're all virgins at business." That idea never appears to have been lost on Branson or his company. Branson's title of chief executive officer doesn't do justice to the culture he's created. A more fitting title would be chief curiosity officer. "My biggest motivation?" commented Branson. "Just to keep challenging myself. I see life almost like one long University education that I never had—every day I'm learning something new." Everyone's curiosity is sparked by different things at varying times (that's state curiosity), but trait curiosity separates the most curious people we know from everyone else.

openness + order = ?

Highly curious people like Branson are different than you might imagine. Think of someone you know who's very open and who loves to engage and explore: the person is adventurous, flexible, artistic, unencumbered, and energized by new ideas. Now think about someone you know who's the opposite—organized, orderly, analytical, logical, structured, and methodical, with everything under the sun in its proper place. Which of the two would you put your money on to have the highest level of curiosity? As it turns out, the answer is neither.

According to decades of research by Dr. David Beswick at the University of Melbourne, people with trait curiosity have a rare, unique blend of openness *and* order. "They have a sufficient sense of security in their world to put their cognitive maps in jeopardy," he said, "without experiencing debilitating anxiety." That blend creates heightened curiosity and the security to work in the intellectual space "belonging at the border between chaos and cosmos." At first glance there appears to be a conflict between order and openness. In fact, when psychologists evaluate personality traits, there is a negative correlation between the two. The "orderly" aren't open enough and resist disruption to their systematic approach or arrangement of things. The "open" undervalue order, and their curiosity is too carefree, easily accepting change without enough thought of the impact.

When order overrides openness, curiosity loses freedom to explore. If left to openness alone, curiosity loses structure and purpose. **The highest concentration of curiosity isn't created by adding an ounce of order to a pound of openness, or vice versa. Trait curiosity requires equal parts of both.** With the right mixture of openness and order, "questions will be asked, calculations will be made, things will be turned over and looked under, there may well be much wondering and doubting," says Beswick, "but after the ball has been kept bouncing for a sufficient length of time some sort of resolution will be reached and . . . a new order of representation of the world is developed." Keeping "the ball" of curiosity bouncing long enough allows time for us to see the world from a slightly different angle.

just one more question?

People with trait curiosity don't see the world differently from the rest of us every minute of the day, but they do see it differently for a few minutes. In those minutes curiosity might catch a glimpse of a subtle difference in what appears routine to everyone else. For example, in the middle of July (Steve recalls) our air conditioner quit working. We couldn't figure out what was wrong, so we called a repairman. Actually, we ended up calling two of them, which is the point of this story.

The first person showed up and after thirty minutes was ready to leave. He showed me his clipboard with twenty items he routinely checks when diagnosing air conditioners. All the boxes on his checklist were checked. "I added more Freon to your system," he said, "so that should take care of it. I couldn't find anything else wrong." While writing the check, I expressed my relief that the problem was only low Freon. "Oh, it wasn't low on Freon," he replied, "but I couldn't find any other problems, so I figured that was probably it. If this doesn't work you'll probably need a new air conditioner." The next day it was still ninety degrees inside our house, so I called the same company—but asked them to send a different technician. They assured me the first person was competent, experienced, and trusted. They even pulled the technician's report and verified that he had accurately completed the twenty-item checklist. She noted that "he added Freon to your air conditioner." I insisted on someone else.

The next repairman arrived wearing the same company uniform, driving the same company van, and clutching a clipboard with an identical twenty-item checklist. He efficiently followed the same diagnostic steps, putting check marks in the boxes as he completed each item. But then something happened that separated him from the first technician. As I walked downstairs to my home office, I noticed he was standing in front of the furnace—staring at it. Fifteen minutes later as I headed back upstairs, I noticed he was still staring, from a slightly different place. With my own curiosity piqued, I asked him what he was doing. "I don't think your problem has to do with what's happened to the air conditioner since you bought the home," he said. "I think it's what happened to it *before* you bought the home." Then he cut into the casing of the furnace to have a look around. What he discovered fixed the problem.

When the construction workers built our home, they used the furnace to stay warm in the winter, but since the ductwork wasn't complete, the casing didn't keep out sawdust and debris. Before finishing our home, they didn't clean the screen that protected the evaporator coil before they encased the furnace. The sawdust and debris made it impossible for the coil to work. If the construction workers hadn't used the furnace the way they did, the problem wouldn't have occurred. This was the first time he had seen this problem. He cleaned the screen, welded the casing shut, and soon our house was a cool seventy-two degrees.

The point here is the twenty items that represented "best practices," no doubt accumulated over years of service repair calls, didn't fix *my* air conditioner. The second repairman's trait curiosity added a twenty-first box. Fixing my problem required a break with routine questions; the mystery wasn't going to be solved by "procedure" or state-induced curiosity from a twenty-item checklist. According to research on curiosity done by Mary Dawn Ainley, also at the University of Melbourne, the first factor driving trait curiosity is a desire to "experience something unique in order to achieve understanding." The second repairman stared and wondered, went back in time in his mind's eye, and reached past the checklist to experience something unique.

In "doing his job," he easily could have completed the same diagnostic checklist and, with the same result as the previous service call, sold me a new air conditioner. I wouldn't have known better, and he would have been perfectly justified in doing so. I asked why he kept trying. "I've always wanted to figure things out," he said. "I want to know how things work, and why they don't. I just have to keep going until something's fixed." That fix is the main purpose of curiosity. The word *curiosity* is related to the words *cure, care, careful,* and *accuracy*. In other words, curiosity drives us to accurately understand what's happening, with the intention of finding an appropriate cure. But sometimes our desire to cure or fix something is the very thing that gets in our way.

what's the cure for the *common* cure?

Our zeal for answers dulls curiosity. As an example of how our initial impulses get in the way, consider a lesson from preschoolers. Imagine that you're only four years old, and an adult offers you your favorite treat. Just before you bite into it, the deal gets sweetened: if you can wait just fifteen minutes to eat your treat while the adult runs an errand, you'll get two treats when the adult comes back. In other words, in as little as fifteen minutes you double your return. What would you do? Remember, you're only four years old. Your answer may have major implications for your future.

Between 1968 and 1974, Walter Mischel of Stanford University conducted a series of studies on what makes it hard or easy for children to delay gratification. One simple experiment included four- and five-year-old preschoolers and a marshmallow. Mischel brought each child into a room, one at a time, and offered the child a marshmallow. But before he allowed the children to eat the marshmallow, he told them if they waited fifteen minutes for him to return, they would get two marshmallows instead of one. Once Mischel left the room, he and his team recorded the behaviors of the children.

For some children, there was no space between stimulus and response. The moment the door closed—*gulp*—the marshmallow disappeared. Some children fought the temptation as long as they could, taking tiny bites off the bottom, hoping their nibbles wouldn't be seen. But their efforts to resist were in vain and they eventually succumbed, happily eating the rest of the marshmallow. A few children pushed the boundaries as far as they could and *licked* the marshmallow, apparently reasoning that licking wasn't technically eating and so was allowed. But alas, licking led to eating.

On the other hand, some children kept their distance using different strategies—ignoring the marshmallow's pleas to be eaten. A few of the children pretended the marshmallow wasn't there and wandered around the room. Others sat in front of the marshmallow with their faces buried in their hands, occasionally peeking between their fingers to see if the marshmallow had escaped. Others talked to themselves as if there was an imaginary friend in the room. One girl sang nursery rhymes to take her mind off the temptation, and then crawled under the table and fell asleep.

Mischel conducted follow-up studies on these children for twenty years after the initial impulse control study. Those with the willpower to outlast fifteen minutes of temptation and wait for two marshmallows were educationally more successful and emotionally intelligent. They showed better skills under stress, embraced challenges, and pursued goals rather than giving up in the face of difficulties. They were more confident, dependable, and willing to take more initiative than those who ate the marshmallow. They scored an average of 200 points higher out of a possible 1,600 on the Scholastic Aptitude Test (SAT) college entrance exam.

Warning: Before you run for a bag of marshmallows to do your own experiment, we recommend you don't try this at home. If your child eats the marshmallow before the fifteen-minute mark, you may slip into a state of depression as your dreams for your offspring vanish before your eyes. Trust us; we know by experience. On second thought, maybe you should try it. At least you'd know whether to start a college fund or take the money and go on an exotic vacation.

is there a marshmallow in the meeting?

As children, we find temptations overpowering. But gaining control over impulses is evidence that we've matured, right? So it would seem. However, our ability to withstand temptation as adults isn't much better; just the "treat" has changed. The venue for the Mischel-like research is a company's conference room. The business version of a marshmallow is an idea (a cure, an answer, a solution) that someone thinks will make a difference. Our impulse, even as adults, is to jump on the idea ASAP because we want results now; we want a fast answer followed by flawless execution. But in pursuit of those results, consider the following from Dr. Thomas Gilovich of Cornell University, who has researched decision making and behavioral economics since 1981: "We humans seem to be extremely good at generating ideas, theories, and explanations that have the ring of plausibility."

Evidence backs his observation; every sixty minutes 101 new patents are applied for, 2,265 new businesses are started daily in the United States alone, and on average 32,000 new products are introduced annually. But there's a second part to Gilovich's findings: "We may be relatively deficient, however, in evaluating and testing our ideas after they are formed." Within the next five years over 90 percent of new ventures will close their doors and 80 percent of new products will fail—most within weeks after launch. As we mentioned earlier in the book, nearly 50 percent of decisions and new projects inside companies fail to deliver anywhere near expectations.

Every day new products are launched, projects initiated, strategies implemented, and objectives set. Too many turn out to be less than we hope for. Some people say the reason for the poor results is a lack of execution. Other arguments include "Hey, at least we're trying," or "We're throwing stuff against the wall, seeing what sticks," or "Nothing ventured, nothing gained." We don't lack the ability to build, or courage to try. Research suggests we don't lack imagination, ambition, or ideas. We lack prebuild, prelaunch, pre-execution curiosity. A failure of curiosity is not the only factor, but it's a major one. Like those children who patiently waited for a better return, when we use discipline and patience to resist our impulse to run with an idea at first glance, we give curiosity time to breathe. In turn, we get better results. But restraint is harder than it sounds.

The problems we face every day pressure us to do something— and we should. But the question of *what* we do and *how fast* deserves more attention than it typically gets. When ego is out of balance, we think we know more than we actually do, and that blocks curiosity. As a result, we invest time, people, and money before we should. For example, a division sales manager had an idea about how training could solve a problem he faced with his sales team. What follows is a transcript of an interview between that manager and Dr. Rosabeth Moss Kanter of Harvard Business School:

KANTER: What resources did you need to proceed with your idea for a sales training program?

MANAGER: None . . . I just wrote out the ideas in a training process.

KANTER: What about information?

MANAGER: I don't know what you mean. I had an idea, and we developed the training.

KANTER: Was anyone opposed or critical?

MANAGER: The manager of a neighboring department.

KANTER: How did you handle this opposition?

MANAGER: I told that manager that this was not his business.

KANTER: Did you win over the "critics"?

MANAGER: No.

KANTER: Did you hit any roadblocks or low points when it looked as if the whole thing would flop?

MANAGER: I never thought about a flop.

Part of his last comment reveals the underlying problem: "I never thought . . ." Proposed "solutions" saturate business conversations, which is why we're used to their presence and they go unnoticed. Even outside of work, we're immersed in advice from all sides of society—politics, religion, community, television, radio, Internet, and so on—and the advice is usually well-intentioned. But whether we're trying to eliminate activity that no longer seems effective, create value by doing something we've never tried, or increase or reduce the level at which we're currently doing something, those cures in their infancy need investigation before they need imagination or execution. With unlimited ideas and limited resources, innovation demands homework first, execution second.

what's our homework assignment?

In the now famous ABC *Nightline* report on the product design firm IDEO, Ted Koppel and crew created the perfect conditions for homework to be ignored. *Nightline* gave IDEO an idea; they asked them to redesign the grocery shopping cart on national television. Koppel's staff could think of no other product that was used by the public so regularly, and yet was so remarkably absent innovation since its invention. It made for a great show and a beautiful new cart, but the reason it makes this chapter is how IDEO responded to the restrictions *Nightline* imposed on the process. For starters, the timeline allowed was only five days, a reduction of about 75 percent of a typical timeline. IDEO had no say in the choice of the project. The entire process was filmed for broadcast on national television. There was nowhere to run, hide, or put on their best face.

What impressed us most was a "small" decision they made early. With 75 percent of the normal development timeline gone, it would be tempting to say, "Look, we have an insane timeline, so let's skip our typical research phase. We're talking about a shopping cart anyway, right? We've all used one—maybe even just last night. We've all probably ridden in one, so we know them inside and out. Let's get creative, brainstorm design possibilities, and build it!" But despite how well they knew shopping carts, they understood that what they "knew" could be a liability. "I don't have a problem getting the people in our company to be curious about things they know nothing about," said one health care executive to us. "It's when they know a lot about something that they close their minds."

With minimal time, IDEO insisted on devoting time up front to exploring the entire reality, not just the one in their heads; they talked to customers, store owners, baggers, repair people, and manufacturers. By looking around, taking pictures, asking questions, and listening, they discovered unanticipated differences that led to genuine innovation. "It is precisely because the unexpected jolts us out of our preconceived notions, our assumptions, our certainties," said Peter Drucker, "that it is such a fertile source of innovation." Because they were anxious to be jolted out of their assumptions, the results of IDEO's efforts were remarkable. In fact, business schools around the world refer to IDEO's shopping cart project as the epitome of the modern-day mechanics for innovation.

If you're not familiar with the makeover of the shopping cart, it was impressive: wheels that turn 360 degrees so you don't have to lift up the rear end of the cart in a tight spot; removable handbaskets that stack into metal frames to reduce cart theft and increase shopping ease; a safer design to prevent child injuries; a lighter, more compact frame for storage; and major improvements all around. "Wherever you are, look around. The only thing not designed by somebody is nature," said IDEO founder David Kelley as he stood in the middle of the produce section of a grocery store. "So the trees are not designed by us, but everything you see . . . every light fitting, every flower vase, every scale, every stand for fruit, everything designed has to go through this process. And they can do a better or worse job of innovating or improving, but everything that is designed has to go through this process."

Kelley's point isn't reserved for product designers and engineers. If we look around our companies, every system, structure, process, strategy, project, or initiative is the product of someone's design. Whatever innovation process we use and no matter what we design, the level of curiosity has a profound impact on the brilliance of the outcome.

four ways to spark curiosity

Because the idea "innovate or die" is etched into the mind of every executive and manager, virtually every company has processes dedicated and designed for innovation and improvement—whether it's Six Sigma, TQM, decision making, problem solving, critical thinking, creativity, or something else. Whatever the process, its value depends on the quality of information that flows from its conversations. A director of a Fortune 500 company's Six Sigma program told us, "We know what boxes to check off. The process is clear, well-defined, and we know what we're doing—technically." He sighed. "But it's the stuff that happens between humans—in the 'white spaces' of those boxes—that makes those boxes actually work."

No matter how clear and well-ordered the steps of a process, the level of curiosity driving the conversations inside those steps can decide the value created by each step. In the white space of those boxes, curiosity is process-neutral. What follows are practices to "jolt us out of our assumptions" and increase the concentration of curiosity in the exchange of ideas and otherwise routine conversations. That curiosity can overcome the liability of what we know—to fluently turn over stones, to open new pages, to keep the ball bouncing so we notice the small openings for insight that pass us by every day. Before we explore those practices, one note of warning is necessary: merely asking questions doesn't mean we're curious. "An estimated forty percent of all questions are really statements in disguise," said William Isaacs, founder of the Dialogue Project at MIT. "Another forty percent are judgments in disguise. Only a small percentage of 'inquiries' are questions."

The number of questions we ask doesn't by itself indicate how curious we are. Curiosity is measured in large part by the willingness it creates in others to give access to what they really think and to embrace different points of view—views that may be unlike those they currently hold. Remember, the perceived intent behind our questions has a major impact on the ceiling of curiosity. If others are suspicious of our questions, we should make our intent explicit: we have nothing to hide. Here are four ways to raise the level of curiosity in daily conversations when we "jump out of our seat and head to the back of the airplane":

1. What do we mean? (clarity)
2. What are we seeing? (context)
3. What are we assuming? (assumptions)
4. What does that lead to? (consequence)

Remember, a characteristic of trait curiosity is that it combines openness and order. These questions are designed to provide both—to give structure to our curiosity, while at the same time opening minds. If we get good at using these questions to induce a state of curiosity, it's more likely over time we'll develop trait curiosity.

1. what do we mean? (clarity)

The first way to spark curiosity focuses on the basic unit of language: a word. Words can either spark our curiosity or, if we're not careful, lull us to sleep. For example, we took five hundred managers and executives from the same organization and separated them into 125 teams, with four people per team. Then we wrote down the word "leadership" on a whiteboard and gave them ninety seconds individually, without talking to one another, to write down as many words as they could that captured what "leadership" meant to them. Next we asked them to compare their lists and see how many words they matched as a team. A word was only considered a match if all four team members had listed it. The winning total?

One.

Only one team had one match. The other 124 teams had a grand total of zero matches. We've conducted this exercise for years in over forty countries using different words, such as *trust, strategy, vision, risk management, branding, customer satisfaction,* and even easier words like *pizza, family,* and *dog.* On a good day, a team will have one or two matches—and only on the easiest words. The mismatch is both good news and bad news.

After completing this exercise in one of our leadership sessions, a manager raised her hand. "I think it's a good thing we didn't have any matches," she proudly exclaimed, "and I'll sit here *all day long* with no matches if it shows we have diversity." She's right. The good news is that there's no doubt we all see things differently, and even less doubt that we need diversity. But what good is diversity if we can't access it because we're not curious enough about something as simple as the meaning of a word? The bad news is we think everyone else knows what we mean. "The danger in communication," said George Bernard Shaw, "is the illusion that it has been accomplished." We throw words and acronyms around as if we'll achieve universal understanding, but meaning is very personal—and varied.

When we assume we're clear about what someone means, we may not be as clear as we think. For instance, as consultants we had a conversation with a group of executives where phrases like "better alignment with our vision" and "we need to be a leader in innovation" were commonplace. At one point, someone said, "It doesn't take much to see the confluence of outside factors driving important change in some of our traditional businesses." Heads nodded in agreement. What? Phrases like these were skipping unnoticed across the surface of a sixty-minute meeting. We were unclear what they meant. "What do you mean when you say 'better alignment with our vision'?" we asked. "What does it mean to you to be a 'leader in innovation'?" The executives had to stop and think about what they meant. It became clear *they* weren't exactly sure either.

One of the most challenging tasks managers face is to get everyone playing from the same sheet of music, whether that song is strategy, vision, alignment, or execution. In an effort to synchronize, many leaders default to repeating a message over and over, hoping it eventually sinks in. While the intent is sincere, and repetition may get the message *repeated*, the message itself rarely gets any *clearer*. "The *more* an organization knows about a term or concept relevant to its business," said Thomas Davenport in his book *Information Ecology*, "the *less* likely it is to agree on a common definition of it."

Repetition isn't the answer. We said earlier that highly curious people notice subtle differences that pass by most of us unnoticed. Words are one of those subtleties. Asking something like "When we say we need better alignment with our vision, what do we mean, specifically?" sounds simple—maybe even simplistic. Given their simplicity, it's surprising how rarely such questions surface. Curiosity about words is a level of detail we miss because it is so simple, and sometimes we think curiosity should be reserved for grander questions and more sophisticated processes. When it comes to curiosity, the devil is in the details.

2. what are we seeing? (context)

The second way to spark curiosity is to explore what's going on around us that affects our decisions. Context is an important part of every situation. In a typical meeting, someone will share an idea. Rather than talk about the idea itself, exploring context requires we suspend our discussion of the idea to get as much information as we can that *surrounds* it. In doing so, we're turning the idea over to exploration, not doubt or disapproval. With an idea in mind, exploration either validates the idea as strong or exposes its weaknesses. Our idea might be "cool" for cool's sake, for instance, but miss market needs completely.

The cofounder of iRobot, Helen Greiner, developed for the army a mine-clearing robot named Ariel that involved dazzling technologies. When the demonstration of the "future" for the army was over, the client's reaction was, "Uh, cool . . . but it doesn't do what we need it to do." The lack of focus on the context of the market earned iRobot an early reputation for being interested in doing "innovation for innovation's sake." To dispel that reputation, iRobot balanced curiosity about technology with curiosity about market needs. In an interview with Jena McGregor of *Business Week*, Greiner reflected on the experience. "After Ariel, I was invited to an Army Rangers demonstration and brought another prototype to solicit input from soldiers. That input led to the design of our Pack-Bot, a bomb-disposal robot which has been credited with saving the lives of dozens of soldiers. We've delivered five hundred of them," said Greiner. "Innovation in our field can lead us in the wrong direction to the most exotic creation. I learned to talk to users and get input before designing." We've been conditioned to quickly move to design after we have an idea. Here's where impulse control can help. It keeps us from skipping past a deep enough understanding of the context that affects the very design of our ideas.

Releasing ideas to explore context first might feel counterintuitive, but it isn't counterproductive. We can explore context by asking questions like "What are we seeing that leads us to believe we need to hire a full-time director of learning and reinforcement?"

Once the question is asked, write down the answers that surface and don't stop at the first one or two. Once we've captured all the answers to the question, argue the opposite: could we, or anyone else, make a case that anything on that list isn't true? What evidence proves what we're seeing or hearing is true or untrue? Then we can invite people to look at the list and challenge our assumptions. As a follow-up question, we can ask what we *don't* know about what we just listed. That usually creates its own valuable discussion for uncovering added context.

Exploring context surrounding an idea may seem intellectually simple, but emotionally it's more challenging. In one study, researchers found groups would rather support the ideas they already have instead of examining those same ideas. The strength of their bias depends on the team's early preferences. The earlier they form conclusions about an idea, the more they only want to consider information that supports their conclusions. In other words, if we search for information to prove our point, we'll exclude evidence to the contrary, either by not seeing it because we're looking for what we want to see or by dismissing it if we do see it.

In the process of asking questions, the four early warning signs might show up at any time. For example, if we see people seeking acceptance by simply going along with whatever is said, argue against what you just said. A true test of curiosity is the ability to take another point of view with as much interest and intensity as we take our own. If our intent is clear, we should be able to set aside our position long enough to fully engage in a different perspective. If someone gets defensive at our question and says, "Are you saying it's a bad idea?" we can clarify our intent. "Not at all. But even though *we* agree we're misaligned, others outside this room may not, and they'll be affected by our decision. From a business perspective, I want to explore as many issues as we can, especially since we'll need buy-in if we move forward with the idea."

3. what are we assuming? (assumptions)

The third way to increase curiosity in conversations is to test assumptions. Testing assumptions is a reality check: do the assumptions that underlie the beliefs make sense? Are they real? For example, let's say we were hiring for a managerial position and someone made a strong argument that candidates must have a master's degree. What are the assumptions? One of the untested assumptions is that a master's degree gives our company the experience we need for the position. We might ask, "If we hire a person for this position who has a master's degree, what does that give us?" We may hear responses like credibility, knowledge, goal orientation, technical expertise, and intellect. To test those assumptions, we could ask the following:

- Is school the best place to learn what a person needs to know for this position?
- If someone has a master's degree, does that mean he or she has the ability to examine real-world problems and think creatively?
- Do we believe a person with a master's degree and no experience is more qualified than a person with on-the-street experience but no master's degree?
- Will a master's degree provide the credibility we need in our culture?
- Does a master's degree ensure that the person is curious?
- If we hire someone with a master's degree, is it more likely we'll hire the right person?
- Does a master's degree ensure the level of intelligence we need?

We can even test our answers to the questions just listed. For example, if we asked, "Does a master's degree ensure the level of intelligence we need?" and the answer was yes, we might test assumptions at a deeper level: "Have we ever known someone who had a doctorate who didn't seem as intelligent as someone with a bachelor's degree?" "How would we know that a person had the level of intelligence we need?" "What specifically would demonstrate intelligence?" Whether our answers are true or not is up for debate. But in testing beliefs, we need to question the validity of the thinking that created them, and question if our particular idea is pivotal in landing on a solution.

4. what does that lead to? (consequence)

The last way to spark curiosity is to take an idea and find what it leads to. Often the reason people hold too tightly to an idea is that they're overly invested not in the idea itself but in the motive behind it. They also may be concerned about what the impact of doing or not doing something might be. When the motive behind an idea isn't clear, we often debate about the wrong topic. To uncover motive, we can use a tool called "cut to the chase."

Cutting to the chase gets to the heart of the matter, but we use the phrase slightly differently from what it commonly means. The phrase comes from early films, where there was typically a long story that led to a chase scene at the end of the movie—cops chasing robbers, aliens chasing earthlings, good guys chasing bad guys, and so on. In the editing room, if the story took too long to get to the chase, and therefore risked losing the audience's attention, the director would tell the editors, "Cut the storyline down and get to the chase." The shorthand version became "Cut to the chase." Today the phrase means get straight to the point, but the modern shorthand is missing the essence of the original meaning. We need enough story to care about the chase scene, and the chase should be worth the wait. Cutting to the chase in conversations gives us the right amount of story and confirms whether the chase is worth it.

The "chase" or impact of an idea may not be apparent at first glance, but it's always there. As we ask questions that reveal the "movie" that's playing in someone's mind, we get the benefit of the "story" along the way that connects the dots between the original idea and the "chase" or motive behind it. There's almost always more than one way to get what we want, and the first idea isn't always the best—or only—way to get there. A personal example of using cut to the chase as a tool played out in one of our workshops.

diver down

The CFO of the company we were teaching asked if our colleague would practice cutting to the chase with her on something she personally wanted but her husband didn't—a boat. Our colleague (Joe) asked her questions to uncover the purpose driving her wish for a boat. To be brief, we'll edit his questions to only those focused on the "chase":

JOE: A boat sounds great. Let's imagine for a moment that you did have a boat; what would that give you that you don't have today?

CFO: Well, it's not really complicated. I just think a boat is a great way to have fun and spend more time together as a family. It's pretty easy to get to the point where you're spending time in the same room or under the same roof, but we're not spending time *together*.

JOE: I can see that. And if you were spending more time together as a family . . . ?

CFO: I'd have more uninterrupted, one-on-one time with my two teenage daughters.

JOE: And if you could spend more time with them—at least the kind of quality time you're hoping to spend with them—what would that give you?

CFO: I'd feel like I was able to have more of an influence on their lives. I guess they're like most teenagers and they're facing some challenges in their lives. I think I could help them through those hard times. A boat would be a great way to spend time together.

JOE: So if you could have the influence you'd like to have, and if you really were able to help them through some tough times . . . ?

CFO: I think I could help them wisely avoid some mistakes. I also think they would be happier and better prepared to be parents themselves when they have children of their own.

JOE: And if they were, what would that lead to?

CFO: *(now visibly emotional)* I'd feel that at the end of my life, I was equally successful a mother as I am a CFO.

After a brief pause, Joe's next question to her was "Is a boat the only way you can get what you want?" The answer was no. She discovered through the discussion that—for her—the fierce debates about the boat weren't about the boat. At the surface, the boat was the topic of discussion, but what she wanted deep down was really driving the intensity, not the boat itself. Her husband didn't know what was driving her interest in the boat, and so they argued about "the boat" when the boat wasn't the issue at all.

Imagine what might have happened if they bought a boat. It's possible her vision of spending quality time with her daughters would come true. It's also equally possible it wouldn't happen the way she hoped. Would her daughters dread boating owing to the heavy cleaning required after each outing? Would they resist going boating because it took time away from hanging out with friends? If they brought friends along, would they ignore Mom and Dad to focus on their friends? It would be a safe bet that two or three years later, there would be unfulfilled expectations from the boat, and yet not a clear understanding why.

By using curiosity to dive deep, we uncover the *real* motivation for an idea, like a boat. That exploration opens us to possibilities— including other ways we can achieve what we want. According to research, 86 percent of gridlock moves to dialogue if we can get to "the dream" or purpose behind an idea. We can more vigorously debate and explore ideas when we understand the motivation behind them.

good intentions pave the road to . . . ?

Making good business decisions daily requires discipline to quickly uncover the purpose behind an idea. With unlimited ideas and limited resources, we can't always afford to be slowed by drawn-out, cumbersome business plans for everything we do. There are hundreds of decisions made every day in a company that require increased business curiosity. Conversational curiosity allows us to test the strategic fit or financial validity of an idea early without detailed financial analysis. For example, let's say the team you're working on proposes an idea they think the company should invest in:

Idea: "We need to build a talent-management platform to launch employer-of-choice initiatives."

While there would be ample room for finding out what different words meant—what is meant by "talent management platform" or "employer-of-choice initiatives"—another way to spark curiosity is to uncover the motive driving the idea rather than leave it a mystery. So the dialogue might flow like this:

CUT TO THE CHASE (C2C):   I like the thinking. Just so I'm clear, if we had that platform as you're envisioning it, what would that lead to for us as a business that we aren't doing today?

COLLEAGUE: I think it would improve our ability to get the right talent in the door and keep them. With the labor market forecasted to tighten over the next five or six years, I'm not sure we'll stay competitive if we don't launch a platform right away. We're already having a hard time filling some positions.

C2C: Let's say we were able to attract and retain top talent, which would be great in this labor market. What do you see that leading to for us as a business?

COLLEAGUE: We could get the right people into the right jobs at the right time. And I'm talking about everyone from doctors and nurses to food services to administration.

C2C: It might be an obvious question, but rather than guess, I'll ask it anyway. Where would the benefits of all that show up?

COLLEAGUE: I think the quality of our care would go up, and we'd be able to improve patient satisfaction scores.

C2C: Good. Anything else?

COLLEAGUE: I think it would also help our reputation in the community. Maybe even decrease our vacancy rates.

Now we know what's driving the talent-management idea, and we can estimate the impact on the bottom line. We also know there's more than one way to improve patient satisfaction, quality, reputation, and vacancy rates, and so we have options. Rather than first debating the merits of what platforms to choose from at the surface level, diving deep opens avenues for a more meaningful, and business-relevant, discussion. Along the way we get the value of connecting the dots—the story behind the idea and the impact at the end. Then a discussion of options regarding talent-management platforms is more useful.

In summary, we've talked about four ways to spark conversational curiosity:

1. What do we mean? (clarity)
2. What are we seeing? (context)
3. What are we assuming? (assumptions)
4. What does that lead to? (consequence)

We can use them in combination or on their own. Each has a different place where it is more likely to free our curiosity.

the soul of curiosity

As with any principle of egonomics, we can go through the motions or passionately devote ourselves to living curious. Techniques without soul are just boxes on a list to be checked off. At five years old, I (Dave) began taking private piano lessons. Like any student, I learned scales, chords, fingering drills, and the like—all designed to make me an accomplished musician. I played in recitals and competitions and did well. One afternoon, I attended a performance given by a cellist I knew from my hometown named John Davis. I was rapt as I listened. He didn't play a particularly difficult or showy piece of music. It wasn't even a piece I recognized. But as he played, I was moved. That's when I realized he had something I didn't. People could hear my music, but they could *feel* his.

At first I thought it was because he had been playing for more years than I, or that he had practiced more—and so I increased my practice time. The more I practiced, the more I became aware that even though I had the technical skill and could play notes with precision, my music wasn't alive. That changed for me one day. Reeling from a painful experience in my life, I sought solace in my music. I went to an old church where there was a grand piano and I knew I would be alone. In the midst of my sadness, I wrote my first song, and, more important, for the first time I felt music come from my soul instead of my fingers. Most songs are inspired by a story that's filled with emotion. Musicians who aren't curious and don't get involved in the story may have impressive technical competence, but the music doesn't come from inside. John Davis had soul, and his soulful playing awakened my soul. Curiosity, when sustained with soul, embeds itself into the very structure of the way we do business.

the résumé of curiosity

Barry Diller is a product of intense curiosity. His accomplishments are nearly unmatched in the business world. Diller was raised in Beverly Hills and started his career in the mail room of the William Morris Agency (a talent and literary agency), after dropping out of UCLA after one semester. He was hired by ABC in 1966 and was soon in charge of negotiating broadcast rights to feature films. Three years later he was promoted to vice president of feature films and program development. There, Diller and his colleagues created the *ABC Movie of the Week* and pioneered the concept of the made-for-television movie. Diller left ABC and served ten years as the chairman and CEO of Paramount Pictures. With Diller in charge, the studio produced multiple hits: *Laverne & Shirley, Taxi, Cheers,* and feature films ranging from *Saturday Night Fever* and *Grease* to *Raiders of the Lost Ark,* to *Indiana Jones and the Temple of Doom,* to *Terms of Endearment* and *Beverly Hills Cop.*

From there he held positions of chairman and CEO at Twentieth Century Fox. Diller quit Fox in 1992 and purchased a $25 million stake in QVC. Diller is currently the chairman of Expedia and the chairman and CEO of InterActiveCorp, an interactive commerce conglomerate and the parent of companies including Home Shopping Network, Ticketmaster, Match.com, and Citysearch. So why the focus on one résumé? Listen to the man whose résumé it is on what created it. "For me, the guiding principle in deciding which route to take in business has always been to follow my own curiosity," said Diller. "Of course, you also need a willfulness to make real, practical use of that curiosity. The one doesn't work without the other." In a quarter-page interview in *Business 2.0*, Diller mentions the word *curiosity* six times, and at his first mention of the word he ties the effectiveness of curiosity to the fusion of openness and order—trait curiosity.

By using one of the four techniques of conversational curiosity, we create an environment that sparks curiosity in the routine of day-to-day business. If sustained with soul, that daily effort leads to the highest concentration of corporate curiosity, catching nuances that go unnoticed by others, and freeing us from investing time, energy, and money in untested ideas and assumptions. We then have more resources available to invest in truly worthwhile projects and products.

As we raise the level of curiosity in the way we think and communicate, we're bound to learn things along the way that won't always be easy to hear or say. That doesn't mean they won't need to be heard or said. But humility's devotion to progress gives us two distinct advantages in saying or hearing them: it 1) builds the capacity to embrace hard-to-hear truth (veracity), and 2) makes us more likely to speak the truth in the most difficult moments. Our appetite for veracity is the third and final principle of egonomics, and the subject of the final chapter.

9: curiosity | key points

- There are two types of curiosity, "state" and "trait." State curiosity—the kind most people have—waits on something to spark it. State curiosity is temporary. Quickly after we're removed from the state that sparked our curiosity, it's finished. Trait curiosity, on the other hand, doesn't wait to be sparked: it does the sparking.

- People with trait curiosity have a rare blend of order and openness.

- When order overrides openness, curiosity loses freedom to explore. If left to openness alone, curiosity loses structure and purpose. Trait curiosity requires equal parts of both.

- Sometimes our desire to cure or fix something is the very thing that gets in our way.

- People don't lack the ability to build or courage to try. Research suggests we don't lack imagination, ambition, or ideas. We do lack prebuild, prelaunch, preexecution curiosity. It's not the only factor, but it's a major one. When we use discipline and patience to resist our impulse to run with an idea at first glance, we give curiosity time to breathe.

- Every company has processes dedicated and designed for innovation and improvement. The value of a given process depends on the quality of information that flows from the conversations inside it.

- No matter how clear and well-ordered the steps of a process, the level of curiosity driving the conversations inside those steps can decide the value created by each step. In the white space of those steps, curiosity is process-neutral.

- Four ways to raise the level of curiosity in daily conversations by combining openness and order include: 1) What do we mean?, 2) What are we seeing?, 3) What are we assuming?, 4) What does that lead to?

10
veracity

On some positions, Cowardice asks the question, "Is it safe?" Expediency asks the question, "Is it politic?" And Vanity comes along and asks the question, "Is it popular?" But Conscience asks the question, "Is it right?" And there comes a time when one must take a position that is neither safe, nor politic, nor popular, but he must do it because Conscience tells him it is right. [Our] lives begin to end the day we become silent about things that matter.

WILLIAM MORLEY PUNSHON

Have you noticed there's often a gap between what executives think is going on and what frontline managers *know* is going on—and vice versa? What about the difference between what marketing thinks the market is ripe for and what sales is convinced clients really want? What about when you and a colleague are on the same team, on the same project, in the same meeting—and yet you hardly see anything the same? What about the gap between someone's actual competence and what that person thinks it is, and what everyone else experiences? What's unsettling is what we don't know, and what we don't know is buried beneath fear of saying what's unknown to someone else or of hearing what's unknown to us. The only way to close those gaps is for both sides to have the courage to say the truth or listen and embrace the truth when said. Veracity bridges the gaps ego creates.

Fused with humility and curiosity, veracity is the third principle of egonomics that keeps the capital of ego working for us rather than against us. *Veracity*'s Latin root, *veritas*, means "truth." But why not say *truth* if that's what we mean? Truth refers to facts or reality; it implies accuracy and honesty. Truth is a destination. Veracity doesn't differ from truth in its destination, but it differs in action. Veracity implies the habitual *pursuit of*, and *adherence to*, truth. Both pursuit and adherence matter immensely: pursuit in arriving at truth, and adherence in making a change once truth is discovered. Let's explore the pursuit of truth first.

In business, veracity is the pursuit of *reality*—the difference between what we think is happening and what's actually going on. That pursuit must be relentless because what's true in business or science today will change. In the 1980s the egg industry was in decline because cholesterol was the mother of all unhealthy food. Then, upon further pursuit, science discovered there was good cholesterol and bad cholesterol, and suddenly eggs were allowed back into good graces. In fact, some now call eggs the "perfect food." In business, it's hard to imagine investing in a product people could get easily and free—like water. If you were an executive at Coca-Cola or Pepsi twenty-five years ago, and someone expressed concern about a new competitor bringing plain water to market, how open-minded would you have stayed? And yet, Americans spend more than $9 billion a year on bottled water, paying 120 to

7,500 times as much per gallon for bottled water as for tap. It out-sells every beverage except pop. That's why the key term in veracity is *pursuit*.

To paraphrase Peter Drucker about pursuit in his book *Innovation and Entrepreneurship*, what we see has to be subjected to rigorous, logical analysis. Intuition isn't good enough. In fact, intuition is no good at all if we use it as another way of merely saying what we *want* something to be. The truth comes from discovering the difference between what most everyone is quite sure is reality and what has become a new reality. Finding the new reality requires the willingness to say, "I don't know enough to analyze, but I shall find out. I'll go out, look around, ask questions, and listen." Those are simple steps—admit you don't know, look around, ask questions, listen—but they're less easy in practice. They are possible.

Kent Thiry, CEO of DaVita, built a culture of veracity and in turn rebuilt a company. DaVita is one of the largest chains of dialysis centers in the United States, helping patients suffering from chronic kidney failure. When Thiry took over DaVita in October 1999, "the company was technically bankrupt," he said. "It was being investigated by the SEC, sued by shareholders, had turnover at over twice the current levels, was almost out of cash, and in general was not the happiest of places. [We] were within three weeks of missing payroll. If the banks had asked for any significant payment, we would have had to shut the doors. The only reason they didn't is they were worried if they did, they would not get their money." With Thiry as CEO, market capitalization grew from $200 million to nearly $5 billion, and stock price over the last five years increased from roughly $10 a share to $47.60 currently. Employee turnover was cut in half, and DaVita exceeds the industry's national average for clinical outcomes.

Thiry is willing to put brutal facts on the table, even when no one else will. In an annual gathering of thousands of employees, he asked if integrating a recently acquired health care company was "fun." The employees said, "Yes!" In disbelief he countered, "Either you're all on drugs or better than me, because integrations are a god-awful nightmare." That honesty sends a clear message: "If you don't say it, I will." Over time, that gives a culture a new level of permission to say what's really happening.

In the pursuit of truth, Thiry is hungry for it—good or bad— even about himself. In his own performance review from thirteen senior executives, he received a "bad grade" for giving too much negative feedback. "They say I'm not harder on them than I am on myself," said Thiry in an article by Carol Hymowitz for the *Wall Street Journal*, "but my negativity isn't constructive." It's the third year he's heard the same feedback, so he implemented a "daily scorecard for feedback to remind himself, and to change." What's impressive is not only the culture of veracity Thiry built, but his openness in an interview in something as public as the *Wall Street Journal* to acknowledge, and embrace, the hard-to-hear truth about himself. It would have been easy to hide it. He doesn't.

got a leak?

To find the difference between our own version of reality and actual reality, how do we invite people to explore what we see, and how do we listen when invited—especially when the truth is hard to say or jarring to hear? There are two questions to answer in that pursuit: 1) when *don't* we want the truth?, and 2) why don't we want it?

The lack of veracity in business is tied to an identity crisis. A quick metaphor explains why. Let's say you're going on vacation. You carefully plan the long road trip and map out the sights you want to see. Before leaving, you check the fluid levels, tire pressure, spare tire, and so on. One-third of the way into your trip you stop to get gas and something to eat. As you walk out of the Chevron FoodMart, someone flags you down. "I think your car is leaking something." What would your reaction be? More than likely it would be interest and appreciation. "Really? Where? Is it leaking a lot? Thanks for pointing that out." Even if you're an expert mechanic and checked everything just before you left, you'd still check to see if the car's leaking or not.

What if on closer inspection you discover your car isn't really leaking, the stranger just thought it was. If it turns out nothing's wrong with your car, you're fine with that as an outcome—in fact, happy. If there was a leak, you're glad someone pointed it out and relieved you didn't discover it later—in the middle of nowhere.

But that changes when we're at work.

For example, let's say you developed a go-to-market strategy and someone said, "This strategy won't work. It doesn't factor in the downturn in that market right now or how buyer preferences are shifting." As opposed to the leak in our car, we're tempted to respond differently to this comment because we don't take it as it's intended—as a helpful observation. We think it reflects poorly on who we are and challenges our identity. **If we don't take it personally when our car is leaking, why do we take it personally when our strategy is?** Part of the reason is we don't control what happens to our car; anything can happen to it at any time. But in a corporate setting, we're supposed to be in control. If someone points out a weakness, it feels like something we should have controlled but didn't. We believe that leak brings our ability into question. The barrier to veracity is not that people are incapable of seeing the truth or even expressing it. So where's the problem? In the reaction to truth when it's revealed.

mum's the word

As a result of typical reaction to candor, most people believe truth telling is risky. In a study by Amy Edmondson of Harvard University and James Detert of Penn State University on why employees are hesitant to speak up, they said, "Employees aren't failing to provide ideas or input because they've 'checked out' and just don't care, but because of fear." Their work was triggered by a survey of over 50,000 employees from one company where nearly 50 percent of all employees from the boardroom to the mail room reported it wasn't safe to speak up or challenge traditional ways of doing things. From 190 interviews of these employees, when asked why they weren't speaking up, here's a sample of what they said:

- I had an idea about improving our production efficiency that I wanted to present to our site manager in a meeting. But I was terrified because he sometimes yells, "That's a dumb idea," like an angry father when people speak up to him. Since I'm a supervisor, I'm not in the union and therefore know that if they don't like what I say, they can easily get rid of me. So I didn't speak up, and I felt angry and disappointed.

- You try to give feedback about a product from what you're hearing in the field. But marketing and others inside don't want to hear [it]. . . . If you speak up in a meeting about this, they think that you are too negative and you are almost not allowed to talk about this. And you think, "They should come with me for a few days and hear what customers are saying," but they don't want to because it's too negative.

- I tried to go further into a market analysis, and the site director started shouting at me. I should have said more but I didn't because you cannot foresee the reactions of that man. Unpredictable. I was fearing a very disturbing incident and I didn't feel like fighting—because I usually have no problem fighting for my ideas. But when you are on ground where you can't control the problem, where it's emotional, I can't do anything.

- I didn't want to push the situation. I didn't want the son of a bitch to fire me. He was liable to take my damned badge right there and fire me. I can't afford to lose my job.

- When I first joined the team, I was very excited. I have tons of experience [and was] looking for ways to make things better—just asking a lot of questions. "So who's responsible for that and how does that work and how come it's not working? And why don't we do it that way?" [starts crying] Because I care a lot about this company. I was told that the comments that I was making, the questions that I was asking were making other people uncomfortable. [My boss] asked me to really think hard about everything that I said. And to me—it isn't safe. If I have to think so hard about what I'm going to say, then it isn't safe.

Emotions like fear, anxiety, frustration, anger, and distrust arise when people don't think it's safe to speak. Situations vary widely, but the feelings behind them don't. People resent giving artificial support to an idea they think will fail, especially if they know something others don't that will stop it from working. If they don't believe anyone will listen if they speak up, they keep quiet while bad projects or corporate inefficiencies keep sucking money from the bottom line. Mum's the word.

turning up veracity

If the pursuit of and adherence to truth is to become habit, we need two specific abilities: *hearing down* and *speaking up*. A client of ours facilitated a workshop for a senior business leader's team. As they were discussing the responsibility to speak up and hear down, one of the vice presidents said, "I don't feel comfortable speaking up all the time. My ideas get shot down most of the time. When I do speak up, I'm seen as the rabble-rouser in the group." His tone was cold and indifferent.

A nervous silence fell over the group. After what seemed like an eternity, the facilitator said, "Well, you just spoke up about how you feel now. Tell me why you did." "It won't make a difference," he said. "Maybe," interjected the general manager, "it's because the ideas you share are so half-baked and unsupported by real research—you think?" The facilitator called a break and pulled the GM aside. "That's one of the guys that just doesn't fit into our culture," the GM complained. "You heard his tone; he doesn't know how to deliver his message in the correct way. I'm the GM—you'd think he could respect that." The facilitator asked if he had considered the content of the messages the vice president delivers, without paying attention to the tone of delivery. "I've been over and over this with him," the GM said. "He's the type that doesn't really listen."

"That really doesn't answer my question," the facilitator replied. In disbelief the GM asked, "Are you saying this is my fault?" "No," our client replied, "I'm not saying it's anyone's fault. I'm just curious about the *content* of his message. If you set the tone aside, have you given any thought to its validity?" "No," the GM stated firmly. "Why should I?" After class, our facilitator talked with the GM and the VP alone. He talked to the GM about how important it is in hearing down to consider the content of the message and, if necessary, disregard the way the message is shared, or the tone with which it's delivered. He reminded the GM to not take it personally. He also talked to the VP about the way he delivers his messages when he speaks up, reminding him not to make it personal. In the end, they both agreed that there was much they each needed to work on, and that their egos got in the way of what should have been the primary focus—the business.

In using the words *down* and *up*, we're referring to reporting relationships at work, not to our value as people. Everyone has someone to whom they report, or someone who reports to them. *Hearing down* means we listen in a way that encourages people who report to us to speak their mind and prevents seeking acceptance from being their—or our—highest priority. *Speaking up* requires candor with those to whom we report, without putting either person in jeopardy. People tend to confuse criticism of their strategy with criticism of their identity. Consequently, we must speak up in a way that doesn't provoke others to be defensive or showcase brilliance to defy what we say. When done right, speaking up opens minds so truth is heard and culled from different points of view.

hearing down

In humility's pursuit of progress, and on the deepest dives of curiosity, we're bound to uncover issues we wish we hadn't. **A major barrier to hearing down is our belief that dissent is disloyalty. If we view dissent as disloyalty, we've closed our mind.** Dissenting from the current point of view, or going opposite the momentum behind an idea, does not mean the dissenter isn't a team player. In fact, the dissenter may be the greatest asset we have.

Let's go back 2,500 years to an era when dissent was usually viewed as disloyalty, and nearly intolerable. In his time, Alexander the Great conquered the most powerful nations of the world. Of those nations, Persia was the most difficult, primarily because of the military power and genius of its king, Darius. After several battles, Alexander finally beat Darius and added the Persian throne to his collection. But only a few years after beating Darius, Alexander died. Shortly after his death, the Greeks retreated from Persia. Since Darius had died in battle, his son Xerxes took the throne of Persia.

First on Xerxes' list of priorities was reestablishing Persia's dominance. He began conquering nations, but despite all his conquests, Xerxes felt Persia would be inferior until he conquered what his father Darius couldn't: Greece. As Herodotus tells it, to reveal his intentions, Xerxes gathered his generals:

> *"For this cause I have now called you together, that I may make known to you what I desire to do. My intent is to . . . march an army through Europe against Greece that thereby I may obtain vengeance from the Athenians for the wrongs committed by them against the Persians and against my father."*

After Xerxes' declaration, a council member named Mardonius responded,

> *"Of a truth, my lord, you surpass, not only all living Persians, but likewise those yet unborn. Most true and right is each word you have now uttered . . . but best of all, your resolve not to let the Greeks who live in Europe—a worthless crew—mock us anymore."*

But not everyone present felt the same as the cheerleading Mardonius. Many of the generals had been with Xerxes' father when he first battled the Greeks, and they recalled the brutal defeats. But despite their memories, most council members were silent, afraid to step out of line with Xerxes' agenda for war. However, a man named Artabanus, who had also fought with Xerxes' father against the Greeks, broke the silence.

> *"O King! It is impossible, if no more than one opinion is uttered, to make choice of the best: a man is forced then to follow whatever advice may have been given him."*

Artabanus then reminded Xerxes of the severe problems Persia had had fighting the Greeks, and the current lack of legitimacy for another war.

> *"Think then no more of incurring so great a danger when no need presses, but follow the advice I tender. Break up this meeting, and when you have well considered the matter, and settled what you will do, declare to us your resolve."*

That was Artabanus's dissent. Now he follows it with loyalty.

> *"If, however, we must go to war with this people, at least allow the king to abide at home in Persia. Then let [Mardonius] and me both stake our children on the issue, and choose your men, and taking with whatever number of troops you would like, lead forth our armies to battle."*

Despite the loyalty, Xerxes wasn't exactly appreciate of the veracity.

> *"Artabanus, you are my father's brother—that shall save you from receiving your due of your silly words [perhaps prison or death],"* he said. *"One shame however I will lay upon you, coward and faint-hearted as you are—you shall not come with me to fight these Greeks, but shall tarry here with the women."*

Then Xerxes broke up the meeting, but the advice of Artabanus "disquieted him." The next morning Xerxes reconvened his leaders.

> *"Men of Persia, forgive me if I alter the resolve to which I came so lately. Consider that I have not yet reached the full growth*

of my wisdom, and that they who urge me to engage in this war
leave me not to myself for a moment. When I heard the advice
of Artabanus, my young blood suddenly boiled; and I spoke
words against him little befitting his years; now however I con-
fess my fault, and am resolved to follow his counsel. Understand
then that I have changed my intent with respect to carrying
war into Greece, and cease to trouble yourselves."

"When they heard these words," records the historian Herodotus,
"the Persians were full of joy." Twenty-five hundred years later, the
same danger of confusing dissent with disloyalty persists.

A call center manager was sharing an initial sketch of a plan for
performance incentives with a large group of employees. She didn't
hear much feedback, good or bad, as she was sharing it. Uneasy
with the silence, she pushed for feedback. At last, two employees
spoke up with concerns about parts of the plan. She thanked them
for speaking up. After the meeting, both came and apologized
for not being supportive. She explained that their feedback was
exactly what she was after and assured them apologies weren't necessary. She realized she had to change the culture's belief that debate, disagreement, and dissent showed lack of support. **Real
disloyalty is keeping silent when something needs to be
said.**

the positivity of negativity

Most dissent is not disloyalty. More often than not, there's positive
intent behind a negative comment or different viewpoint. When
those who report to us speak up, we can find it hard to listen if we
perceive what they're saying is bad news. However, most hard-to-
hear truths, no matter how negative, are in another way an expression of positive value. If people complain that red tape and
bureaucracy get in the way, at the same time they're expressing a

desire for freedom to get things done. Creating a culture where truth is heard requires we see the positive side of negative facts.

speaking up

Hearing down is only half the equation in our pursuit of truth. If we want those "above" to hear down, those *speaking up* have a responsibility equal to those who should be listening. There are many people we could point to as examples of speaking up, but few would be better than Edward R. Murrow. He may be the most distinguished figure in the history of broadcast journalism. His career began at CBS in 1935 and crossed radio and television news. In 1961, Murrow left CBS to become director of the United States Information Agency for the Kennedy administration. By that time, his colleagues were already referring to him as a "legend of courage, integrity, social responsibility, and excellence and emblematic of the highest ideals of both broadcast news and the television industry in general." Pulitzer Prize–winning journalist David Halberstam observed in his book *The Powers That Be* that Murrow was "one of those rare legendary figures who was as good as his myth."

At a time when Senator Joseph McCarthy was publicly accusing dozens of American citizens of being Communists—with little or no evidence—and getting away with it, Murrow spoke up despite the risk that he could be McCarthy's next target. But it's important to note that Murrow didn't save speaking up for those he disagreed with or who were at a distance. On October 15, 1958, at a celebratory dinner held in his honor, and surrounded by peers whom he loved and with whom he collaborated, he delivered a veracious assessment of his own industry. As you read an excerpt of his speech, notice how he chooses his words to speak up.

> *This just might do nobody any good. At the end of this discourse a few people may accuse this reporter of fouling his own*

comfortable nest, and your organization may be accused of having given hospitality to heretical and even dangerous thoughts. [It] is my desire, if not my duty, to try to talk to you journeymen with some candor about what is happening to radio and television. [If] what I have to say is irresponsible, then I alone am responsible for the saying of it. [T]here exists in mind no reasonable grounds for personal complaint. I have no feud, either with my employers, any sponsors, or with the professional critics of radio and television. But I am seized with an abiding fear regarding what these two instruments are doing to our society, our culture, and our heritage.

[O]ur history will be what we make it. And if there are any historians about fifty or a hundred years from now, and there should be preserved the kinescopes for one week of all three networks, they will there find recorded in black and white, or color, evidence of decadence, escapism and insulation from the realities of the world in which we live. [T]elevision in the main insulates us from the realities of the world in which we live. If this state of affairs continues, we may alter an advertising slogan to read: LOOK NOW, PAY LATER.

Murrow spoke up to those he worked with, to his employer, and to anyone else who needed it—including himself. He didn't shrink for fear of what others would think. He spoke candidly and directly and opened minds to truth.

If we want people to open their minds to truth, we need as much humility and courage to speak up as others need in hearing down. When speaking up, what we say, how we say it, and what we intend play a big part in where the conversation goes. While it's true that some things are better left unsaid, too often silence stifles progress. Most of us have been in a meeting where silence prevails even though everyone knows the truth is being avoided. There are dozens of reasons we keep quiet: "silence is golden," "better safe than sorry," somebody else will speak up, they probably already know, it won't make a difference anyway, they have seniority, you're new, they're new, we fear the unknown, and on and on.

One of the main reasons we don't speak up is fear. There are two primary fears that keep us quiet: fear of being labeled and fear of saying what we're not afraid to think.

fear of being labeled

We don't speak up for fear others will label us. We're afraid that bringing up a negative equals being a negative person, or that if we say something brutally honest, then we're not "nice." Or it could be we think if we state the obvious or ask an obvious question, we'll seem uneducated or stupid. When we strain to manage perceptions others have of us, that effort kills truth in the process. The fear we feel that prevents us from speaking up was clearly illustrated to me (Steve) while I was a freshman in college.

My psychology 101 class was held in an auditorium that seated a thousand students. The professor was onstage with a microphone and a slide show, cruising through the day's lecture. Rarely did anyone ask questions; we just took notes and tests. One day as the professor lectured, I couldn't understand what he was talking about. I looked around the room to see if anyone else was in the same boat. But everyone, even my friends sitting next to me, looked like they were getting it. So I continued to stare blankly toward the stage below. Since no one seemed to be taking a lot of notes, I assumed this was either pretty straightforward or unimportant stuff. What's more, I told myself I was probably the only one in the auditorium who didn't get it.

A couple of minutes later I still couldn't follow the ideas. Finally, out of desperation, I raised my hand from the balcony, told him I didn't understand, and asked a question about what he was saying. My question didn't come without fear that I would look "dumb" or that it would seem like I hadn't been listening. The professor thanked me and began to reexplain the ideas in a different way. Not only did I start to understand, but I noticed nearly everyone else frantically taking notes. I wasn't the only one in left field. When we're feeling peer pressure, self-imposed or not, we don't ask questions or say what's on our mind for fear we'll be labeled. Losing veracity is often the price we pay to maintain an image—ours, or someone else's.

In one of many experiments on how we misperceive what others think of us, Kenneth Savitsky of Williams College and Nicholas Epley and Thomas Gilovich of Cornell had participants attempt to solve a set of anagrams—words whose letters are jumbled in random order—in full view of another person who would observe their performance. Before working on the word puzzles, the solvers were asked to estimate how the observers would judge them on things like intelligence, competence, honesty, and so on, both before and after the task. On the other hand, observers were told to state their *actual* impressions with no premeditated thoughts either way. Before taking the test, solvers were told, "Those who do well on tests such as this one tend to be individuals who are clear thinkers and who are highly intelligent" and that "few people get all the answers correct, but most people tend to do well."

As the solver attempted to unscramble the word puzzles, the experimenter responded out loud "correct" or "incorrect," while the observer looked on. When finished, the experimenter revealed the score. What neither the solver nor the observer knew was that the test was designed to be very difficult, with only two or three easy answers—so difficult in fact that the average "solver" only solved 2.6 anagrams of the 16.

The research discovered solvers *over*estimated the extent to which observers were thinking badly of them, and *under*estimated charitable thoughts in their behalf. Solvers also overestimated how harshly observers would judge them if they did poorly on the test *before* they had even taken the test. In other words, we're harder on ourselves than others are on us, even when we make mistakes. Fear of what others will think is often unrealistic. "One may refrain from speaking in public, from expressing one's true feelings . . . all because of an unnecessarily strong fear of how others would react if things did not go as well as one hoped," the researchers said in conclusion. "People's excessive fear of social censure often comes back to haunt them, as research has documented that with hindsight the biggest regrets in people's lives tend to involve things they had not done but wished they had, rather than things they had done and wish they had not." Let's not allow exaggerated fear to persist as a barricade between us and veracity.

fear of saying what we're not afraid to think

The second reason we don't speak up is a different kind of fear. I (Dave) learned that the hard way. In a performance review, I asked for specific suggestions on what I could do to get promoted. I was given a few general suggestions and told, in so many words, "It's just a matter of time. Your future is bright in this company." Subsequent performance reviews weren't any different. But in the meantime, I saw three peers on other teams get promoted ahead of me. That made me mad—at my boss. I thought, "He has to know why others are advancing. If they're doing something I'm not, why won't he say something—especially when I specifically ask for feedback?" Because it was frustrating not to get feedback, I decided to get good at *giving* feedback to others. That's when I learned about a fear I had never fully appreciated.

To be meaningful, feedback has to be specific and real. What surprised me—and this is the unexpected reason we don't speak up—is how *afraid* I was to say what I was not afraid to think. It's hard to say to a colleague, "I don't think you deserve credit for the success of this project. In fact, you're more of an obstacle than a contributor." It's not hard to think those things, but it's a different story when we have to say them. As it turns out, even leaders have a hard time speaking up—including to those they lead.

two prerequisites for speaking up

A major factor in getting people to listen is their perception of our motive. Let's return to our gas station analogy for a moment. If we tell strangers their car is leaking, there are two main reasons they're open to our speaking up: 1) our comment is prompted by concern rather than a self-serving motive or judgment (we have nothing to gain or lose by speaking up), and 2) our observation, which may or may not be accurate, isn't about their identity. It's about an object—their car—and something we've seen that they haven't.

Now, imagine how their reaction changes if we approach them and say, "You really did a lousy job of tying down that load. You're liable to cause an accident when that all comes undone. You should fix it." Now they'll perceive their ability, intelligence, judgment, or whatever is under attack: their identity is in danger. Now we're in different territory. Our perceived motive in speaking up, and the way we do it, either increases or dramatically decreases the likelihood that our message will be heard and respected.

the language of speaking up

When speaking up, say hard truths in a way that won't create harsh responses. In other words, deliver the brutal facts without *being* brutal. The language of speaking up doesn't eliminate fear, but it does allow us to say what's on our mind in a way that reduces risk. Here are three steps designed to keep minds open when speaking up:

1. Establish permission.
2. Make your intentions clear.
3. Be candid.

You may not need all three, depending on the context of the situation and your relationship with the people in the room, but you're likely to need at least one.

1. establish permission

According to research by Dr. John Gottman, the tone of the first three minutes of discussion predicts how a problem will end, even five years from the time it surfaced. He has a rule: "If it starts negative, it stays negative." If people detect we're on the hunt to blame or judge, they get defensive. Remember, the more dangerous we think a situation is, the more likely *we* are to shut down and protect identity. The same is true of others. Establishing permission is simple, like ringing the doorbell at a close friend's home before you walk in; no matter how well you know your friend, let your friend invite you in. Here are some examples:

- Could I share something that's been on my mind that I can't seem to shake?
- At the risk of sounding like I just don't get it—and maybe I don't—could I ask a question?
- I've thought a lot about this, and there's something I need to put on the table. Maybe it will be tough to talk about, maybe it won't. I don't want the fact that it may be tough to get in the way of at least thinking it through.
- It could just be me, but it seems we're missing something in our discussion. Maybe we're not, and we can quickly move past it. And maybe there's something to it.

2. make your intent clear

Once we've established permission to say what's on our mind, making our intent clear increases the odds others will hear our message without misinterpretation. "What stronger breastplate," said Shakespeare's Henry VI, "than a heart untainted?" Remember, humility's intent is devotion to progress. Now is a good time to remember that. There are at least three reasons we should make our intent clear:

1. We let others know why we're bringing up a question; it keeps them from guessing about our intent or assigning us a negative one.
2. We reduce the chance that words will interfere with our message.
3. A public statement of our intent reminds *us* to be committed to that intent.

Sometimes, especially in tense situations, we can't find the right words. Even when we find the right words, sometimes they're misread. But if our intent is right, it keeps identity safe and the conversation focused on ideas. Here are examples of gaining permission combined with making our intent clear:

- I'd like to put something on the table that's bothering me. Right now, I'm not convinced the logic behind this is sound. At first I put off saying anything, thinking my comment might come across as negative. It may seem like that, but I want the best idea to win, whether it's my idea or not. If there's a hole in my rationale, point it out and I'll let go of it. If your logic is faulty, I expect the same from you. If we're all wrong, we can come up with another idea.

- I like the way we challenge ideas as a team: it's healthy. At the same time it doesn't seem like we challenge ourselves *enough* when it comes to whether our ideas will benefit the company as a whole even though *we* like them. I think the proposal on the table might hurt the business unintentionally. Maybe I'm wrong, but it seems to me that in our enthusiasm, we're overlooking something.

- I think we should kill this. That doesn't mean we should, but I'm more and more convinced that's a very real option. That's hard for me to say, especially since I've been such an advocate of this project, but I don't think it's going to meet customer needs the way we want it to.

In the examples above, instead of saying, "We're wrong," we said, "I'm not sure the logic behind this idea is sound." Rather than saying, "We're making a mistake," we said, "The proposal on the table might hurt the business unintentionally." When intent is clear, it's easier for others to focus on the message rather than question our intent or misconstrue it as an attack on their identity.

3. be candid

Candor is our effort to assert the facts, as best we can, and put them on the table for examination. This is the moment of truth— when we say what's on our mind as clearly and candidly as possible.

One manager we interviewed in our research shared a story about candor in a critical meeting with the CEO and the vice president of sales. The meeting was prompted by a sudden, behind-the-scenes withdrawal of resources. Three weeks before the meeting, the manager received approval to hire two people critical to the business unit's new strategy. The management team interviewed several candidates and were ready to make offers. Before extending offers, the necessary paperwork was sent to human resources. The requests were rejected. When the manager asked the reason for the rejection, he was told, "[The CEO] called last week and canceled these requisitions."

With repeated conflicting messages, the management team felt the CEO had become nearly unreachable. His elusiveness sapped enormous energy from the entire business unit. The CEO had once referred to this group as an "island of excellence in a sea of mediocrity," but his actions didn't back up his words. Since these positions were critical to their strategy, the manager arranged a meeting with the CEO to find out why he had reversed his position and pulled support.

The meeting, scheduled for two hours, began at 10:00 a.m. sharp. "My purpose in agreeing to this meeting is to understand your concerns and talk through your proposal," the CEO said. "My whole purpose is to listen to you. I have no other agenda. I wonder, however, if you would allow me just a few minutes to set some context for our meeting." The team agreed. For the next thirty-seven minutes the CEO talked without taking a breath. Complete with whiteboard diagrams, he rehearsed what seemed like every line he had delivered the previous two years. The team sat in disbelief, waiting their turn. At 10:38 a.m. he sat down from his lecture and said, "The time is now all yours. I'm all ears."

One team member, on his way to a client engagement, was attending the meeting via cell phone over the conference line. His time was cut short because he had to board an airplane. "I respect your message, and at this point I don't have much to say," he began. "And even if I did, I don't have much time to say it. My concern is this meeting is an example of your style and how you run our company. This meeting is the last time we're going to talk about our proposal. You've taken almost half our allotted time to rehearse your ideas about the direction of the company. What I don't understand is how you expect to understand our proposal if you don't allow us adequate time to present it. You acknowledged up front your purpose was to listen, and now I don't see how that's possible."

The room was silent. Stunned by the candor, the CEO looked around the room to see if the speaker was joking or serious. Hoping to recover, the CEO turned the remainder of the meeting over to those left in the room. Given that this was the meeting where the CEO had committed to make a final decision one way or the other, he had pledged to read the proposal before the meeting. As the team dove into the content of their proposal, it became clear he hadn't read it in any depth, despite his promise. "I've read the proposal," he said, "but I don't see the connections to our strategy." When asked what specifically didn't fit, he couldn't answer. His amnesia didn't match his extraordinary mind for numbers or near-photographic memory at other times. "You have one of the brightest minds I know," said the general manager, "and yet you don't seem to recall any specifics about our proposal. That makes us think you're not really listening or interested."

The agreement before the meeting was that the CEO would make a decision. But the CEO refused to say what he was really thinking and made another "delay" move. "Before I make a decision," he said, "I'll read your proposal one more time." In yet another candid response, one colleague said, "I'm not sure I understand what difference reading it again will make. We've talked through all the key elements today. When we talk to you, we get head nodding and a noncommittal answer. We're equally okay with a yes or no decision, but we didn't come here looking for another 'maybe.' "Another colleague, who had a reputation for being patient and able to open and advance difficult conversations, stepped in. He tried being "nice," asked open-ended questions, used

Socratic reasoning, showed understanding, and so on. Then, suddenly, rather calm discussion transformed into confrontation.

The same man interrupted the CEO, challenged his strategy, questioned his logic, contested his points, and drew out both guns for high-IQ shooting. He aggressively questioned the CEO and escalated the intensity of the conversation. After the meeting his surprised colleagues asked him why he had done so. "Well," he responded, "if what you're doing isn't working, try something different. This was as different as I knew how to go, and we still couldn't reach him. We still didn't get an answer." Finally, a decision came.

No.

So what's the good news about the candor of that interaction? The answer is a *decision*. This management team turned an eternal yellow light to red by advancing the discussion. In doing so, they created two green lights; the CEO could focus resources on what he really believed in, and the business unit was no longer distracted by continuing a discussion that didn't have support and resources.

When we're candid, we can't expect the world to shift in our direction because we've broken the cold silence with tough facts. Veracity also doesn't assume we're unbiased. Our perceptions may be right, and they may just as easily be wrong. In either case, companies are better off when people speak up.

adherence

As we conclude the book, let's talk about the second meaning of veracity: adherence to truth. That usually means change, and change is the very point of egonomics. While it's true that knowledge is power, there is a clear difference in the power of knowing versus the discipline of becoming. If our pursuit reveals truth, and we don't change, the pursuit was worthless. If we resist truth when faced with it, we build egotistical scar tissue that makes future resistance more likely. Not long ago we were in a taxi in Boston. The driver wanted to talk. We didn't. He won.

TAXI DRIVER: . . . had quadruple bypass about a year ago.

US: Wow. How did it go?

TAXI DRIVER: Oh, it went well. I'm taking stress classes, trying to eat right, trying not to get too wound up when I'm driving.

US: That's good. Congratulations.

TAXI DRIVER: I can't quit that damned smoking, though. My doctor says it's going to kill me, but I just can't do it. I'll probably die with a cigarette in my mouth.

He probably will.

But before ego tempts us to place ourselves above the discipline of the taxi driver, imagine for a moment that over the last few months you've experienced numbness in your left arm and occasionally a slight tightness in your chest. Concerned enough to check it out, you set an appointment with your physician. Upon your arriving at the hospital, your doctor expresses enough concern that she decides to run some tests. After an EKG, an angiogram, and stress tests you return to your doctor's office for the results.

She informs you there's good news and bad news. You want the bad news first, so she delivers it: you need triple bypass surgery. It's more serious than you thought. After a moment to absorb the bad news, you ask for the good news. "From everything I can tell," the doctor says, "this isn't hereditary. You don't have a genetic predisposition to this problem. Once we perform the surgery, this can be prevented from ever happening again if you take care of yourself, specifically by your diet and exercise." If you heard those words directly from your doctor, would you adhere to them?

Yes?

Maybe you would, but here's something to consider before you answer. Not long after our cab ride, Alan Deutschman wrote an article on change for *Fast Company* entitled "Change or Die." "What if you were given that choice? For real. What if it weren't rhetoric that confuses corporate performance with life or death, but actual life or death? Yours. What if a doctor said you had to make tough changes in the way you think and act—or your time would end soon? Could you change? Here are the scientifically studied odds: nine to one. That's nine to one against you."

In the article, Deutschman cites Dr. Edward Miller, dean of the medical school and CEO at Johns Hopkins University. About 600,000 people have bypasses every year in the United States, and 1.3 million heart patients have angioplasties at a total cost of about $30 billion. Approximately 50 percent of the bypass grafts clog up in a few years, and the angioplasties in a few months. According to Dr. Miller, the way to decrease the number of patients returning for repeat surgery is a simple change to a healthier lifestyle, but that change is rare. "If you look at people after coronary-artery by-pass grafting two years later, 90% of them have not changed their lifestyle," Miller said, "and that's been studied over and over and over again. And so we're missing some link in there. Even though they know they have a very bad disease and they know they should change their lifestyle, for whatever reason, they can't."

So now what's your answer—would you change?

It's probably still yes. We haven't asked that question of a group yet and had someone answer, "No. I prefer open-heart surgery or death." But even under the threat of life or death, the majority stays the same. And if people don't change under the threat of life or death, what are the odds they'll change the way they work?

when no change *is* change

Because the odds are so ominous, here's something to think about. If we don't make the choice to change, we will change anyway. We change every day—without any effort. People who stay the same move backward. When we stand still, people pass us, and so our status changes. The early warning signs are signals we're stuck in neutral or—more accurately—in reverse as the world passes us. The business world grades performance on a curve, and someone is pushing that curve upward right now. Even if it's just one person who pushes that curve, everyone else will be measured by a higher standard.

It's also possible our world isn't changing. Maybe it's static, and what we've written doesn't apply. Certainly the oil industry doesn't appear to change as dramatically as technology. Maybe we're safe. In the economics of change, we won't change unless what we're earning (money, growth, opportunities, contribution) isn't good enough—unless we're not satisfied. No amount of rhetoric can force people to progress. A decision to take the next step is an individual choice, and we will make that choice when the pain is intense enough that relief becomes a high priority. Or it could be that the opportunity in front of us makes us restless with the current state of affairs.

Organizations—and people—most interested in change generally fall into two categories: already great or dying. It's the ones who are "good enough" who rarely make a move and opt for mediocrity. But wherever we are, if we want to change, now is the time. "This is no time to engage in the luxury of cooling off," said Martin Luther King, Jr., "or to take the tranquilizing drug of gradualism."

The point of departure for change is irrelevant. It's the departure itself that matters—one moment at a time.

Note: A free survey to assess your team's effectiveness on the principles of humility, curiosity, and veracity is available at www.ego nomicsbook.com.

10: veracity | key points

- Veracity doesn't differ from truth in its destination, but in action. Veracity implies the habitual pursuit of, and adherence to, truth. Both pursuit and adherence matter immensely, pursuit in arriving at truth, and adherence in making a change once truth is discovered.

- In business, veracity is the pursuit of reality—the difference between what we think is happening, and what's actually happening. Pursuit must be relentless because what's true in business or science today will change.

- Veracity in business suffers when identities are threatened.

- The barrier to veracity is not that people are incapable of seeing the truth or even expressing it. The reaction to hard-to-hear truth when revealed isn't usually favorable. As a result of the typical reaction to candor, most people believe truth telling is risky.

- If the pursuit of truth is to become an individual and cultural habit, we need two specific abilities: *hearing down* and *speaking up*.

- A major barrier to hearing down is our belief that dissent is disloyalty. If we view dissent as disloyalty, we've closed our mind. More often than not, there's positive intent behind a negative comment.

- If we want those "above" to hear down, those *speaking up* have a responsibility equal to those who should be listening.

- We need as much humility to speak up as others need in hearing down. When speaking up, what we say, how we say it, and our intent plays a big part in where the conversation goes. While it's true that some things are better left unsaid, too often silence stifles progress.

- One of the main reasons we don't speak up is fear. There are two primary fears that keep us quiet: fear of being labeled and fear of saying what we're not afraid to think.

- There are three steps for speaking up effectively: 1) establish permission, 2) make your intentions clear, 3) be candid.
- The second half of veracity's meaning is *adherence* to truth. That usually means change. While it's true that knowledge is power, there is a clear difference in the power of knowing versus the discipline of becoming.

appendix

early warning signs—beliefs

Most of us are influenced by more than one of the early warning signs of ego. We may have tendencies toward one sign, like being defensive, but everyone has experienced more than one sign at different times. The signs show up in the moment and turn our strengths into counterfeits. Since we make decisions based on beliefs, breaking the habit of any early warning sign—even momentarily—requires we examine beliefs that drive our tendencies. Our beliefs are based on an equation—a series of "this plus this equals this" or "if-then" logic. But the math we do in our heads doesn't always add up: the beliefs we have may be anything but true. If we can identify the faulty equations in our minds, we can break bad habits.

The first item under each early warning sign lists healthy viewpoints when our level of that sign is about right. Next we list indications we've crossed the line and several questions that test beliefs that could be pushing us over the line. While we may not have all these beliefs, we probably have at least one.

early warning signs—primary emotions or attitudes

There is often a difference between what we say or do and what we're thinking or feeling. Even though we might say the right words, sometimes we feel different. While what we feel or think can be masked by the right words or actions, our intentions and feelings are always true, although not always revealed. What we're feeling lets us know if our ego is causing us to feel an inappropriate level of a particular warning sign. Finally, we list the primary emotions or attitudes related to that early warning sign. If we feel one or more of the related emotions or attitudes for that sign, we should double-check to make sure we're not preoccupied with that particular warning sign.

early warning sign 1: being comparative

when it's about right: internal competition

I want and expect to win.

when we cross the line

- I see nearly everyone as a rival.
- I have a hard time when others are recognized for their performance.

beliefs we can test

- Will competition discourage talented but less-competitive people from contributing?
- Does competition always equal better team performance?
- Have you seen competition hurt team performance?
- Do all team members value competition equally?
- Will all team members respond to competition in a positive way?
- Will competition hurt collaboration?
- In this situation, is competition the best way to elevate team performance?

primary emotions/attitudes

aggressive	defeated	envious
complacent	demoralized	inferior

jealous	ruthless	uncooperative
rationalizing	scarce	unlucky
resentful	superior	

early warning sign 2: being defensive

when it's about right: my ideas

Good ideas are worth defending.

when we cross the line

- I shouldn't have to defend my ideas.

beliefs we can test

- If people challenge the idea, are they really challenging me personally?
- Will the challenge hold up?
- If the challenge prevails, will I be seen as a loser (dumb, less capable, or hasty)?
- Is challenge negative?
- Will challenge take away any credit I deserve for my effort?

primary emotions/attitudes

accusing	indignant	protective
bitter	inflexible	resentful
cynical	jealous	sarcastic
envious	judgmental	unforgiving
evasive	justified	
excusing	justifying	

early warning sign 3: showcasing brilliance

when it's about right: expertise

I have unique perspective and expertise.

when we cross the line
- I give advice, even when I'm not asked.
- I have all the answers.

beliefs we can test
- If I give advice, even when not asked, is my expertise *always* relevant?
- Is now the best time to share my expertise?
- Is this the best way to share my expertise?
- Is my advice true, or is there some bias in what I'm saying?
- Just because I give my opinion, does that mean it will be heard and others will value it?

primary emotions/attitudes

annoyed	disdain	irritated
autocratic	impatient	patronizing
condescending	insensitive	self-satisfied
contempt	intolerant	superior
controlling	invincible	unappreciative

early warning sign 4: seeking acceptance

when it's about right: disagreement

I want people to like my ideas but, disagreement can be productive.

when we cross the line
- Disagreement is another form of attack.
- I'm troubled when someone disagrees with my point of view.

beliefs we can test
- If people disagree with an idea, does that mean they don't like the person who shared the idea?

- If people don't like my idea, does that mean they think less of me?
- If people like my idea, does it always mean they like me?
- If people disagree with an idea, is it always because they're objective?
- If people disagree with part of my idea, does that mean the whole idea is bad?
- If people disagree with my idea, does that mean they have a better idea?
- If a few people disagree with my idea, does that mean everyone will have the same reaction?
- Don't all of the best ideas require some modification before they're truly great?

primary emotions/attitudes

conflicted	offended	tentative
embarrassed	rejected	unpopular
insecure	resentful	

notes

1. ego and the bottom line

1 *"Every good thought that we have":* William Law in *The Forbes Book of Business Quotations,* ed. Ted Goodman (New York: Black Dog and Leventhal Publishers 1997), 682.

2 *Over half of all businesspeople estimate ego costs their company:* MarcumSmith, LC survey of 837 businesspeople. "Considering the effect of ego on conversations, decisions, and meetings, how much would you estimate ego is costing your organization as a percentage of annual revenue?" Revenue cost estimate: 0 percent: 3 percent; 1 percent to 5 percent: 17 percent; 6 percent to 10 percent: 34 percent; 11 to 15 percent: 19 percent; 16 percent to 20 percent: 27 percent. Error rate + or −5 percent. Employee size: fewer than 250 employees, 38 percent; 251 to 500 employees, 9 percent; 501 to 1,000 employees, 9 percent; 1,001 to 2,500 employees, 10 percent; more than 2,500 employees, 34 percent. Annual revenue: less than 25 million, 43 percent; 25 to 100 million, 10 percent; 100 to 500 million, 14 percent; more than 500 million, 31 percent. Rank distribution: individual contributor, 22 percent; manager, 34 percent; senior manager, 12 percent; executive, 21 percent; C-suite, 3 percent; board member, 7 percent.

2 *Fannie Mae was listed as one of only eleven companies:* Jim Collins, *Good to Great* (New York: HarperCollins, 2001), 25.

3 *"Fannie Mae reaches $400 million settlement":* Reuters, *CNNMoney,* May 23, 2006, http://money.cnn.com/2006/05/23/news/companies/fannie.reut/index.htm.

3 *"Fannie Mae thought itself so different, so special, and so powerful":* Bethany McLean, "The Fall of Fannie Mae," *Fortune,* January 24, 2005.

4   *Roy Baumeister . . . and Liqing Zhang . . . conducted a series of experiments:* Liqing Zhang and Roy F. Baumeister, "Your Money or Your Self-Esteem: Threatened Egotism Promotes Costly Entrapment in Losing Endeavors," *Personality and Social Psychology Bulletin* 32 (2006): 881–93.

5   *Over one-third of all failed business decisions are driven by ego:* "Smart Companies, Dumb Decisions," *Fast Company,* October 1997, 160; Paul C. Nutt, *Making Tough Decisions* (San Francisco: Jossey-Bass, 1989).

6   *News articles berate ego-trippers:* "Don't Let Ego Kill the Startup," *Business-Week Online,* Special Report, October 25, 2005, http://www.business week.com/technology/content/oct2005/tc20051025_043783.htm; "Ego Slams T.O.," *USA Today,* November 8, 2005, http://www.usatoday. com/news/opinion/editorials/2005–11–08-owens-edit_x.htm.

8   *"I believe what you say":* Collins, *Good to Great,* 35–36.

14–15   *"In a certain sense, they may have been playing chicken up there":* Jon Krakauer, "True Everest: Into Thin Air,"*Outside,* http://outside.away.com/outside/ destinations/199609/199609_into_thin_air_11.html.

15   *"Other businesspeople can do that":* Carol J. Loomis, "Why Carly's Big Bet Is Failing," *Fortune,* February 7, 2006, 60.

16   *"It must watch for clues":* Marcus Buckingham and Donald O. Clifton, *Now Discover Your Strengths* (New York: Free Press, 2001), 5.

16–17   *In getting full access to that talent:* MarcumSmith, LC survey of 837 businesspeople. "At work, how often do you observe ego negatively affecting conversations, decisions, or meetings?" hourly, 15 percent; daily, 48 percent; weekly, 31 percent; quarterly, 3 percent; annually, 0 percent; never, 3 percent. Error rate, + or –5 percent. Employee number: fewer than 250 employees, 38 percent; 251 to 500 employees, 9 percent; 501 to 1,000 employees, 9 percent; 1,001 to 2,500 employees, 10 percent; more than 2,500 employees, 34 percent. Company revenue: less than 25 million, 43 percent; 25 to 100 million, 10 percent; 100 to 500 million, 14 percent; more than 500 million, 33 percent. Position distribution: individual contributor, 22 percent; manager, 34 percent; senior manager, 12 percent; executive, 21 percent; C-suite, 4 percent; board member, 7 percent.

17   *"If those cultures are as prevalent":* Anne Fisher, "Starting a New Job? Don't Blow It," *Fortune,* March 7, 2005, http://money.cnn.com/magazines/ fortune/fortune_archive/2005/03/07/8253411/index.htm. Fisher was referencing a study by Right Management Consultants.

17 *we shouldn't be surprised:* "65% of Workers Looking Around Says Survey," Reuters, *CNNMoney,* January 30, 2006, 1.

17 *"While there are certainly other factors":* Gardiner Morse, "Hidden Harassment," *Harvard Business Review* (June 1, 2005): 28. Morse was referring to research by Christine Pearson of the Garvin School of International Management at Thunderbird and Christine Porath at USC's Marshall School of Business that studied "uncivil experiences" of more than 2,400 workers, managers, and executives in the United States and Canada.

17 *"at $50,000 per employee":* William G. Bliss, "Cost of Employee Turnover," *The Advisor,* http://money.cnn.com/magazines/fortune/fortune_archive/2006/02/06/8367928/index.htm; Calculations were also made using the U.S. Census Bureau's Statistics about Business Size (including Small Businesses); Employers and Non-Employers, 1997, Employment Size of Employment Firms, 2001; and U.S. Annual Employment Turnover Rates by Industry and by Geographic Region through August 2004.

18 *scarcest, most valuable resource:* Geoffrey Colvin, "Catch a Rising Star," *Fortune/CNNMoney,* January 30, 2006, http://money.cnn.com/magazines/fortune/fortune_archive/2006/02/06/8367928/index.html.

18 *By the year 2010:* Louis E. Boone and David L. Kurtz, *Contemporary Business 2006* (New York: Thomson South-Western, 2006), 24.

18 *"There's an imminent leadership crisis":* Colvin, "Catch a Rising Star."

2. the ego balance sheet

21 *"Ego is our silent partner":* The Forbes Book of Business Quotations, ed. Ted Goodman (New York: Black Dog and Leventhal Publishers, 1997), 238.

21–22 *"The competitor to be feared":* The Forbes Book of Business Quotations, 160.

22 *A meta-analysis of 265 studies:* Alfie Kohn, *No Contest* (Boston: Houghton Mifflin Company, 1986), 47–48.

23 *"We should take care":* Albert Einstein, quoted at http://www.bartleby.com/66/87/18587.html.

25 John Gottman and Julie Gottman, "The Art and Science of Love," marriage retreat in Seattle, Washington, February 11–12, 2006; John M. Gottman and Nan Silver, *The Seven Principles for Making Marriage Work* (New York: Three Rivers Press, 2000), 4.

28 *In one survey:* "Integrity Matters," *Fast Company,* September 2005, 52.

30 *"Truth, when not sought after":The Forbes Book of Business Quotations,* 858.

32 *"Jeff, I'm your biggest fan":* John A. Byrne, "The *Fast Company* Interview: Jeff Immelt," *Fast Company,* July 2005, 61–64.

3. early warning sign 1

38 *"Every man in the world":* Jerome Agel and Walter D. Glanze, *Pearls of Wisdom: A Harvest of Quotations from All Ages* (New York: HarperCollins, 1987), 30.

38 *"[Competition] is here; we cannot evade it":* Andrew Carnegie, quote at, http://www.bartleby.com/66/60/10560.html.

39 *"A foe by being over-heeded":* Jean de La Fontaine, *The Original Fables of La Fontaine,* trans. Frederick Colin Tilney, (Teddington, UK: Echo Library, 2006).

40 *"That's a classic mistake":* Elizabeth Esfahani, "How to Extend a Franchise," *Business 2.0* (December 2004), 102; available at http://money.cnn.com/magazines/business2/business2_archive/2004/12/01/8192532/index.htm.

40 *In one study, researchers asked people to rank:* J. K. Beggan, "On the Social Nature of Nonsocial Perception: The Mere Ownership Effect," *Journal of Personality and Social Psychology* 62 (1992): 229–37.

40 *In another study, researchers found that we're influenced:* Brett W. Pelham, Matthew C. Mirenderg, and John T. Jones, "Why Susie Sells Seashells by the Seashore: Implicit Egoism and Major Life Decisions," *Journal of Personality and Social Psychology* 82 (2002): 469–87.

40 *how likely particular celebrities were to reach heaven:* Douglas Stanglin, "Oprah: a Heavenly Body?" *U.S. News & World Report,* March 31, 1997, http://www.usnews.com/usnews/politics/whispers/articles/970331/archive_005829.htm.

41–42 *rank increased happiness:* Colin Allen, "Rank Determines Job Satisfaction," *Psychology Today,* October 6, 2003, http://psychologytoday.com/articles/pto-20031006–000002.html.

42 *"Pride gets no pleasure out of having something":* C. S. Lewis, *Mere Christianity* (San Francisco: HarperSanFrancisco, 2001).

43 *"disheartened and depressed":* Oprah Winfrey, "What I Know for Sure," *Oprah Magazine Supplement,* Fifth Anniversary Edition, May 2005, 22–23.

45 *"What it looks like now"*: Sydney Finkelstein and Shade H. Sanford, "Learning from Corporate Mistakes: The Rise and Fall of Iridium," *Organizational Dynamics* 29 (2000): 138–48.

46 *"Competition whose motive is merely to compete"*: Henry Ford, *The Forbes Book of Business Quotations,* ed. Ted Goodman (New York: Black Dog and Leventhal Publishers, 1997), 160.

46 *"If you base your strategy"*: Melanie Warner, "How to Think Competitively," *Business 2.0* (December 2004): 111.

46 *"He's welcome to say whatever he'd like"*: John Battelle, "The 70 Percent Solution," *Business 2.0* (December 2005): 136.

46 *"Everyone engaged in creative work is subject to persecution"*: Frank Lloyd Wright, *Testament* (New York: Horizon Press, 1957), 15.

47 *2002 revenue:* EDS financial results gathered from www.eds.com, 4Q 2002; and FY Earnings Results, February 6, 2003. Strategies reported were from interviews with EDS managers at the time of the story.

48 *"If anything, Donovan provided clear-cut evidence"*: Ives Galarcep, "Donovan Needs to Leave His Comfort Zone," ESPNSoccernet (June 23, 2006), http://soccernet.espn.go.com/columns/story?id=372268&root=world cup&cc=5901.

49 *Until Toyota . . . world's largest automobile manufacturer:* Micheline Maynard and James Brooke, "Toyota May Top G.M. as Biggest Car Maker in 2006," *New York Times,* December 20, 2005, http://www.nytimes.com/2005/ 12/20/business/worldbusiness/20cnd-toyota.html?ex=1292734800& en=52ce2c484a4bcbaf&ei=5088&partner=rssnyt&emc=rss.

4. early warning sign 2

55 *"Men often oppose"*: Alexander Hamilton, *The Federalist* 70 (March 15, 1788), http://constitution.org/fed/federa70.htm.

56 *"I look for bright people with strong personalities"*: Kay Barnes, "Fast Talk: The Business of Politics," *Fast Company,* October 2004, 57.

57 *"I'm sure that I'm supposed to act all sorry or sad or guilty"*: Mike Dodd, "Recognizing 'I'm 14 years late,' Rose Admits He Bet on Baseball," *USA Today,* January 5, 2004, http://www.usatoday.com/sports/baseball/2004– 01–05-rose_x.htm.

58 *"anyone I offended"*: Alan Ehrenhalt, "The Art of Apology," *Governing* (January 18, 2000), http://www.governing.com/view/vu011800.htm.

58 *"guys with Confederate flags on their pickup trucks"*: "Dean: 'I apologize for flag

remark,' "CNN.com (November 7, 2003), http://www.cnn.com/2003/ALLPOLITICS/11/06/elec04.prez.dean.flag/index.html.

59 *"Receives negative feedback"*: Stephen R. Covey, *7 Habits* 360 Research, 1989–2002.

60 *"I am not a crook"*: Carroll Kilpatrick, "Nixon Tells Editors, 'I'm Not a Crook,' " *Washington Post,* November 18, 1973, A1.

60 *"It depends on what the meaning of the word 'is' is"*: President William J. Clinton, Grand Jury testimony, 1998, http://www.library.unt.edu/Gov Info/impeach/answerpr1.pdf.

60 *"I wish you would have given me this written question ahead of time"*: "President Addresses the Nation in Prime Time Press Conference," the White House, press conference of the President; the East Room, President George W. Bush, April 13, 2004, http://www.whitehouse.gov/news/releases/2004/04/20040413–20.html.

61 *"It's an excellent question"*: Mike Allen, "Next Question Please," *Washington Post,* December 1, 2004, C1.

62 *the more positive we are about ourselves:* Shelley E. Taylor and Jonathan D. Brown, "Illusion and Well-Being: A Social Psychological Perspective on Mental Health," *Psychological Bulletin* 103 (1988): 193–210.

63 *Holding an overly flattering view of one's personality:* Mark R. Leary, *The Curse of the Self* (New York: Oxford University Press, 2004), 71.

64 *You can't shut out the world:* Arnold Glasgow, *The Forbes Book of Business Quotations,* ed. Ted Goodman (New York: Black Dog and Leventhal Publishers, 1997), 935.

69 *"Do we have to change"*: David Leonhardt, "McDonald's: Can It Regain Its Golden Touch?" *BusinessWeek,* March 9, 1998, 70–77.

70 *"The company was considered to be lost"*: Todd Benjamin, "Carlos Ghosn: Nissan's Turnaround Artist," CNN.com (June 6, 2005), http://edition.cnn.com/2005/BUSINESS/04/20/boardroom.ghosn/.

70 *Nissan is on track:* "Nissan Turns Around!" *ICFAI: Center for Management Research,* 2003, http://www.icmr.icfai.org/casestudies/catalogue/Busi ness%20Strategy1/BSTR073.htm.

71 *"You're not missionaries"*: Jeremy Cato, "Industry Update: A Conversation with Nissan President, Carlos Ghosn," *Canadian Driver,* http://www.canadiandriver.com/articles/jc/ghosn.htm.

5. early warning sign 3

74 *"This woman said I was acting like God"*: Attributed to Woody Allen.

76 *In a study of over 10,000 real-time working relationships:* Tiziana Casciaro and Miguel Sousa Lobo, "Competent Jerks, Lovable Fools, and the Formation of Social Networks," *Harvard Business Review* (June 2005): 92–99.

76–77 *"gives the segregator a false sense of superiority":The Papers of Martin Luther King, Jr.: Desegregation and the Future,* vol. 3, *Birth of a New Age, December 1955–December 1956* (Berkeley: University of California Press, 1997), http://www.stanford.edu/group/King/publications/papers/vol3/561215.004-Desegregation_and_the_Future,_Address_at_the_Annual_Luncheon_of_the_National_Committee_for_Rural_Schools.htm.

77 *"He embraced his authoritative nature"*: Seth Mnookin, *Hard News* (New York: Random House), xvii, xx, 227.

78 *Many accident investigations do not go far enough: Columbia* Accident Investigation Board; Report, vol. 1 (2003): 97.

80 *"The larger the island of knowledge"*: Ralph W. Sockman, quoted at www.brainyquote.com/quotes/quotes/r/ralphwsoc104775.html.

81 *In times of change:* Eric Hoffer, *The Ordeal of Change* (New York: Harper, 1967), 237.

81 *"The illiterate of the 21st century"*: Alvin Toffler, quoted in *Educational Technology in the 21st Century. Joint Hearing before the Committee on Science and the Committee on Economic and Educational Opportunities. House of Representatives,* 104th Cong., 1st sess., 1996, 240.

81 *"There's good evidence that once physicians leave their residency"*: T. DeAngelis, "Better Self-assessment Equals Better Medical Judgments," *APA Online* 34 (February 2003), http://www.apa.org/monitor/feb03/better.html. DeAngelis was referring to research by Larry Gruppen, University of Michigan Medical School.

84 *"Our individual differences"*: Scott E. Page, *The Difference* (New Jersey: Princeton University Press, 2007), i–ii.

85 *"high-power group were almost three times more likely":The Science Daily,* January 11, 2007, http://www.sciencedaily.com/releases/2007/01/070110124121.htm.

85 *"The research has wide-ranging implications"*: Adam D. Galinsky, Joe C. Magee, M. Ena Inesi, and Deborah H. Gruenfeld, "Power and Perspectives Not Taken," *Psychological Science* 17 (December 2006): 1068–74.

85–86 *To put it another way:* Paul C. Nutt, *Why Decisions Fail* (San Francisco: Berrett-Koehler, 2002), xi.

86 *Steve Jobs's picture is on the cover:* Brent Schlender, "How Big Can Apple Get?" *Fortune,* February 21, 2005, http://money.cnn.com/magazines/fortune/fortune_archive/2005/02/21/8251769/index.htm.

6. early warning sign 4

89 *"Here is a secret that no one has told you":* "Tom Brokaw's Commencement Address," May 15, 2000, http://www.providence.edu/About+PC/College+News/Hidden+Press+Kit+Items/Brokaw+Address.htm.

90 *Nearly three hundred adolescents were surveyed:* Mark R. Leary, *The Curse of the Self* (New York: Oxford University Press, 2004), 126–27.

90 *Performance on video games:* Leary, *The Curse of the Self,* 138–39.

91 *Those who told corporate recruiters what they love to hear:* Kim Girard, "The Fine Art of Sucking Up: Brownnosing, at Least in Its Milder Forms, Can Work Wonders as a Short-Term Career Booster. Just Don't Overdo It," *Business 2.0* (April 1, 2003), http://money.cnn.com/magazines/business2/business2_archive/2003/04/01/339807/index.htm. Girard was referencing Jenny Chatman's research.

93 *I'm really excited about your proposal:* Girard, "The Fine Art of Sucking Up," 120.

94 *"Exit champions need to be fearless":* Isabelle Royer, "Why Bad Projects Are So Hard to Kill," *Harvard Business Review* 81 (February 2003): 56.

96 *"If I tell you who I am":* John Powell, *Why Am I Afraid to Tell You Who I Am? Insights into Personal Growth* (Texas: Thomas More Association 1995).

7. humility

100 *"True humility is intelligent self-respect":* Ralph W. Sockman, quoted at http://thinkexist.com/quotes/ralph_w._sockman.

101 *Our experience is that people are hungry for the answers:* MarcumSmith, LC survey of 837 executives, managers, and individual contributors. "Do you wish your organization were more humble?" Yes, 83 percent; no, 17 percent; error rate + or −5 percent.

102 *"You can say this much for Disney CEO Bob Iger":* Peter Lauria, "Iger's Apparent Humility Seen as Strength," *New York Post,* January 22, 2006, 27.

105 *"One of the most difficult things for God to do":* Scoop Jackson, "One Defining Moment," *ESPN Page 2,* May 9, 2006.

107 *58 percent of workers believe most top executives:* Betsy Morris, Rutgers and University of Connecticut poll, *Fortune,* July 11, 2006, http://money.cnn.com/2006/07/10/magazines/fortune/rule5.fortune/index.htm.

111 *Economists have long assumed:* Jerry Useem, "How to Build a Great Team," *Fortune,* June 1, 2006, http://money.cnn.com/2006/05/31/magazines/fortune/intro_greatteams_fortune_061206/index.htm.

113 *"That man over there says that women":* Sojourner Truth (Isabella Baumfree), "Ain't I a Woman?," 1851: Account by Frances Gage, 1881. Available at http://www.fordham.edu/halsall/mod/sojtruth-woman.html.

115 *"Despite their proven success":* Roderick Kramer, "The Great Intimidators," *Harvard Business Review* 84 (February 2006): 96.

116 *"For the first time in my life":* Taylor Hartman, *The Color Code* (New York: Fireside, 1999), 19–20.

119 *"Many of the more conventional books on leadership":* Janet Zich, "Genius & Folly," *Stanford Business* 69 (May 2001), http://www.gsb.stanford.edu/community/bmag/sbsm0105/features_genius_folly.html. An interview with Dr. Roderick Kramer.

119 *"by force of personality":* Kirk H. Beetz. "Steve Jobs," http://www.referenceforbusiness.com/biography/F-L/Jobs-Steve-1955.html. Beetz is an expert encyclopedia writer.

120 *"And then I got fired":* Steve Jobs, Commencement Address, *Stanford Report,* June 14, 2005, http://news-service.stanford.edu/news/2005/june15/jobs-061505.html.

121 *"Every year he's mellowed and matured":* Katherine M. Hafner and Richard Brandt, "Steve Jobs: Can He Do It Again?" *BusinessWeek,* August 25, 1997, 5.

121 *Although he was still certain:* Beetz, "Steve Jobs."

121–22 *"I'm pretty sure none of this would have happened":* Jobs, Commencement Address.

123 *"We haven't written it yet":* Edna Gundersen, "U2: How to Dismantle a Ticking Time Bomb," *USA Today,* June 30, 2005, 3D.

123 *"Cars now spend 8 hours in paint":* Charles Fishman, "No Satisfaction at Toyota," *Fast Company,* December 2006/January 2007, 82, http://www.fastcompany.com/magazine/111/open_no-satisfaction.html.

125 *"only the paranoid survive"*: Andrew S. Grove, *Only the Paranoid Survive* (New York: Currency, 1996).

8. humility, part ii

137 *"What the eye is to the body"*: John Wesley, "On a Single Eye," Sermon 118, 1872.

137 *"Unless one considers alternatives"*: Peter F. Drucker, *The Effective Executive* (New York: HarperCollins, 1966), 148.

138 *"You need executives"*: Jim Collins, *Good to Great* (New York: HarperCollins, 2001), 60.

141 *"Then I propose"*: Drucker, *The Effective Executive*, 148.

142 *"All right, Rogers"*: U.S. Senate, Committee on Commerce. Subcommittee on Communications, *Hearings on S. 1242, Extension of Authorizations under the Public Broadcasting Act of 1967, 1969 National Educational Television Hearings,* 91st Cong., 1st sess., April 30 and May 1, 1969, Y 4.C 73/2 (Washington, D.C.: U.S. Government Printing Office, 1969), 91–95.

143 *"diffuse physiological arousal"*: "The Mathematics of Love: A Talk with John Gottman," TheEdge.org., April 14, 2004, http://www.edge.org/3rd_culture/gottman05/gottman05_index.html.

143 *"neural tripwire"*: Daniel Goleman, *Emotional Intelligence* (New York: Bantam, 1995), 16.

144 *"cool down"*: John Gottman and Julie Gottman, "The Art and Science of Love," marriage retreat in Seattle, Washington, February 11–12, 2006.

149 *"It's tough for guys like Brett Favre"*: Colin Cowherd, "The Herd," ESPN-Radio, May 11, 2006.

149 *"I'd just like to talk"*: U.S. Senate, *Hearing on S. 1242 . . . 1969 National Educational Television Hearings.*

152 *"When Lego decided in 1999"*: Nelson D. Schwartz, "One Brick at a Time," *Fortune,* June 6, 2006, http://money.cnn.com/magazines/fortune/fortune_archive/2006/06/12/8379252/.

153 *Carl Rogers was one of the most influential psychologists*: Carl Rogers's works include *On Becoming a Person, Client-Centered Therapy, Freedom to Learn for the 80's, A Way of Being, Carl Rogers on Personal Power,* and *Becoming Partners: Marriage and Its Alternatives.* Biographical sketch provided by Rogers's daughter, Natalie Rogers.

157 *"Here's the scene"*: Brent Schlender, "Pixar's Magic Man," *Fortune,* May 17,

2006, http://money.cnn.com/2006/05/15/magazines/fortune/pixar_ futureof_fortune_052906/index.htm.

9. curiosity

168 *"Genuine ignorance is profitable because"*: John Dewey, quoted at http:// www.en.thinkexist.com/search/searchquotation.asp?search=genuine+ ignorance&q=author%3A%22John+Dewey%22.

170 *"So, you're onto a winner?"*: "Got a Big Idea?" accessed at www.virgin.com/ aboutvirgin/gotabigidea.

172 *"We're all virgins at business"*: Richard Branson, "Losing My Virginity," http://www.virgin.com/aboutvirgin/allaboutvirgin/richardsauto biography/default.asp.

172 *"They have a sufficient sense of security"*: David Beswick, "An Introduction to the Study of Curiosity," Centre for Applied Educational Research, University of Melbourne, May 10, 2000, http://www.beswick.info/psy chres/curiosityintro.htm.

173 *"questions will be asked"*: Beswick, ibid. Beswick's relevant writings also include "From Curiosity to Identity: Wonder, Curiosity, Purpose, and Identity; The Function of Identity in the Psychology of Intrinsic Motivation," http://www.beswick.info/psychres/CuriosityIdentity.htm.

176 *Between 1968 and 1974, Walter Mischel of Stanford University:* Yuichi Shoda, Walter Mischel, and Philip K. Peak, "Predicting Adolescent Cognitive and Self-Regulatory Competencies from Preschool Delay of Gratification," *Developmental Psychology* 26 (1990): 978–86.

178 *"We humans seem to be extremely good"*: Thomas Gilovich, *How We Know What Isn't So* (New York: Free Press, 1991), 58.

178 *101 new patents are applied for:* Statistics drawn from U.S. Patent Office, Small Business Administration, Dun and Bradstreet, U.S. Department of Labor; Robert McMath and Thom Forbes, *What Were They Thinking?* (New York: Times Books, 1998); Don Debelak, "Want Some of This?," *Entrepreneur,* June 2002, http://www.entrepreneur.com/magazine/entrepre neur/2002/june/51926-2.html; "Overdue and Over Budget, Over and Over Again," *The Economist,* June 9, 2005.

179 *"What resources did you need"*: Rosabeth Moss Kanter, *The Change Masters* (New York: Simon & Schuster, 1983), 213–14.

181 *"Wherever you are, look around"*: David Kelley, "The Deep Dive," *ABC Nightline,* February 9, 1999.

182 *"Jolt us out of our assumptions"*: Peter F. Drucker, *Innovation and Entrepreneurship* (New York: Harper & Row, 1986), 50.

185 *"The* more *an organization knows"*: Thomas Davenport with Laurence Prusak, *Information Ecology,* (New York: Oxford University Press, 1997).

186 *"Uh, cool . . . but it doesn't do what we need it to do"*: Jena McGregor, "Fabulous Failures of Successful People," *BusinessWeek,* July 10, 2006, http://www.businessweek.com/magazine/content/06_28/b3992001.htm.

195 *"For me, the guiding principle in deciding"*: Duff McDonald, "How to Find the Hidden Value," *Business 2.0,* December 2004, 102.

10. veracity

199 *"On some positions, Cowardice asks the question"*: Martin Luther King, Jr., quoting nineteenth-century preacher William Morley Punshon in a personal letter to Gene Patterson, the Pulitzer Prize—winning editor of the *Atlanta Constitution;* Roy Peter Clark, "Correspondence: The Preacher and the Editor," *St. Petersburg Times,* January 19, 2003, http://www.sptimes.com/2003/01/19/Perspective/Correspondence__The_p.shtml.

199 *"Our lives begin to end the day"*: Martin Luther King, Jr., "A Proper Sense of Priorities," February 6, 1968, Washington, D.C.

200 *If you were an executive at Coca-Cola:* Michael Shermer, "Bottled Twaddle," *ScientificAmerican,* July 2003, http://www.sciam.com/article.cfm?articleID=000007F0-6DBD-1ED9-8E1C809EC588EF21.

201 *"I don't know enough to analyze"*: Peter F. Drucker, *Innovation and Entrepreneurship* (New York: Harper & Row, 1986), 50.

201 *"The company was technically bankrupt"*: Carol Hymowitz, "Executives Who Build Truth-Telling Cultures Learn Fast from What Works," *Wall Street Journal,* June 13, 2006, B1; Ray Pelosi, "Corporate Spotlight: DaVita," *American Health Executive, Supplement,* November 2004, RedCoatPublishing.com, http://www.redcoatpublishing.com/spotlights/sl_11_04_he_DaVita.asp.

204 *"Employees aren't failing to provide ideas"*: James R. Detert and Amy C. Edmondson, "Latent Voice Episodes: The Situation-Specific Nature of Speaking Up at Work," Harvard Business School Working Paper Series, no. 6–024, October 31, 2005.

208 *"For this cause I have now called you together"*: Herodotus, *The Histories* (New York: Everyman's Library, 1952).

211 *"legend of courage, integrity, social responsibility"*: David Halberstam, *The Powers That Be* (Urbana: University of Illinois Press, 2000).

211–12 *"This just might do nobody any good"*: Edward R. Murrow, Keynote Address, RTNDA Convention, Chicago, October 15, 1958, Museum of Broadcast Communications.

215 *"One may refrain from speaking in public"*: Kenneth Savitsky, Nicholas Epley, and Thomas Gilovich, "Do Others Judge Us as Harshly as We Think? Overestimating the Impact of Our Failures, Shortcomings, and Mishaps," *Journal of Personality and Social Psychology* 81 (2001): 44–56.

217 *"If it starts negative"*: John Gottman and Julie Gottman, "The Art and Science of Love," marriage retreat in Seattle, Washington, February 11–12, 2006.

218 *"What stronger breastplate"*: William Shakespeare, *Henry VI,* Part II, III, ii.

224 *"What if you were given that choice?"*: Alan Deutschman, "Change or Die," *Fast Company,* May 2005, 54.

225 *"This is no time to engage in the luxury of cooling off"*: Martin Luther King, Jr., "I Have a Dream," August 28, 1963.

acknowledgments

Stanford Professor Coit Blacker once said each of us is the "elaborate construction of others." Not only are we personally the elaborate construction of loving, wise teachers, so is this book. Our work exists because time and again, people went out of their way to help, with no obligation. This book tapped every ounce of mental, physical, and spiritual energy we possessed. When we were perplexed and exhausted, business leaders, scholars, colleagues, clients, and friends liberated us through encouragement, hard-to-hear feedback, granted interviews, swiftly answered emails, completed surveys, challenged our ideas, and added insight and—candidly—prayers. Many of our greatest breakthroughs were the direct result of the humility, curiosity, and veracity of hundreds of people—not two.

With deep gratitude, we thank: Tatiana Christensen, Esq.; Nancy Hancock; Timothy Bothell, PhD; Lisa Harkness; Greg Link; Ron Beck; Greg Steed; Christie Shaw; Greg Hartle; Stephen Quesenberry, Esq.; Wallace Goddard, PhD; Cherise Davis; Iyar Koren; Molly Takeda, PhD; Kathryn Moon; Jason Pierson; Claudia Simon; Bill Goodwin; Nancy Spencer; Gerry Spence, Esq.; Bryan Huddleston; Crickett Willardsen; Natalie Dew; Jahn Prince; Lisa Bearnson; Simon Billsberry; Ivan Cage; Stephanie Ashton; Dr. James Parkin; Jim Thyen; Jack Welch; Angela Habingreither; Mindy Hunter; Daynia Lewis; Bridget Penney; Madonna Elsbury; Gregg DeWaele; Mahan Khalsa; Robin Beck; Ben Johnston; Mark Matheson; Catherine McCann; Eric Nuttall; Blake Modersitzki; Steve Moreschi; Edith Strommen; Jeff Thomas; Paul Peterson; Hal Howard; Dr. Todd Nilson; Chris Willardsen; Einar Schow; Deon Lewis; Paulie Measom; Dave Harkness; Charles Lynn Frost; Lahn Simmons; Paul Jackson; Steve Schade; Denise Snyder; Bryce Thacker; Kirk Hall; Gordy Janiec; Kyle Hunter; John Davenport; Stephen M. R. Covey; Ian Edwards; Lisa Hartle; David Moon; Les Barber; Shelly Thacker; Les McGuire; Giselle Fox; Micah Christensen; Terry Johnson; Bret Van Leeuwen; Keri Anderson; Dr. Aaron Jensen; Steve Robinette; Michael Simon; Debbie Orton; Mindy Hall; Susan Stoll; Alice Cogdill; Alex Pulsipher; Morgan Ashton; Julie Hall; Craig Peterson; David Lamping; Ben Pratt; Dave Senior; Garrett Lyman; Jared Lundquist; Jim Hopkins; Malcolm Burt, Esq; Joe Thomas; Mark Dalley; Greg Pyper; Bruce Dew; Todd Stephens; Allie Davenport; Paul Coon; Von Orgill; Perry Santia; Glen Steinman; and Barry Bauer.

We also thank everyone who sent chapter reviews and personal stories to our Review Board blog. We learned something from each one shared.

Special thanks to Amy Edmondson of Harvard University, Scott Page at the University of Michigan, and Jim Detert of Penn State University for sharing their insightful work and research with us. You don't always get the privilege of meeting those who shape your work; that doesn't mean we're any less grateful to William Zinsser, Jim Collins, and Peter F. Drucker for their profound affect on our thinking and writing.

Last, but not least, we thank our families and express our love and appreciation for their amazing support and sacrifice, especially during our 24/7 disappearance of July 2006. Thank you, Karen, Lindsay, Jeff, and Spencer. Thank you, Kitty, Alec, Caden, and Nickolaus.

September 1, 2006

index

acceptance, seeking: beliefs about, 232–33; and comparisons, 52; and costs of ego, 97–98; and culture, 94–95; and curiosity, 169, 187; emotions/attitudes about, 233; and humility, 111, 115, 117, 135, 145; and insincerity, 93–94, 99; junior high school analogy about, 89–90, 91–92, 99; key points about, 99; and popularity over candor, 94–95, 99; reasons for, 95–96; and respect, 96–97; and validation, 24, 36; as warning sign, 16, 20, 21, 24, 26, 36, 89–99, 232–33
air conditioner story, 173–75
alcoholism, 105–6
anagrams research, 214–15
apologies, 23, 57–58, 73, 120, 210
Apple. *See* Jobs, Steve
assumptions, 183, 187, 188–89, 194, 198

being comparative: and beliefs, 52–53, 230; and "better than," 21–22, 36, 42, 48, 49–50, 54; and bias, 40–42, 44; and complacency, 45, 48–49, 54; and costs of ego, 97–98; and creativity, 45–47; and curiosity, 168; and defensiveness, 52;

emotions/attitudes of, 230–31; and first among, 50–53; and fox-turkey analogy, 39–40; and goals, 44–48, 54; and humility, 102, 111, 115, 117, 131, 135, 145; key points about, 54; and "more or less" campaign, 44–45; and perfection, 44, 46; and seeking acceptance, 52; and self-perception, 50–53; and showcasing
beliefs, 52–53, 188–89, 229–33
Beloved (film), 43
Beswick, David, 172, 173
"better than," 21–22, 36, 42, 48, 49–50, 54
bias, self-, 40–42, 44, 63
Blair, Jayson, 77–78
boat story, 190–92
Branson, Richard, 169–72
Bride of Chucky (film), 43
brilliance, 52; and unfair/inaccurate comparisons, 41–42, 43, 52, 54; as warning sign, 16, 20, 21–22, 26, 36, 38–54, 97–98, 230–31
brilliance, showcasing: beliefs about, 232; and collaboration, 81–87, 88; and comparisons, 52; and costs of ego, 97–98; cultural signs of, 77–79; and curiosity, 169; and diversity,

brilliance, showcasing (*cont.*)
83–87; emotions/attitudes about,
232; and half-life of brilliance, 79–
81; and humility, 111, 114–16, 117,
135, 136, 145; and identity, 77–78;
and isolation, 75–76, 88; key points
about, 88; and learning curve, 79–
81, 88; reactions to, 74–77, 88; and
sharing brilliance, 76-77; and
spotting brilliance, 74–75, 88; and
taking credit, 81–83; and veracity,
207; as warning sign, 16, 20, 21,
23–24, 26, 36, 74–88, 97–98,
231–32. *See also* duality
Bush, George W., 60–62

candor, 94–95, 99, 217, 219–22, 227,
228
career-altering decisions, 50–52
CEO, candor story about, 219–22
Challenger space shuttle, 79
change, 222–26, 227, 228
children, curiosity of, 176–77
clarity/clarification, 183–85, 187,
194, 198
collaboration, 24, 81–87, 88, 111,
132
Collins, Jim, 2, 8, 125–26, 138
Columbia space shuttle, 78–79
communication, key ideas of, 152–59,
166
competition, 20, 131. *See also* being
comparative
complacency, 45, 48–49, 54
confidence, 22, 28, 41, 80, 96, 97,
99, 118, 138
consequences, 183, 189–92, 194, 198
"constructive discontent," 27, 30, 36,
101, 107, 122–26, 136, 168
context, 183, 185–87, 194, 198, 217
creativity, 29, 30, 45–47
culture, 77–79, 94–95, 151–52, 172,
201–2, 206, 210, 211
cures, and curiosity, 175, 176–77,
197

curiosity, 168–98; and assumptions,
187, 188–89, 194, 198; of
children, 176–77; and clarification,
187, 194, 198; and consequences,
189–92, 194, 198; and context,
194, 198; and creativity, 29; and
cures, 175, 176–77, 197; and
defensiveness, 168, 187; and doing
homework, 180-82; dulling/lack
of, 176–77, 197; functions of, 168,
175; and humility, 164, 168; and
impulse control, 176–80; and
intensity, 187; and intent, 183,
187, 189–94; key points about,
197–98; measurement of, 98; and
moments, 31, 33; and openness,
172–73, 183, 196, 197, 198; and
order, 172–73, 183, 196, 197,
198; as principle of egonomics, 19,
20, 29, 37, 98; and questions,
182–83, 186–87, 188-89; raising
level of, 172, 182–94, 197, 198;
résumé of, 195–96; and seeking
acceptance, 169, 187; and
showcasing brilliance, 169; soul of,
194–95, 196; types of, 169–72,
197; and veracity, 207; and
warning signs, 168–69, 187
"cut to the chase," 189–93

Davis, John, 194, 195
DaVita, 201–2
defensiveness: and apologies, 23, 57–
58, 73; beliefs about, 230; and bias,
63; and comparisons, 52; and costs
of ego, 97–98; and curiosity, 168,
187; emotions/attitudes about,
231; evasiveness as, 60–62; and
fear, 64; and feedback, 23, 58–59,
62–63, 64, 73; and Ghosn, 70–72;
and he said, she said, 66–69; and
humility, 62, 111, 115, 117, 135,
145, 161; and image, 59–63, 73;
key points about, 73; and logic, 23,
57, 63, 64, 73; and McDonald's,

69–70; in marriage, 25; and perfection, 59–62; and spin, 64–65, 66–69, 73; and veracity, 207, 217; as warning sign, 16, 20, 21, 22–23, 26, 36, 55–73, 97–98, 231

delayed gratification, 176–77

devotion to progress. *See* "we, then me"

Dickerson, John, 60–62

Diller, Barry, 195–96

Disney, 102, 121, 157–59

dissent, as disloyal, 207–10, 227

diversity, 83–87, 130–31, 138, 140, 165

DPA (diffuse physiological arousal), 143–45, 159, 160–67

Drucker, Peter, 7, 77, 137, 138, 181, 201

duality, 101, 107, 114–22, 130, 136, 168. *See also* ego: dual nature of

Edmondson, Amy, 203–5

EDS, 47

ego: as asset, 1, 4–9, 10, 20; balance of, 21–37, 179; control of, 3, 13–15; costs of, 2, 6, 12–13, 17–18, 20, 97–98; definition of, 7; dual nature of, 1–2, 7–9, 20; as free radical, 9–10, 26–27; and how it works, 9–10; importance of, 4, 15; as liability, 4–9, 10–13, 19, 20; management of, 9, 18, 100; negative, 1, 4, 5–6, 7–9, 10–13, 20, 26; of others, 19; power of, 10, 135, 143; threats to, 4–5, 143-45, 148, 166; too little, 1, 95–96, 99, 100, 103, 135; too much, 100, 135. *See also specific topic*

egonomics: definition of, 9, 34; function of, 222; three principles of, 19, 20, 26–30, 36–37, 97–98. *See also* curiosity; humility; veracity

Eisner, Michael, 102, 157–58

emotions/attitudes, 53, 204–5, 229–33. *See also* fear

Enron, 2, 3

EPA (elevated physiological arousal), 159–60, 161, 162–64, 167

exaggeration, 65, 68, 73

ex-convict, Smith's meeting with, 154–56

fabrication, 65, 69, 73

Fannie Mae, 2–3

fear, 64, 204–5, 213–16, 227–28

feedback, 23, 58–59, 62–63, 64, 73, 202, 204, 210, 215–16

Fiorina, Carly, 14, 115

Foot Locker, 91–92

Ford, Henry, 22, 46, 81, 82–83

"four horsemen of the apocalypse," 25–26

fox-turkey analogy, 39–40

funeral (example), 34–35

gas station analogy, 202–3, 216

GE, 32–33

Ghosn, Carlos, 70–72

Gillette, 33

Gilovich, Thomas, 178, 214–15

GM, 206

goals, unrealistic and wrong, 44–48, 54

Google, 46

Gottman, John, 25–26, 143, 144–45, 217

Greiner, Helen, 186

Hartman, Taylor, 10, 116–17

he said, she said, 66–69

hearing down, 205–10, 212, 227

heartbeat, in a, 143–45

heart surgery, and change, 223–25

Hewlett-Packard, 14, 33

homework, doing, 180–82

humility, 100–136, 137–67; characteristics of, 101–7, 122; color of, 116–17; and comparisons, 111, 115, 117, 131, 135, 145; and curiosity, 164, 168;

humility (*cont.*)
  and defensiveness, 62, 111, 115,
    117, 135, 145, 161; and defining
    moments, 31, 33; definition of, 28,
    101, 103; equilibrium of, 100,
    103–4, 114, 118, 119–22, 126,
    130, 135; and intensity and intent,
    137–67, 218; key points about,
    135–36, 165–67; measurement of,
    98; misunderstanding of, 28; as
    principle of egonomics, 8, 9, 19,
    20, 27–28, 36, 98, 100–134;
    properties of, 100–101, 106–7,
    135, 136; reputation of, 137, 165;
    and respect, 100, 103, 135; and
    seeking acceptance, 111, 115, 117,
    135, 145; and showcasing
    brilliance, 111, 114–16, 117, 135,
    145; and survival, 110–11; traction
    of, 126–34; as unfinished business,
    119–22; and uniqueness, 105–7;
    and veracity/truth, 112–14, 196,
    207, 212, 227; and warning signs,
    104, 115, 117, 125, 143, 145, 147,
    159, 164, 165, 167; and winning as
    losing, 109–10. *See also*
    "constructive discontent"; duality;
    we, then me
Hurricane Katrina, 65

IBM, 92, 108
identity: and humility, 116–17, 138,
    145–52, 153, 157–66; and
    intensity and intent, 138, 146–52,
    153, 157–64, 165–66; power
    station analogy of, 145–47, 151,
    165–66; and showcasing brilliance,
    77–78; and veracity, 202–3, 216,
    217, 218, 227. *See also* image
IDEO story, 180–82
Iger, Bob, 102, 157, 158–59
image, 50–53, 59–63, 73, 96, 97,
    130. *See also* identity; labels
Immelt, Jeffrey, 32–33
impulse control, 176–80

insincerity, 93–94
intensity: and curiosity, 187;
    definition of, 138; and humility,
    137–67; key points about, 165–67;
    in moment, 141–43; and veracity,
    222
intent: clarification of, 187, 217,
    218–19; and curiosity, 183, 187,
    189–94; and humility, 143, 159,
    162, 164, 218; key points about,
    165–67; and veracity, 210, 212,
    216, 217, 218–19, 227, 228
Iridium, 45
iRobot, 186

Jobs, Steve, 86–87, 102, 119–22,
    157, 158
junior high school analogy, 89–90,
    91–92, 99

Kanter, Rosabeth Moss, 179
Kimball International, 126–33
King, Martin Luther, Jr., 77, 225
Koppel, Ted, 180–81
Krakauer, Jon, 13–15
Kramer, Roderick, 115, 119

labels, 154–57, 213–15, 228
Lasseter, John, 157–59
leaders/leadership: crisis of, 18; good
    versus exceptional, 30–31; and
    humility, 28, 132; imperfect,
    32–34; Level 5, 8, 9; meaning of,
    184; qualities of, 115
leaks, 202–3, 216
learning curve, 79–81, 88
Lego, 151–52
Leonardt, David, 69, 70
logic, 23, 57, 63, 64, 73
"Love Lab," 25–26

McDonald's, 69–70
manipulation, 65, 68–69, 73
marriage, 25–26
marshmallow story, 176–78

Microsoft, 46
Mnookin, Seth, 77, 78
Molly (example), 50–52
moments: decisions in, 30–31;
    defining, 32–34; great, 126;
    managing intensity in, 141–43;
    perfect, 32–34
momentum, 18, 34–35, 157
"more or less" campaign, 44–45
Mount Everest expeditions, 14–15
Mudd, Daniel, 2, 3
Murrow, Edward R., 211–12
music lessons story, 194–95

NASA, 78–79
National Educational Television, 141
New York Times, 77–78
NeXT, 120–22
niceness, 140–41, 165
Nightline (ABC-TV), 180–82
Nissan, 70–72
Novations Group, 18

one more thing. *See* "constructive
    discontent"
openness: and curiosity, 29, 172–73,
    183, 196, 197, 198; and
    defensiveness, 22–23, 57, 70; and
    defining moments, 34; and
    humility, 27, 36, 131, 144, 151,
    153, 156, 158, 159, 160, 164; and
    intensity and intent, 144, 151, 153,
    156, 158, 159, 160, 164; and
    order, 172–73, 196, 197, 198; and
    veracity, 30, 212, 216
order, 172–73, 183, 196, 197, 198

Packard, David, 33, 120
Pastore, John, 141–43, 147–51
peer pressure, 89–91, 213–15
perfection, 44, 46, 59–62, 119, 123
performance reviews, 215–16
permission, establishing, 217, 228
Persia, story about, 207–10
personality, 116–17, 173

Pixar, 120–22, 157–59
popularity, 94–95, 99
power, 23, 71, 85, 95
power station analogy, 145–46, 151,
    165–66
premature judgment, 19
Prince, Jahn, 105–6
progress. *See* devotion to progress
projects, success and failure of, 94–95
Public Broadcasting System (PBS),
    141–43, 147–51

questions, and curiosity, 182–83,
    186–87, 188–89

reality, and veracity, 200–201, 227
regard. *See* UPR
rejection, 91, 96, 99
reporting relationships, 206–7
respect, 96–97, 100, 103, 135.
    See also UPR
"risk, reward," 11–13, 16–17
Rogers, Carl, 153, 154
Rogers, Fred, 141–43, 147–51
r.o.i. (return on investment), 9,
    16–17

sacrifices, 112–14
sales training story, 179
September 11, 2001, 60–62
shopping cart project, 180–82
Six Sigma, 182
Sockman, Ralph, 80, 100
Sousa Lobo, Miguel, 76
speaking up, 196, 205–7, 211–22,
    227–28
spin, 64–65, 66–69, 73, 102
state curiosity, 169–72, 197
Sunbeam, 3
survival of the fittest, 110–11

talent, 10–13, 16, 17–18, 20, 104.
    See also brilliance, showcasing
Thiry, Kent, 201–2
Thyen, Jim, 126–33

Toyota, 123–24
trait curiosity, 169–75, 183, 197
triathlon (example), 50–52
truth, 65, 112–14, 222–25, 227, 228.
   See also veracity
Truth, Sojourner, 112–14
turnover, job, 17
Tyco, 3

understatement, 65, 69, 73
uniqueness, terminal, 105–7
University of Michigan, students at,
   29
UPR (unconditional positive regard),
   152, 153–59, 161, 164, 166
U2 band, 123

veracity, 199–228; as adherence to
   truth, 222–25, 227, 228; and
   candor, 217, 219–22, 227, 228;
   and change, 222–26, 227, 228;
   culture of, 201–2, 206, 210, 211;
   and curiosity, 207; and
   defensiveness, 207, 217; and
   defining moments, 33; definition
   of, 29–30, 200; and delivery of
   message, 206, 216–17, 227; and
   dissent as disloyal, 207–10, 227;
   and fear, 204–5, 213–16, 227–28;
   and feedback, 202, 204, 210,
   215–16; function of, 200; and
   hearing down, 205–10, 212, 227;
   and humility, 196, 207, 212, 218,
   227; and identity, 202–3, 216, 217,
   218, 227; and intent, 210, 212,
   216, 217, 218–19, 227, 228; key
   points about, 227–28; and
   moments, 31; and positivity of
   negativity, 210–11; as principle of

egonomics, 19, 20, 29–30, 37, 98;
   as pursuit of truth, 200–201, 227;
   and reality, 200–201, 227; as risky,
   203–5, 227; and showcasing
   brilliance, 207; and speaking up,
   196, 205–7, 211–22, 227–28; and
   warning signs, 225
violence, 138–40, 141, 165, 166
Virgin Airways, 169–72

warning signs: awareness of, 16, 26;
   and beliefs, 52–53, 229–33; and
   costs of ego, 97–98; and curiosity,
   168–69, 187; of ego as liability, 16,
   19, 20; and emotions/attitudes,
   53, 229–33; and humility, 104,
   115, 117, 125, 143, 145, 147, 159,
   164, 165, 167; and r.o.i., 16;
   tipping points for, 26; and veracity,
   225. *See also* acceptance, seeking;
   being comparative; brilliance,
   showcasing; defensiveness
"we, then me": and "constructive
   discontent," 123–26; and curiosity,
   168; economics of, 111–12; and
   equilibrium of humility, 101; and
   intensity and intent, 161, 162, 164,
   165, 166; as property of humility,
   101, 107–14, 136, 168; and
   sacrifice, 112–14; and survival,
   110–11; and Thyen-Kimball
   example, 126–33; and veracity,
   196; and winning as losing, 109–10
weakness, 10–13, 20, 104, 135
Welch, Jack, 32–33
winning, 102, 109–10
WorldCom, 3

"you versus me," 44–45

about marcumsmith, lc

David Marcum and Steven Smith founded MarcumSmith, LC, in 2002. We travel the world helping organizations utilize the corporate asset of ego while limiting its liabilities. MarcumSmith, LC, works with organizations in a variety of industries: conglomerate, high tech, government, insurance, service, finance, utilities, telecommunications, health care, and media. Our client list includes companies from the Fortune 500, America's Most Admired Companies, and the 100 Best Companies to Work For. In each case, we deliver our content from the top of the corporate ladder to the watercooler in a professional but very uncorporate way. When we go to our graves, we hope to be compared to Apple or Virgin—insightful, unique content, stylish design, and pure business relevance. Imagine a leadership class designed by people who hate to waste time and drag themselves through leadership training as much as you do. We think of humility, curiosity, and veracity as the playbook for a new generation of businesspeople, or an old generation ready to think differently and reach for the next level of leadership. We teach techniques and deliver tools for optimizing that playbook.

At MarcumSmith, LC, we acknowledge our ambitious goal to raise every business's awareness to the truth about ego—what it costs and what return it delivers when managed effectively. Fifty-one percent of businesspeople estimate that ego costs their company 6 to 15 percent of annual revenue; 21 percent say that cost ranges from 16 to 20 percent. But any cost to a company is too high. To deliver on that ambition, we offer on-site teaching and train-the-trainer certifications. Participants in our workshops, and teams we consult with, credit us with a 48.9 percent improvement in their effectiveness. We also deliver keynotes, public workshops, executive coaching, and consulting. If you're curious, reach us at 877.EGO.INSIGHT (877.346.4674), www.marcumsmith.com, or www.egonomicsbook.com.

Index

3. positives
4. $3.71 experiment
8. Good to Great/Level 5
8-9 Dual nature of ego
9. Free radical analogy, 26-7
15. Perception
16. early warning signs
17. egotistical culture
19. Ideal "Google" culture
21-22 Henry Ford on competition
22, collaboration vs. individualism
22. decision making
23,24 ones ideas vs. self
24, decision making
25, marriage and ego